THE
ARNOLDS

THOMAS ARNOLD AND HIS FAMILY

THE
ARNOLDS

Thomas Arnold and His Family

Meriol Trevor

THE BODLEY HEAD
LONDON · SYDNEY
TORONTO

Contents

Acknowledgments

Very grateful thanks to the Birmingham Oratory and to Fr Charles Stephen Dessain for permission to quote from material in the Archives and for much kind assistance; to Oriel College and the Librarian, Dr W. E. Parry, for most kind loans from the Orielensia; to Pusey House and the Librarian, and to Mrs Mary Moorman, for permission to quote from the unpublished correspondence of Mrs Humphry Ward; to Mrs Moorman for permission to quote from the unpublished correspondence of the younger Thomas Arnold with Newman, and from his letter to his daughter Mary in 1876; to Professor James Bertram for permission to quote extensively from his excellent edition of *The New Zealand Letters of Thomas Arnold the Younger*, a model of its kind; to The Clarendon Press, Oxford, for permission to quote from *The Letters of Matthew Arnold to Arthur Hugh Clough*, edited by Howard Foster Lowry; to Mr Arnold Whitridge of New York for information kindly sent by letter on his grandfather, Matthew Arnold, and his family; and to many friends who have taken an interest and assisted in collecting information, especially to Mrs Barbara Vincent, a descendant of Dr Arnold of Rugby, who supplied me with answers to my first questions about her family.

M.T.

Illustrations

THE
ARNOLD FAMILY

THOMAS ARNOLD   =   MARY PENROSE
(1795–1842)   (1791–1873)

JANE, b. 1821
Married William Edward Foster. Childless;
adopted William's orphans.

MATTHEW, b. 1822
Married Fanny Lucy Wightman. Children: Tom, Trevenen
(Budge), Richard, Lucy, Eleanor, Basil.
Died, 1888.

TOM, b. 1823
Married (1) Julia Sorell. Children: Mary (later Mrs
Humphry Ward), William, Theodore, Arthur,
Lucy, Frank, Julia (Judy), Ethel.
(2) Josephine Benison.
Died, 1900.

MARY, b. 1825
Married (1) Aldred Twining, (d. 1848)
(2) The Rev. J. S. Hiley (in 1858)

EDWARD, b. 1826
Children: Edward.
Died, 1878.

WILLIAM, b. 1828
Married Fanny Hodgson. Children: Edward,
Florence, Hugh, Frances.
Died, 1859.

SUSANNA, b. 1830
Married John W. Cropper. Children: Frances.

FRANCES, b. 1833
Unmarried.

WALTER, b. 1835
Children: Nelly.

Introduction

THE NINETEENTH CENTURY:
LIGHT AND THE LORD

People have ideas – but people are always more than the ideas they have. We all know this from our own friends and relations. 'She's a nice person but she's got some funny ideas' – as if they were a mild disease. 'He can't think of anything but Reds under the bed.' Or, 'Everything turns into a lecture on the Revolution.' Nevertheless everyone agrees that people must have some ideas to be human at all, even if these are only reflections of primitive folk-wisdom or the daily news pulp.

For this reason I have written this book about people, and their ideas as part of their lives; not about their ideas, with themselves appended as mere identification badges. It is about a family, chiefly about two of the sons of Dr Arnold, with the daughter of one of them, who became a novelist, as an interested observer towards the end of the century.

Thomas Arnold, who became headmaster of Rugby, was five years old when the nineteenth century began, and his son, another Thomas, died just before he was seventy-seven, in 1900; so between them they spanned a hundred years. It was their century, in many ways. They came of an East Anglian family of farmers and fishermen, who, by their intellectual ability, launched themselves into the middle class, once mainly composed of traders and manufacturers, but spreading during the nineteenth century into the professions, including the rapidly increasing forms of civil service. Here they mixed with the less well-off members of the gentry, who nowadays are generally included in the middle class, but certainly did not so include themselves during the first part of the nineteenth century, perhaps not for the whole of it. Of old it was 'upper classes' – descendants of arms-bearers, whether rich or poor – and 'lower classes'; though we all know that in any age 'money talks' so that there was a continual process of infiltration going on.

The Arnolds were typical of the new middle class, which itself was the typical product of the period and at the same time the chief moulder of the Victorian England we remember. They had no inherited wealth, no lands – since they had ceased to be farmers in the generation before the elder Thomas. They had to make their living and they made it by means of their intelligence. Thomas Arnold was a clever boy who was sent to Oxford; he made his own career as a schoolmaster and his sons too went to Oxford, but also had to make their own careers. Money was always a problem but they never set out simply to get money. They were all dedicated to ideas, to learning, to public service, to the community – their own nation and the future of humanity. But all of them thought out what they were doing and why, questioned their own assumptions and those of others. The lives of none of them were lived by inherited routine. These were just the kind of men who made the expanding England of their day.

In nothing were they more typical of their age and class than in the searching of heart and mind they went through, on the great questions of religion. In reading nineteenth century memoirs it is surprising how often we find, in the same family, a variety of religious belief or lack of it; nearly every educated family had its dissenter, its freethinker, its Roman Catholic, as well as its members, more or less committed, of the established Church of England. When I first thought of this book it was to be a study of several such families – one could take the Froudes, the Gladstones, the Pattisons, the Newmans, and many others. But people need elbow room if they are to show themselves as they really were, and in the end the Arnolds have more than filled the space required for one book. And as well as being representative of their own era they seem to me to have more to contribute to our own than most of the others. The influence of Dr Arnold, and in another way of Matthew Arnold, has been very great and the effects continue. The younger Thomas is little known, yet he brings into the picture the figure of John Henry Newman, whose life and work interpenetrated his own at so many points; and through Tom's descendants the Arnold strain continues to influence the intellectual life of our time – for instance, through his grandsons, Sir Julian Huxley and Aldous Huxley.

Dr Thomas Arnold of Rugby was a liberal of the Church of England whose strong moral influence led so many of his pupils into lives of dedicated public service. His son Matthew, the poet and critic, took his own original line with regard to the religious problems and doubts of the time. The younger Thomas, becoming a Catholic in the fifties, slid out of the organization during the polemic sixties, but returned to the fold for the later part of his life. His daughter Mary, Mrs Humphry Ward, published in 1888 a novel, *Robert Elsmere*, about a clergyman losing his faith in traditional Christianity, which became a best-seller, talked of everywhere and reviewed by Gladstone in the magazine *The Nineteenth Century*.

Was not the nineteenth the first century in which a serious popular magazine could call itself just that? It was the period during which people acquired the general idea of development: of biological evolution and of historical process, and acquired it through a mental revolution which necessitated a complete re-thinking of ideas on the nature of the universe, of humanity, and of God – if there was such a being. Doubt of God had, of course, appeared much earlier, but even during the French Revolution most people agreed with Robespierre at least in his conviction that there was a 'Supreme Being'. In the reaction that followed the Revolution there was a general revival of the idea of Christianity *as a religion*, seen as the shaping genius of civilization – which then meant European civilization. But this was something different from the almost unconscious acceptance of Christianity *as the truth about life* which prevailed, except for the fashion of Deism, well into the eighteenth century.

In the course of the nineteenth century everything came into question, and among a much wider group of people than before. Although this began to happen in certain circles in the early decades it was not till the late forties that religious doubt really assailed the younger generation, and even then, so much was their interest taken up with revolution, political and social, that it was only in the second half of the century that intellectual scepticism, or agnosticism, became common in England among the intelligent of the middle and upper classes. (The 'practical atheism' of the urban working class is a different, though equally important, matter.)

This is why the controversies of the thirties, on the Church, which seemed out of date in the late forties and fifties, could suddenly, through the medium of Newman's *Apologia*, find a large new public in the sixties and seventies. 'On what authority do you ministers preach to the people?' had been the demand of the Tracts. In the sixties and after, this was seen as the first form of the question that teased the later generations: 'On what authority do you believe that Christianity is true?' Newman's penetrating mind had always seen this second, more radical, question behind the other, which was the reason why his writings were read by many who had no intention of becoming Roman Catholics.

Darwin's *Origin of Species* appeared in 1859 and T. H. Huxley became his prophet, and the prophet of scientific agnosticism. In 1860 there was published a book of essays on religious topics, including the new Biblical criticism, by various learned members of the Church of England: *Essays and Reviews*, the first of many such controversial collections. The reaction to this was so excited that legal proceedings were instituted against some of the authors, and these, with the verdicts of one court reversed by another, went far to show how muddled was the supposed authority behind established orthodoxy. People thought they knew what religious authority was till they appealed to it and found it crumbling under their hands. The organs of the State failed to determine the standards of truth for the national Church. 'Hell was dismissed with costs,' was the *bon mot* which aptly summed up this attempt.

It was chiefly historical criticism of the Bible which destroyed the old simplicities of belief, perhaps more than the scientific criticism of the received ideas of creation. If the world was not created in six days with every species perfect and separate, the Old Testament authors were not relaying the direct truth from God when they said it was. But when the New Testament writers spoke of the miracles of Jesus and of his resurrection, could they be trusted any more than other writers of their day, who also told histories full of miraculous happenings which no one now believed? But if God was not talking through the mouths of the evangelists, what became of the unique revelation in Jesus Christ? And, looking at this from another angle, if the Bible was not a true account either of creation or of salvation, what authority was there for believing in God at all?

I have put these questions in simple form because by the second half of the nineteenth century they pressed upon so many people, not merely the intellectual. Matthew Arnold was one of the few in his day who did not think the truth of Christianity depended on the literal acceptance either of miracles or, as he put it, of metaphysics. He saw, what is quite true, that the central *experience* of Christianity is a certain way of living, and that people can believe the most anthropomorphic notions about God while living to the full the life of self-sacrificing love which Jesus inaugurated. Whether he was right in concluding that it simply did not matter what intellectual (theological) explanation was given so long as this moral and spiritual life was lived, is another matter. Christians of the tradition will suspect that it cannot be lived without the participation of the mind, in the sense that believing *in* Christ entails believing something *about* him, and that it must make a difference to conduct what this something is.

However that may be, Matthew Arnold's way of 'standing aloof from revelation' as Newman put it politely in a letter to him, is certainly of interest as a halfway house between belief and disbelief, and is in some ways akin to modern forms of 'secular Christianity'. What he had to say about the literary forms of the Bible and its moral and poetic, rather than scientific, truth, was an insight which has had a great and continuing development in our own century, as one of the bases of modern Biblical scholarship.

Dr Arnold was a liberal within an unbroken Christian tradition: his son Thomas, growing up in the forties, had to lose his faith before he could find it, and is typical of many in later generations who have had to *discover* the Church as the community of Christ, the witness to him, as the eternal become the historical. Tom was a liberal Catholic in the sense of accepting the authority of the whole Church, while learning the hard way to distinguish this from the mere authoritarianism sometimes displayed by its leaders – never more so than in his day, so that the organization played its part negatively in his temporary lapse out of communion.

His daughter Mary started from further outside the tradition than he had done, though her agnosticism was to become gradually more like the non-supernatural faith of her uncle Matthew. It was hard for any Arnold to take negative views. They were all positive by nature, full of energy, mental and physical, and this is what constitutes much of their charm, for I think them an attractive family. It is the vitality that counts, the exuberance, the strong will and the good humour. People are apt to think of the Victorians as gloomy and certainly their photographs reveal a stern race, but then having one's photograph taken was a serious business. The Arnolds might be obstinate, might be pugnacious, but they were not gloomy. This makes for great refreshment in reading their books and letters now, when even the apostles of freedom and love seem to feel an obligation to be savage and surly.

The shifts of thought on religion in our own century have often only repeated, in different circumstances, those of the nineteenth – we are not as modern as we think we are. The only real change seems to lie in a vague feeling that religion does not matter all that much anyway. But when a crisis occurs, in society or in individual lives, people discover that it does matter to them very much whether life has a meaning or not.

Happy the man who can say, in the psalmist's words that lie in the open book which is the emblem of the university of Oxford:

DOMINUS ILLUMINATIO MEA: the Lord is my light.

I

Dr Arnold of Rugby

I

Thomas Arnold was the seventh and youngest child of William Arnold and Martha Delafield and he was born on 13th June 1795 at Cowes in the Isle of Wight, where his father was then Collector of Customs and Postmaster. The family came from Lowestoft but William's father had gone into the Excise and after a period in the General Post Office, William did the same. The Delafields came from Aylesbury, where Martha and William had played together as children; they were married, after a long engagement, in April 1779. Martha was well on in her forties when Thomas was born and William over fifty.

Soon after the arrival of the new baby the family moved to East Cowes, then less fashionable but nearer to William's work, and built a new house known as Slatwoods, never forgotten, though Thomas Arnold left it when he was only a boy. The Arnolds were always devoted to home places.

Young Thomas began early to take notice of the world about him. From the garden of the house he could watch the shipping, and his father often took him to the harbour, teaching him to identify the different ships and the flags of all the nations. The little boy made a catalogue of ships of the Royal Navy with their registration numbers. England was at war with revolutionary France, so there was plenty to see. His father taught him history by means of pictures of famous people and gave him prizes of history books and a set of geographical cards of the world.

But quite suddenly, in March 1801, William Arnold collapsed with severe pains in his chest and died almost at once. Only a little over forty years later his son Thomas was to die in the very same way.

Martha Arnold, left suddenly to manage alone, was given the job of Postmistress in place of her husband, and with two daughters running the farm contrived to stay on at Slatwoods; her daughter Patty married John Ward, William Arnold's deputy and successor as Collector of Customs. The eldest son William, who had turned out rather wild, had been sent off to the Customs in St Pierre, Martinique; the second, Matthew, did well enough at Warminster Grammar School to go on to Oxford. In September 1803, when he was only eight, Thomas was sent to the same school.

The first Viscount Weymouth had built it in 1707, 'to the Glory of God and the Advancement of Religion and Learning'. In spite of his tender age Thomas was full of confidence, boasting that instead of starting at the bottom of the school, 'I am got into Delectus so that all the grammar boys are below me'. He played cricket and fives, bathed in the river and raised radishes and cress in his garden. He also learned dancing and enjoyed it.

The second master, a clergyman called James Townsend Lawes, was a friend of the family who had stayed at Slatwoods, and he took the boy home to tea. 'I stuffed as full as I could hold with cake tea and plumb pudding,' he wrote home, in Tom Brown-ish style.

But the little Warminster school was not really good enough for this exceptional boy and when he was twelve, in 1807, he was sent to Winchester. Both the masters at Warminster were Wykehamists and explained to Mrs Arnold that if her son could get elected as a scholar the fees would be very little more. Actually Thomas had to enter as a Commoner but transferred to College at the beginning of his second half. (The school year was then divided into two unequal 'halves' – the short from autumn till Christmas, the long from January till about midsummer.) Scholars and Commoners lodged separately, though they worked together. The school day was long, beginning at 5.30 a.m with chapel at 6 and then hours of work on an empty stomach and not much to fill it with when the meal times did come round.

If the boys were treated rough by the schoolmasters, they treated each other even worse. New boys had their hands burned, their heads hit with wooden platters; they were tossed in blankets or roasted, as in the famous scene in *Tom Brown's Schooldays*.

Arnold suffered another form of attack which appears often in school stories of the nineteenth century: when he knelt to say his prayers at night he received a volley of boots from the other boys.

Arnold's love of intellectual work earned him some suspicion from his schoolmates, but he was not unpopular, made some life-long friends, boated and swam and went for long walks which sometimes ended with cherry brandy at an inn. He took zestful part in midnight dormitory battles, produced Saturday plays on a stage made of chests and even as a prefect was caught playing a forbidden game of cards for money. But he found disgusting the wild behaviour of some of the boys who, on one occasion, not only cut down some trees but threatened with a bayonet a soldier's wife who tried to stop them.

Thomas Arnold was not yet sixteen when he left Winchester for Oxford, in 1811, the year that Shelley was sent down for atheism. Failing to get into New College, Thomas became a scholar of Corpus Christi College, where his brother Matthew had been before him. With his usual exuberance he threw him-self into social life, and the fun of furnishing his rooms, so that he was soon obliged to write home for more money. But he con-tinued to work hard; it was a small college and the standard was high. In those days only Classics and Mathematics were studied for a degree.

Among those who were up with him and became friends were John Keble, later a founding father of the movement Arnold so much disliked, and John Taylor Coleridge, nephew of the poet, who became a judge. Coleridge afterwards remembered young Arnold's pugnacity, his attacks on the Tory opinions he found current in the Common Room – he was full of radical ideas and was known as a Jacobin. But as he did not resent opposition he was liked in spite of his argumentativeness. He always had tre-mendous energy, physical and mental, jumping hedges and ditches in his long walks, learning French and reading Wordsworth as well as the necessary classics. In 1814, before he was nineteen, he had gained first-class honours, and in celebration went off on a tour of the Wye valley with his friend Trevenen Penrose.

They returned to Oxford just as the victory celebrations over the defeat of Napoleon spilled from London to Oxford, where on 14th June the Prince Regent and the Duke of York entertained the Tsar of Russia, the King of Prussia and General Blücher. They were met by the Chancellor and heads of Houses in academic dress and that evening there was a dinner at the Radcliffe Library where Blücher got very drunk. Next day the Sheldonian Theatre was packed, ladies in the front rows wearing court dress with feathers, and squeezed in among the crowd young Thomas Arnold who wrote home: 'for ten minutes there was nothing heard but one continued roar of applause: caps waving in the air, cheering and clapping.' Degrees and diplomas were presented to the foreign rulers and *in absentia* to the Duke of Wellington; and 'at that glorious name' the enthusiasm was redoubled.

Meanwhile, Slatwoods had had to be given up, in 1812, so that Susannah Arnold, who had been stricken, at twenty-five, with paralysis, could follow a treatment advised by a London specialist. Her mother and sisters moved to Kensington, where Thomas Arnold spent his vacations while he was at Oxford. He went about with his sisters Lydia and Frances, and a cousin, Joe Delafield, saw *The Beggars' Opera*, the Covent Garden pantomime and Edmund Keane as Othello at Drury Lane.

In August 1814 Lydia, rather surprisingly, married the Earl of Cavan; two years later Frances married Arnold's friend John Buckland – an event which was to influence his life rather more, for Buckland opened a small private school at Hampton on the Thames. Mrs Arnold, the invalid Susannah and aunt Susan Delafield all removed to a cottage near the school. In 1815 Thomas had been elected to a fellowship at Oriel College, owing it mostly to the advocacy of Richard Whately, one of the outstanding figures then at Oxford, a logician, an eccentric and a liberal type of churchman who was later to be Archbishop of Dublin. And the same year Arnold won the Chancellor's Latin Essay prize.

Waterloo was hardly won before Thomas Arnold rushed off to tour the battlefields, visit Paris and sail down the Rhine from Mainz to Cologne. After that he went abroad almost every year, in 1816 travelling along the Meuse, in 1817 on the Moselle from Trèves to Coblentz. In 1818 he visited the Lake District and met Wordsworth for the first time, sowing the seeds of a long friendship with the poet and a love affair with the country which was to flower in the most beloved of all Arnold homes, Fox How in Ambleside.

That same year, on 20th December, Thomas Arnold was ordained a deacon of the Church of England in Oxford Cathedral, after some weeks of painful worry as to whether he could subscribe to the Thirty-nine Articles. He had always wanted to be a clergyman and yet now his conscience prevented him from proceeding to priest's orders, for although his Oriel friends had persuaded him out of his scruples they afterwards returned and he decided he must find other work.

This was how he came to take up schoolmastering, almost accidentally. His brother-in-law John Buckland suggested he should join him; but the house at Hampton was too small and they spent some fruitless weeks in the summer of 1819 looking for two houses suitably situated. They found them at last at Laleham, near Staines, on the Thames, and Arnold brought his mother, aunt Delafield and sister Susannah to live with him.

But not for long. For at the time of his move to Laleham Thomas Arnold had become engaged to Mary Penrose, whom he had met for the first time in the New Year of 1819; she was the sister of his friend of Winchester and Oxford days, Trevenen Penrose. Mary, born on 21st August 1791, was four years older than Thomas Arnold, though she had four sisters older than herself. Her father was a clergyman of a clerical west-country family and her early childhood had been spent in Cornwall, at Carwythenack, or Crannick, as it was called. In 1801, however, the year Arnold's father died, the family migrated to Fledborough in the flat country near Nottingham. They were a happy family, acting plays and reciting poems from their earliest years, and Mary was an intelligent clear-minded young woman, more calm and stable than Arnold. He could not have chosen better, for Mary was to be a real partner in his life, whom he consulted on everything, and who shared his interests and ideals without being so easily carried away by enthusiasm.

As usual, once he had made up his mind, Arnold could not bear to wait. He had to borrow £1000 to start with, on an interest of 5%, without much prospect of ever being out of debt. But he went up to Fledborough to propose to Mary in August 1819 and married her in the same month the next year: 11th August 1820.

In the May of that year his brother Matthew, who had been for some time an army chaplain, was tragically drowned sailing near Gosport. As William, the eldest, had already died out in the West Indies, Thomas was now the only remaining son. The house next door to the Bucklands was rented for his mother, aunt and invalid sister, and Thomas cheerfully left them to achieve their own removal, and to see to the redecoration of his own house, while he went north to spend a holiday month with his betrothed. In spite of this casual treatment Mrs Arnold liked Mary, and once he was married, Thomas became a more dutiful son, visiting his mother every day while they all lived at Laleham.

He certainly knew what was best for him, for it was not till after his marriage, that he really put his heart into the school; till now he had taken as much interest in parish work, though he was still only a deacon – the Thirty-nine Articles would not disappear. But now he flung himself heart and soul into education, full of his own ideas, sure he knew what was best for boys, turning the school into an extension of his family, for he boated with his pupils, bathed with them, played cricket and took them on long walks, jumping the hedges as of old.

Thomas Arnold was twenty-five in 1820, the year of his marriage and he was to spend eight years at Laleham; Mary was twenty-nine and in those years she bore seven children, of whom six lived. Three more were to be born after the move to Rugby. The first child was a girl, Jane, born in 1821; the second was Matthew. In December 1822 Mary was thrown from her pony on to the frozen ground and nine days later, on Christmas Eve, she bore her first son.

Matt's inauspicious arrival was the first of many difficulties of his childhood, the worst of which was a curving of the legs which the doctors insisted could only be cured by putting him in irons. He was not yet two when this was done and he struggled through fifteen months in them and then fell off the sofa in Arnold's study and cut his head open on the foot of a table. The wound took so long to heal that there were some fears of a serious injury. But Matt survived this, and the next summer, when he was three and a half, his parents, in defiance of the doctors, took off the leg irons. No ill effects occurred, though the poor little boy was clumsy and slow for months afterwards. It was probably from this episode that Matt earned his nickname of 'Crab'. As in most large families the children soon acquired nicknames. Jane was 'K', Matt was 'Crab'. Tom, born only eleven months after his brother, was 'Prawn'.

After Tom came another girl, who lived only a few days; however, in March 1825 a daughter was born who survived, the sturdy Mary. Edward Penrose was born in 1826 and William Delafield in the spring of 1828. Mary's nickname was 'Bacco' and the little boys were 'Didu' and 'Widu'.

Jane, Matt and Tom, who developed a stammer when he began to talk, played together and were close allies. Matt always remembered Laleham with deep affection; it was home to him, more than Rugby perhaps ever was, although he was only six when the move took place. But then he went back to school there with his uncle John Buckland, which reinforced his early memories. And Tom went too. Tom did everything with Matt. They were very different in temperament but always fond of each other.

Arnold had pronounced Matt bad-tempered, as a baby. Bad-tempered later he certainly was not, but he was always a great one for doing as he pleased, puzzling his good serious mother by his carelessness, his tricks and whims. Matt had thick black hair and light blue eyes, a full-lipped mouth; he was quick and imaginative but lazy in the way creative people sometimes are lazy, unable to work until their interest is wholly engaged.

Tom was gentle and dreamy; dark-haired and dark-eyed, Matt later saw in him Cornish traits. He was shy, but with strong feelings and deep. At work he was more persevering than Matt; he was impulsive, but not so aggressive.

In spite of his exacting standards Arnold was not a stern or frightening father; proof of this lies in his sons' respect and affection which long outlasted his early death – they were all of them proud of him, and liked to think in later life that they would have earned his approval, even Tom, who in joining the Catholic Church seemed to have gone furthest from the parental line.

Arnold's school was small but in it he was completely free to follow his own ideals; he refused a position at Winchester because of this. Besides, it left him time to write; it was at Laleham that he began work on Roman history, first as articles for the *Encyclopaedia Metropolitana* (a useful starting ground of the day: Newman too began writing with articles for it) which were later made into a book. In 1821 he started on what was to prove a ten-year task: the *Lexicon of Thucydides*. He taught himself enough German to read the scholars writing in that language; at that period, in almost every field, German scholars were in the forefront.

Arnold continued his travels abroad, keeping journals from which extracts were afterwards published. He travelled in the energetic enthusiastic way in which he did everything, talking to as many people as possible, finding out their way of life and opinions and comparing them with the English. In 1825, for instance, he thought the peasants in Italy better off than those in England, and though in Italy Catholicism looked like 'old Heathenism', in France he thought the Catholics 'Christian and daily becoming more so'. He was much less prejudiced than most English travellers of the day about religion, and appreciated the festivals and processions and wayside Calvaries of Catholic countries.

He also took shorter holidays in England, sometimes with Mary, though she was so often pregnant she had to stay at home with her mother-in-law at Laleham more often than not. When he was at home Arnold accompanied her every day for a walk, she on a quiet pony and he striding along beside, occasionally leaping up banks or into ditches after flowers, in which he took a keen interest, both botanical and poetic. Mary's brother, Trevenen Penrose, was often Arnold's companion on his travels, as of old. And he kept up with the friends who remained at Oxford. John Keble became Matthew's godfather, but Edward Hawkins, Provost of Oriel, and Richard Whately were his closest Oxford friends. He shared many of their liberal views – with Keble he shared only his Christian piety and love of poetry; he was a great admirer of Keble's hymns – *The Christian Year* came out in 1827.

It was Hawkins and Whately who pressed Arnold to stand for the headmastership of Rugby; he had at first determined to retain his freedom at Laleham. Hawkins recommended him so strongly to the trustees that he was chosen out of fifty candidates, in December 1827, almost to his surprise. In the January following they paid a brief visit to Rugby, Mary too, though she was in an advanced state of pregnancy and had to stay a few days with the Whatelys on the way home for fear her fatigue would bring on a premature birth. The child to be born, on 7th April 1828, was William, the son who went to India.

The Trustees, contrary to Arnold's expectation, did not insist that he should be in priest's orders, but as he intended to found all his educational policy on his Christian faith, he himself decided that he would like to be able to administer the sacrament in the school chapel. He visited Dr Howley, then Bishop of London, who reassured him that his views on certain of the Articles did not render him ineligible, and was ordained priest by him in June. He took his BD in Oxford, disputing with Newman (who became Vicar of the university church of St Mary the Virgin, this year, at the age of twenty-seven). Arnold was now thirty-three. Later in the year he was made Doctor of Divinity. Mary thought it strange, almost ridiculous, to call him 'Doctor'. But soon he was to be 'the Doctor' to a whole generation of boys.

It is typical of Arnold, though not common at the time, that he should have written to a friend in March, 'Both Mary and myself, I think, are well inclined to commence our work.' *Our* work, he said, regarding her as a partner, as indeed she was, becoming the ideal headmaster's wife to a succession of boys invited to her drawing room where they could feel as if they were at home.

The family migration took place in August; the household goods were sent by the Grand Junction Canal and they left themselves on the 5th, staying the night in Oxford. The next day was heavy and rainy, necessitating 'a rare stuffing' of children inside the coach, as their father cheerfully recorded. They had all been sad to leave Laleham, where they had been so happy, little Jane crying dismally, but now they settled into the splendid house, as Arnold called School House at Rugby, with prayers for the future offered in his usual hearty manner by the new headmaster.

2

At Laleham Arnold had about twelve pupils; at Rugby he had a hundred – and the fact that these were so few, for a public school, was one reason why the trustees had appointed someone recommended as an energetic man who would put the place on its feet. The retiring headmaster, Dr Wooll, had been an autocrat who ruled by force and ignored what did not come to his notice. He had expelled boys for rape, but took no steps to protect them from each other. Boys were severely punished if caught in any misdemeanour, but little attempt was made to prevent the same thing happening again. Some of the Sixth Form spent as much as £100 a year on wine – now and again someone was expelled for drunkenness. Farmers complained of poaching and stealing but nothing was done to make the boys aware of the rights of others.

There was at that time a good deal of talk about the evils of public schools, the antiquated forms of teaching, the lack of moral guidance and the consequent horrors of laissez-faire; as a result, the more responsible parents had their boys educated at home or at small schools like Arnold's own at Laleham, or the one at Ealing which Newman and his brothers attended. The trustees wanted Rugby improved so that numbers would increase and at first they were somewhat startled by Arnold's methods, especially his frequent use of expulsion.

It was a considered policy. There were two types of boy whose presence he deplored and he invented two types of expulsion to deal with them. The hardened criminal who would only corrupt others was publicly expelled in disgrace. But the intellectually backward, physically overgrown boy, who had committed no serious offence, he would quietly 'superannuate', writing to the parents to explain that he thought it useless to keep the boy any longer at school, but suggesting methods of continuing his education. Some of these superannuated boys Arnold even invited to his home in the holidays, so he did not consider them in any sense disgraced. George Hughes, elder brother of the author of *Tom Brown's Schooldays*, was one of them.

Arnold's methods were drastic but effective. The first thing he did was to get the trustees to increase the fees; with the proceeds he raised the salaries of the assistant masters and by 1829 was able to ask them, in consequence, to give up the curacies they held in the district and concentrate on teaching. He treated his masters as equals and had started at once a system of weekly staff councils, which was a complete innovation. From the beginning Arnold treated the school as a community and this was the secret of his success.

There was already a system of praepositors; Arnold made every member of the Sixth a praepositor but gave them duties as well as privileges and began the practice of inviting four to dinner each week. These were the youths who had been getting drunk the year before at great expense; Arnold treated them as responsible young gentlemen and most of them responded. Certainly the next batch did. And local inns were put out of bounds.

Again, there had been an overflow of boys living in lodgings in the town. Arnold started the house system by asking the chaplain, Anstey, to take boys into his own new house. When Anstey retired in 1831, Arnold asked for the post, waiving the fee of £60 a year. The trustees not only gave it to him but insisted on his accepting the fee – which he used to improve the school library. He had not at first preached often but now he preached almost every Sunday at the afternoon service – short talks of from fifteen to twenty minutes, written on the same day, on topical subjects, and he knew how to hold the interest of the boys. Arnold was unmusical (Matthew inherited his tone-deafness) and to him all psalm-tunes sounded the same; his voice was metallic and harsh, nor did he go in for oratorical eloquence; but he meant what he said and said it with passion. The boys were impressed; his words had a powerful effect.

That same year, 1831, in an effort to make himself more available to others besides Sixth Formers, Arnold had an outside stair constructed to his study and a pole put up, where he flew a flag when he was at home to any boy who cared to come. At first he had to invite them, but those who went spread the word that the new headmaster was not as stern as he looked and presently anyone felt free to call at such times.

Arnold could look and sound severe, when angry he went 'ashy pale', as Arthur Stanley noticed, and his temper was so irritable that he often sent boys who had annoyed him out of the room, to give himself time to calm down. But basically he was a just man, and actively concerned for the welfare of all the boys, taking an interest in each as an individual. With the youngest he was even paternal, taking them on his knee and teaching them by pictures as his father had done to him. This was exceptional; generally he taught only the Sixth Form, though he presently introduced tests and viva voce examinations all through the school, which enabled him to write half-yearly reports on progress to the parents.

In the bad old days boys slept five or more in a bed and their fathers had to pay extra if they wanted single beds. Arnold insisted on separate beds for all boys without any charge. And no one, not even a master, not even himself, was to enter a boy's study without knocking. His principle was to trust the boys and for the most part they responded. 'It is a shame to tell Arnold a lie,' they said, 'for he always believes you.' This was in contrast to the earlier tradition when it was considered all right to lie to a master since he was a boy's natural enemy. But after one crisis Arnold said to the assembled school, 'If I am to be here as a gaoler I will resign my office at once.'

As for punishment, he disliked the old custom of flogging for everything. For most offences impositions were set and he introduced rules for what should merit a beating (administered by the praepositors) and ordained that normally no more than three strokes should be given; six was the maximum. As early as 1829 he told a friend that birchings had been reduced to only seven in the last half-year. Right at the start of his Rugby career, in September 1828, he wrote, 'I believe that boys may be governed a great deal by gentle methods and kindness, and appealing to their better feelings, if you show you are not afraid of them; I have seen great boys, six feet high, shed tears when I have sent for them up to my room and spoken to them quietly, in private, for not knowing their lessons; and I have found that this treatment produced its effects afterwards, in making them do better. But of course deeds must second words when needful, or words will soon be laughed at.'

The truth was that Arnold ruled by his powerful personality, and by the time a boy reached the Sixth, he was usually already under the spell, or sufficiently in awe of 'the Doctor' to wish for approbation rather than risk defiance. Many, of course, became his devoted disciples for life. One of these, Arthur Stanley, afterwards his biographer, came to the school the year after Arnold's appointment. He was the second son of the Reverend Edward Stanley, brother of the Sir John who was to become Lord Stanley of Alderley in 1839. Arthur was a small, fair, delicate and sensitive child but mentally tougher than he looked; he was not only clever but persevering and sensible, so that, although he was hopeless at games, he suffered very little bullying and became as popular in the school as he was in later years as Dean of Westminster. Arthur's father was Rector of the family living at Alderley till he became Bishop of Norwich, and it was at Alderley that Arthur was born, in December 1813. He was just thirteen when his father took him to Rugby on the last day of January 1829.

He wrote to his sister Mary, three years his senior, a few days later, describing his arrival. 'Papa and I then walked to Dr Arnold's and presently Mrs Arnold came in – she was very nice indeed. At last came the Doctor himself; but I certainly should not have taken him for a Doctor. He was very pleasant and did not look old. When Papa asked him whether I should be examined, he said that if I would walk into the next room, he would do it himself; so of course in I went with him, with a feeling like that when I am going to have a tooth drawn. So he took down a Homer, and I read about half a dozen lines, and the same with Virgil; he then asked a little about my Latin verses, and set me down without more ado in the great book as placed in the Fourth Form.'

Stanley soon worked his way through the Fourth Form and by the end of the half was promoted to the Fifth, where he was exempt from fagging for the older boys. The next year Arnold made the Fifth Form praepositors in their own houses, so Stanley was able to boast that in one year he had moved from fagging for others to having boys fag for him. In 1830 he was already in the Sixth and spent the next four years under Arnold's direct guidance – though even before that he had been examined by him. 'Oh! How particular he is; but at the same time so mild and pleasant,' he had told Mary.

With his Sixth Form round him, Arnold would sit on a wooden kitchen chair, which the boys wondered at, because it seemed 'undignified'. He was always ready to confess his own ignorance and admit mistakes, which made the boys respect him; and he held that a man had no business to teach unless he himself were learning all the time.

Although in his famous list of educational aims Arnold put religious and moral principles first, gentlemanly conduct second, and intellectual ability only third, in practice he reformed this side of the school as much as the others. For generations at public schools Latin and Greek had been taught with little reference to history or modern literature; some Mathematics was thrown in as well. Arnold taught the classics in a live way, using ancient history to illuminate modern politics; he increased the Mathematics side and added French. He regarded French as very important and it was thus that he got modern history into the curriculum. History was Arnold's great interest; his letters are full of the reading he was doing for his Roman History and of comments on Guizot and the history of France. 'Never read history without a map at your side,' was a maxim of his – and so geography found its way in too. In 1835 he succeeded in getting a Frenchman appointed to teach French, and German lessons were added, since the chief scholars of the day wrote in German.

Thus for a school in the eighteen-thirties the curriculum was thoroughly modernized; but Arnold did not expect a boy to excel in every subject. He instituted many prizes, even giving consolation prizes for effort, which he paid for out of his own pocket. If anyone won a university scholarship he would give a half holiday. Thus the prestige of intellectual work rose and when

Stanley won the first scholarship to Balliol in 1834 the whole school cheered him to the echo. He was so loaded with prizes that he had to get two fags to carry them back to his House.

Other boys from Rugby were already at Oxford but Stanley was the first to gain the coveted Balliol Scholarship. Balliol had by then begun to overtake Oriel, which never really recovered from its internal battle in 1830, when the Provost, Hawkins, had prevented Newman from carrying out his reform of the tutorship by removing his pupils. Newman's method was that personal tuition which became such a feature of the university and for which, at Balliol, Benjamin Jowett was famed.

Arthur Hugh Clough, who was to be such a friend of Arnold's two eldest sons, also went to Rugby in 1829, in the autumn of that year when he was between ten and eleven, for he was born on New Year's Day, 1819. Three years younger than Arthur Stanley, he was another quiet, reserved boy, but dark, with almost black hair waving over his large forehead and a small mouth and chin. Because his parents were for much of the time in America, where his father was trying to run a business, without much success, Arthur Clough spent his holidays with Welsh cousins or, later, with the Arnolds at Fox How. As a boy he was deeply devoted to Arnold, and became over-conscientious in following out his ideals. Arnold demanded high standards of work and conduct and communicated his own enthusiasm and reforming energy. But he was aware of the dangers of overwork and overstrain and often invited Sixth Formers to Fox How expressly so that they could relax, ramble in the Westmorland country, fish and shoot with himself and his sons.

Even at Laleham Arnold had told his friends that he himself needed 'absolute play, like a boy' for relaxation, and in 1829 he wrote to his friend Cornish, 'My spirits in themselves are a great blessing, for without them, the work would weigh me down, whereas now I seem to throw it off like the fleas from a dog's back when he shakes himself.'

So he expected others to be able to relax similarly. But some people are born without the capacity and Clough seems to have been one. Because his family were so far away he lived too much for the school and his friends were mostly older than himself. He followed Stanley in carrying off prize after prize till, as Arnold said, he had won everything Rugby could offer, and ended with the Balliol Scholarship in the autumn of 1836. He stayed on at school till the end of the following summer and went up to Oxford in the autumn of 1837, at eighteen already emotionally worn out by the intensity of his conscientious dedication to the Rugby community.

Stanley and Clough were outstanding boys of unusual quality but there were many others who went on to Oxford and Cambridge during the thirties, intellectually and morally more developed than most of their contemporaries from unreformed schools, to carry off prizes and fellowships, and to go on to become dons and deans, missionaries, lawyers, administrators and, most significant of all, schoolmasters in England and overseas, carrying Arnold's ideals to the colonies of the expanding Victorian empire. The combination of scholarship and 'manliness' – that quality then so much admired – impressed the older generation and as the young men were mostly hero-worshippers of 'the Doctor' Arnold's fame spread and still more boys were sent to the school. The numbers jumped up and up, to three hundred and beyond, and the Rugby Trustees, for a long time suspicious of Arnold's methods, and still more of his radical views, which he freely expressed all through the thirties, came to the point where they could make public their confidence in their unusual, lively, but highly successful headmaster.

Arnold made Rugby by his personality, but he did it by taking immense trouble with the personalities of others.

Meanwhile, however, Arnold was not at all anxious to send his own sons to someone else's unreformed school. In 1831 he sent Matt, then not quite nine, to his brother-in-law Buckland, at Laleham – and Tom went too. John Buckland pronounced Matt backward; he did not do well and in 1833 came home again (with Tom) and they were taught by a private tutor, Herbert Hill, a cousin of the poet Southey. The parents were still worrying about Matt's legs and engaged a sergeant to come and drill him. A speech therapist, Mr Bull, came for a fortnight to try to cure Tom's stammer, in which he failed, for Tom was still worrying about it years later. Then Matt, Shelley-like, got burned with phosphorus fire and it was thought he might have to lose his arm – fortunately it survived, for the older Matt, keen fisherman that he was, would have been lost without it.

The younger children had their accidents too, Willy falling into the schoolroom fire and sustaining burns on his head and neck.

The school problem remained. 'I am a coward about schools,'

said Arnold, who knew too well what they could be like. However, at the end of August 1836 Matt and Tom were despatched to Winchester. They did not stay there long, for in 1837 Arnold finally decided his own school was best and both of them came back to School House, Rugby, where they stayed out the rest of their school career. Matt was fifteen at the end of that year and Tom fourteen.

By this time their holiday home, Fox How, was well established. After coming to Rugby Arnold continued his habit of travelling abroad; he did so both in 1829 and in 1830, the latter being the year of the birth of Susanna, the third daughter. Susannah the sister died in 1832 at Laleham. Old Mrs Arnold had died in 1829 and Susan Delafield, at the age of eighty, a few years later. The older generation were going – Mary's father also died in 1829 – and perhaps this made Arnold feel he would like to build a home for his retirement. They had already returned to Westmorland several times, visiting the Wordsworths; the site in Ambleside was recommended by the poet, who kept an eye on the building of Fox How. Arnold had bought twenty acres and the house was ready by the spring of 1834. Many are the references thereafter to this beloved place, in the letters of all the family.

Dorothy Wordsworth had always taken an interest in the Arnold children. 'Little Willy is such a funny thing,' she wrote. Mary was 'as queer as ever'. Matt and Tom did not appear to have grown on that occasion; Jane was as sweet and gentle as ever and 'Edward the same clever, wayward thing'.

In 1832 Mary Arnold had lost a baby, which had lived only a few days, and had been near to death herself; nevertheless in 1833 she bore another daughter, Frances, known as Fan, the daughter who was to spend all her life at Fox How. In 1835 came the last child, a boy who was christened Walter; Mary was forty-four at his birth. There were now nine Arnold children and going off for the holidays was a major expedition.

They all adored the country home, the mountains, the streams. Arnold used to go shooting snipe with Matt; there was boating on Rydal water and bathing in summer; in winter it often froze hard as a rock. In January 1841 Arnold wrote to a friend, 'Four of my boys skate, Walter is trundled in his wheelbarrow, and my daughters and I slide, for I am afraid I am too old to learn to skate now.'

The children dammed the stream in the garden, acted plays and wrote *The Fox How Magazine*, which Jane illustrated with lively sketches – Mary falling on the ice, the boys, in top hats, knee deep in water, and so on. Verses were written by the children and rules by Papa, who called them 'the dogs'. The first rule was 'that all Dogs do strictly observe hours, that they be down to breakfast by ½ past 8 o'clock. . .' And there was to be no mistake about that, for Arnold woke them himself, boisterously pulling off the bedclothes and applying hair-brushes – a treatment they did not appear to resent, to judge by the cheerful description in the magazine verses. The Dogs' rules were mostly for safety – the younger children were not to go out alone in boats, and so on.

One of the plays was 'Beauty and the Beast' and Matt was Beast, 'with my cloak as his furry garment,' wrote his mother, 'and a boa to complete his equipment as tail.' Jane, she said, made a straightforward Lady Beauty, and 'Tom was so good as the Papa, at once business like and pathetic.' The parts of the hard-hearted sisters were taken by 'Mary and Co.'

Arnold wrote a memorandum to his brother-in-law Trevenen Penrose about the upbringing of his children in the event of his death. The document was not in fact discovered till thirteen years after his death when Matt, himself then a father, was surprised by his father's care for their education and character while they were still so young. In this memorandum Arnold said that he would rather they had an Evangelical foundation than nothing but that he did not hold with the Evangelicals' way of over-strictness, which tended to lead children into hypocrisy 'and then to desperate outbreak'. In moral and religious training his common sense was strong and is refreshing in an era when theory and practice were both heavily overloaded for the unfortunate children of the good.

3

Almost as soon as he came to Rugby, Arnold began to gain a national reputation as a trenchant writer on political and ecclesiastical affairs – at that time still closely enmeshed together. His friends were familiar with his bold hard-hitting style, but the educated public was not, and thought him more revolutionary than he was. He published, in 1829, a pamphlet entitled *The Christian Duty of Conceding Roman Catholic Claims*, which was sold out within a few weeks and caused great annoyance in clerical circles because in it he freely criticized the clergy's ignorance of history and their feebleness in politics. As he observed, in a letter to his invalid sister Susannah, the prophets of Israel denounced the rich and their oppression of the poor; why did not the clergy of England denounce the Game Laws for their savage penalties against the poor man's 'hunting'?

Oxford friends were 'pained' at his tone, which they had heard called arrogant; Arnold replied that he disliked paining his friends but did not consider it arrogant to say what he thought on a subject he had deeply considered – in this case, Christian tolerance of different opinions. Owing to his pugnacious manner of expressing himself, Arnold was always having to explain to Provost Hawkins, J. T. Coleridge and others, that slanging their opinions did not mean he was attacking *them*. He did not regard an opinion different from his own as a moral fault. And, he thought, dear Keble was inclined to do just that. Unorthodoxy was due to a bad conscience; doubts had a moral origin. In repudiating this attitude, Arnold, curiously enough, was on the same side as Newman, who, while emphasizing the necessity for a purified conscience, gave intellectual answers to intellectual questions.

In the summer of 1830 there was a revolution in France which put an end to the reactionary régime of Charles X (the last brother of Louis XVI). The king fled to England and after some days of renewed republicanism, France accepted the compromise rule of Louis Philippe, of the Orleans branch of the royal family, who became the constitutional King of the French, adopting once more the tricolor of the Revolution and saluting it, as the 'Citizen King'.

Arnold was as delighted with this revolution as his sons were later by that of 1848, when it was Louis Philippe's turn to flee across the Channel. 'It seems to me a most blessed revolution,' he wrote to his friend, George Cornish, on 24th August 1830, 'spotless beyond all example in history, and the most glorious instance of a royal rebellion against society, promptly and energetically repressed, that the world has yet seen. It magnificently vindicates the cause of knowledge and liberty, showing how humanizing to all classes of society are the spread of thought and information, and improved political institutions; and it lays the crimes of the last revolution just in the right place, the wicked aristocracy, that had so brutalized the people by its long iniquities, that they were like slaves broken loose when they first bestirred themselves.'

This romantic view of revolutions not only pained his friends but alarmed them; in November Arnold was explaining to Hawkins that he did not in the least want a revolution in England, but he did admire the recent one in France and was convinced that every English clergyman should not only think so but say so. Of course it was just this desire for political commitment from the clergy that pained those Oxford conservatives. Arnold ended this letter, 'There is not a man in England who is less a party man than I am, for in fact no party would own me.'

This was perfectly true, and continued to be so, for though many of Arnold's views were radical, the radical party could not do with his Christian fervour, any more than the Church-and-King Tories could do with his shouts for democracy and against oppressive laws. 'I cannot understand what is the good of a national Church if it be not to Christianize the nation,' Arnold wrote, 'and introduce the principles of Christianity into men's social and civil relations, and expose the wickedness of that spirit which maintains the Game Laws, and in agriculture and trade seems to think that there is no such sin as covetousness, and that if a man is not dishonest, he has nothing to do but to make all the profit of his capital that he can.'

These were the views which led him to start a weekly newspaper in the summer of 1831 – and it must be remembered that these were the years immediately preceding the famous Reform Bill, years of unrest, riot and fear. Arnold called his paper *The English-man's Register*, in imitation of Cobbett; he wanted it, he said, to be 'Cobbett-like in style – but Christian in spirit'. The venture lasted only a few weeks, running at a loss, and on 11th July 1831, he had to report to Provost Hawkins: 'The *Register* is now dead, to revive however in another shape; but I could not afford at once to pay all, and to write all . . .' The revival in another form was due to the editor of the *Sheffield Courant*, who had copied extracts from Arnold's articles on the labourers, and now offered to take articles direct. He was to publish thirteen, signed 'A' – and Arnold's friends became more pained than ever. Here was the man they had recommended to the Rugby trustees getting a name for himself as a radical agitator.

Arnold was attacked in the county newspapers (Tory in

principle) and the publicity was not good for the school, even though he always insisted that he did not force his opinions on the boys. Many Sixth Formers picked them up, all the same. The trustees were indeed suspicious at this time.

Arnold did not expect much from the Reform Bill (to extend the franchise down the social scale) but when it became law it did have some effect in quietening political unrest. Whereupon the Israelite prophet at Rugby immediately involved himself in the next big controversy of the thirties – the question of the Church. He wrote another pamphlet, on *The Principles of Church Reform*, published early in 1833. Now his Oxford friends were not merely pained, they were seriously 'overset', especially Keble, who, in this very year, was to preach the sermon on *National Apostasy* which Newman counted as the beginning of the Oxford Movement. Newman, back from a severe fever which had prostrated him in Sicily, and burning with the conviction that he had 'a work to do in England', was present at Keble's sermon in July, but it was the first *Tracts for the Times*, written and distributed by him, which were the real beginning of the battle. Arnold always called the Tractarians 'Newmanites'. He knew that Keble, saintly conservative that he was, could never be the leader of a movement.

Church Reform, as Arnold conceived it, was a very different thing from the Catholic reformation planned by Newman, Hurrell Froude, Keble, Edward Bouverie Pusey and their friends – not all Oxford men, but all young, with many lawyers among the laymen. Hawkins, their inveterate foe, all the same did not agree with Arnold's views, which were too liberal for him; he must have suggested that Arnold had rushed forward to express his opinions without sufficient consideration, for Arnold wrote him two letters, insisting that this was a subject he had been considering for years, and that he knew rather more about it than most people.

It annoyed Arnold that one proposal, made in passing, about the sharing of churches with Dissenters, should be picked on and remembered as the only suggestion he had made, and very widely laughed at. But it did express Arnold's conviction that except for the Unitarians (who did not believe in Christ's divinity), all Christians were already united in fundamentals and differed only in theological opinions which he thought of secondary importance. The omission of the Unitarians is interesting because it shows that Arnold did hold a criterion of orthodoxy; as usual

(34)

with him it was a Christological doctrine, but it was a doctrine none the less. However, after the carefully agreed statements of basic doctrine issued in recent years by the World Council of Churches, and after the experiments of shared churches, Arnold's attitude should find more understanding in our day than it did in his.

The new Catholics, or Apostolicals, as Froude christened them, certainly saw no future in that direction; Newman was one of those who laughed at the church-sharing idea, suggesting, in a letter to Froude, that Mohammedans and Jews could easily be accommodated too, on Fridays and Saturdays. He saw no point in getting under one roof people who disagreed violently over what they believed; he did not think it merely a matter of opinion, but of truth. There was the truth about Christ somewhere to be found; how and where? It was the search which eventually landed him in St Peter's net.

Arnold had added to his second book of published sermons an essay on the interpretation of the Old Testament. This was something much needed, as Arnold, in constant touch with young minds, knew well. But his method was highly individual, consisting largely of Arnoldian common sense, applied with more force than delicacy. Discussing the subject with Newman and Froude when they were in Rome, someone had instanced an interpretation as possible for a Christian to hold, because Arnold had defended it. Word came back to Rugby that Newman had laughed and said, 'But is Arnold a Christian?' When taxed with this, Newman could not remember it, but thought he might have said something like 'But Arnold must first show he is a Christian.' He meant 'show he is orthodox', but Arnold took it as a slur on his character and was very annoyed indeed. Letters were exchanged through a third party but no better understanding emerged and the whole quarrel began again over the question of admitting Dissenters to the university. Arnold's friend, Renn Dickson Hampden, a pluralist and a liberal theologian, was angry when Newman's friend, Henry Wilberforce, the son of the great Wilberforce, attacked him. Arnold sympathized with Hampden because he thought that the Church of England must become more comprehensive or the establishment could not fairly be maintained. He believed firmly in the royal supremacy for the interestingly Arnoldian reason that it meant that the Church was controlled by (Christian) society, and not by the clergy.

When Lord Melbourne appointed Hampden Regius Professor of Divinity in Oxford, he united every church party against him; there was an almighty row, in which the Apostolicals provided the intellectual ammunition in the form of attacks on Hampden's theological orthodoxy. Arnold was so angry that he wrote an article for the *Edinburgh Review* (unsigned, according to custom), headed *The Oxford Malignants*, which appeard in April 1836. In his hardest-hitting style he let fly against the moral wickedness of the revivers of priestcraft in Oxford. By using the Puritans' term 'malignants' he identified the Apostolicals with the High-Church tradition stemming from Laud and the Caroline Divines, supporters of the Divine Right of kings and the sacred alliance of throne and altar. Keble, who really was a spiritual descendant of this school, was so pained by Arnold's Round-headedness that he never could feel the same towards him afterwards, in spite of being Matthew's godfather. But Newman's Anglo-Catholicism was not based on the seventeenth-century Caroline divines, but on the Fathers of the early Church. And he was more distrustful of the State than was Arnold; he did not think the altar benefited by alliance with the throne, and though he no more wished the clergy to tyrannize over the laity than Arnold, he saw the royal supremacy as a threat to the spiritual autonomy of the Church.

Arnold, on the other hand, was not a puritan, nor an Evangelical. Some people called him latitudinarian – he repudiated that as an insult. He once said his view of the Church was high, but not of the priesthood. Like Newman he took an historical view of the Church, but his conclusions as to which it was and what it should be were different. What he hated about Catholicism, Roman or Anglican, was *priestcraft*, clericalism, the division of the Christian community into two classes, clergy and laity, with the clergy assuming all the power. He called the Newmanites idolaters because he thought they put the Church, the Sacraments and the Ministry, in the place of Christ himself. The reason why he was so bitter against the Anglo-Catholics was because they seemed to him to be *introducing* a narrower clericalism into the Church of England just when the time seemed ripe to reform the structure towards more lay participation.

The great religious quarrel of the eighteen-thirties was about the nature of the Church and the authority of the Christian faith it mediated. At this distance of time one may discern right on both sides. Newman and his friends were not, in their own view, advocating clerical power but asserting the necessity for the Church to be a self-determining body, with power to define and defend its traditional teaching, independently of civil governments and with a collective (conciliar) authority, undistorted by the opinions of individual theologians or by different national prejudices. The Oxford Movement was in origin a rediscovery of the *community* of belief and witness, of the fact that the Church was *not* just the nation at prayer, but a body with a structure ordained, it was believed, by Christ himself, when he sent out his apostles as leaders of the new people, gathering them to the sacrificial feast of the coming kingdom. Priesthood was a function within the community – the Apostolicals did not study, or even realize, the dangers of clericalism.

But Arnold, and many others, were so angry at what they saw as a revival of priestcraft and the domination of one set of men over the rest, that they could see no apostolic intention behind the movement. Arnold himself had views on the Church which emphasized its community aspect; with so political a mind he could not fail to think of it as an institution and to study it as such. He studied it as he saw it functioning, in England and in Europe – for on his travels this was a prime interest – with the aid of the New Testament, as interpreted by his own common sense. He looked on the early ages with a critical but fairly sympathetic eye. He did not, like Newman, trace the principles of development from the writings of the Fathers – but after all, Newman was the pioneer in that field. Arnold looked at history with the classical eye of a man formed before the theory of evolution and observing human nature and the way institutions are corrupted and reformed. He had the natural reformer's confidence that he knew what was, and what was not, corruption. And like so many reformers he thought that those who wished to preserve were less concerned with truth and right than he.

When he died, so suddenly, in 1842, Arnold was working on a pamphlet or book about the Church which Mary Arnold published after his death under the title *Fragment on the Church*. It gives Arnold's considered views without the polemical setting of his occasional articles and essays, written in haste and often in anger. In this book he makes a distinction between the Christian Religion and the Christian Church.

'By Christian Religion I mean that knowledge of God and of Christ, and that communion of the Holy Spirit, by which an individual is led through life, in all holiness, and dies with the confident hope of rising again through Christ at the last day. This knowledge being derived, or derivable at any rate, from the Scripture alone, and this communion being the answer to our earnest prayers, it is perfectly possible that Christian Religion may work its full work on an individual living alone, or living amongst unbelieving or ungodly men – that here, where the business rests only with God and the individual soul, God's glory may be exalted and the man's salvation effected, whatever may be the state of the Church at large.

'But, by the Christian Church, I mean that provision for the communicating, maintaining, and enforcing of this knowledge by which it was to be made influential, not on individuals, but on masses of men. This provision consisted in the formation of a society, which by its constitution should be capable of acting both within itself and without; having, so to speak, a twofold movement, the one for its outward advance, the other for its inward life and purification; so that Christianity should be at once spread widely and preserved the while in its proper truth and vigour, till Christian knowledge should be not only communicated to the whole world, but be embraced also in its original purity and bring forth its practical fruit.'

It is typical of Arnold that he should immediately decide that Christianity had succeeded as a religion but failed as a church, because greatly corrupted. 'Christianity contains a divine philosophy, which is its religion,' he declared, 'and a divine polity, which is its Church.' Both could suffer corruption.

We can compare this twofold division into philosophy and polity with Newman's threefold division into prophetical, sacerdotal and ruling elements, inherited from the offices of Christ as Prophet, Priest and King. Newman aligned theology and the teaching office of the Church with the prophetical element, the sacramental and mystical side with the priestly element, and the hierarchical order with the kingly rule – remembering that this king was the Suffering Servant of Israel predicted by the prophet Isaiah. This triple division, traditional in origin, was pondered by Newman all his life and his finest exposition of it is in the preface he wrote in 1877 for the re-issue of those lectures on the Prophetical Office of the Church, which had so excited the young men of Oxford when he delivered them in the side chapel of St Mary's in 1837. Newman, as much as Arnold, was aware of the corrupting influences always at work in the Church, composed as it is of a multitude of human beings. He saw that one or other of the three elements was always getting the upper hand, to the disadvantage of the mission of the Church. The priestly, sacramental side was inclined to degenerate into superstition; the kingly, ruling hierarchy to become domineering and worldly; and the prophetical, theological office, which should regulate the others, could lose the living freedom of true reason and become a deadening academic system.

Arnold's division of the Church into a divine philosophy and a divine polity leaves the sacramental life between the two and fully admitted by neither. To one with a great understanding of the act of communion, as Arnold believed the Eucharist to be, this omission was not apparent; it was due to his intense dislike of what he called priestcraft. But by leaving it out of his scheme he unintentionally presented the Church as a social organization motivated by a complex of beliefs about Christ. And then he was left with the problem of authority for these beliefs. Arnold seems never to have questioned certain beliefs about Christ 'derived or derivable' from the New Testament, but his sons, with so many others of their generation, were to realize that these as well as others which he refused to recognize, were developed by the Church over a period of years and stood or fell with the authority of that body. This became more clear as textual and historical criticism of the Biblical documents progressed with the century. And in fact most of Arnold's disciples, whether or not they remained in the Church of England, became increasingly sceptical of all the component elements of the Christian tradition, retaining only the moral fervour which, even to him, was the most important part of Christianity.

Newman was to assert that, intellectually, he must be allowed the theory of the development of doctrine if he was to accept even the earliest creeds; there was more evidence for papal supremacy than there was for the doctrine of the Trinity in the New Testament. Arnold died before Newman published his essay on this subject and he seems not to have realized either the necessity for theology, or its limitations. He could not see theology as the common intellectual effort of the Christian community.

Yet in the *Fragment on the Church* he writes finely on the social aspect of Christianity and how it is served and nourished by the

Eucharist. 'The direct object of Christian co-operation was to bring Christianity into every part of common life; in Scriptural language, to make human society one living body, closely joined in communion with Christ, its head.' And, he says, 'the meal of an assembly of Christians was made the sacrament of the body and blood of Christ' so that 'Christians at their very social meal could enter into the highest spiritual communion; it taught them that in all matters of life, even when separated from one another bodily, that same communion should be preserved inviolate; that in all things they were working for and with one another, with and to Christ and God.'

'In all matters of life' Arnold had an unerring instinct; it was because his Christianity was so active, so real a thing for everyday, that he exercised so great an influence over the younger generation. One of his moments of greatest joy and satisfaction was when all members of his Sixth Form stayed to partake of the Sacrament – something that was left to their own decision.

Arnold thought that the perfect and sovereign commonwealth of the Church was destroyed by two things, the division into a few active rulers and a passive mass – clergy and laity; and by any distinction being made between the spiritual and the secular. He called these plagues Popery and 'the more open Antichrist of dissoluteness'; both antichrists, he maintained, had ever prepared the way for each other. Divide the sacred from the secular and you tend to leave religion to priests and the world to the worldly. But the duty of Christians was precisely to reform and purify the world.

Arnold saw the priest in the old Protestant way as simply an interferer between God and the individual. 'His interference makes the worshipper neither a wiser man nor a holier than he would have been without it; and yet it is held to be indispensable. This unreasonable, unmoral, unspiritual necessity is the essence of the idea of the priesthood.' Of *his* idea, perhaps; but it is a caricature of even the most sacerdotalist view of the Catholic priesthood, where the priest has always been regarded as the minister of the body, acting for Christ, as the apostles did, in building together the new and living temple of the spirit. Certainly there is always a danger of priests becoming a caste and dominating the life of the Church too much, but their function is communal and as necessary as is a doctor's to the health of a society.

But with this reservation, no modern Catholic would quarrel with Arnold's social view of the Church, his insistence that Christianity was intended to penetrate every part of common life, and that communion was meant to be the inspiriting bond between all Christ's followers.

Much of the rest of the *Fragment* is devoted to attempts to explain passages in the New Testament which suggest that the early Church was more 'Catholic' than Arnold wanted it to be. In the history of the Church he distinguished three phases: (1) the first and perfect state, where the forms of the institution were subordinate to the spirit; (2) the state where forms become necessary, for without them the spirit will be lost; (the centuries of the Councils, when the Creeds were formed, exemplify this); (3) the third, unfortunate, state in which, after the storms have passed, the forms are clung to which should have been allowed to pass with them. Arnold was kinder to the second state than most of his Protestant contemporaries, who saw no need for 'forms' at any time. But it is noticeable that this scheme does not allow for a future. Arnold simply assumed that now (from about 1830 onwards, presumably) the spirit of Christianity is self-evident and so forms are unnecessary. Arnold thought the truth must be apparent to all who could read; he died before the doubts about the truth of the Bible really began to bite. Matthew and Tom, Clough and the rest, had to struggle with these problems.

Yet Newman had seen these storms coming, and in 1838 had earned himself some unpopularity in clerical circles with Tract 85, on *Holy Scripture in its relation to the Catholic Creed*, in which he pointed out that the sort of criticism certain liberals were then making of the statements of doctrine in the Creeds could be equally well applied to Scripture. The truth of Christianity does not rest upon words but upon the communion of witnesses: the Church. And for Newman, the history of the Church was not simply how the spirit was kept alive through times of stress, but the development of the original idea through the guidance of the Spirit in the human understanding of generations of believers.

Newman, in his Anglican days, was studying and defending the *idea* of the Church which he found within the ancient tradition; but Arnold's criticisms of the actual institution were often justified. He annoyed not merely Oxford Malignants – who soon had more powerful opponents – but all the establishment men, ecclesiastical or political, who disliked his defence of the rights of

Roman Catholics and Dissenters. He and his liberal friends and disciples were for a time almost as unpopular with the great central mass of the Church of England as the Apostolicals, with their strong views on the autonomy of the Church, were unpleasing to the inheritors of the Elizabethan compromise (which subordinates Church to State).

From Arnold's letters, as printed in Stanley's *Life*, which appeared in 1844 (before Newman had left the Church of England) it is easy to see how Arnold's irritation with the Anglo-Catholic party intensified over the years. On 30th October 1841 he wrote to an old pupil then at Oxford: 'You seemed to think I was not so charitable towards the Newmanites as I used to be towards the Roman Catholics, and you say that the Newmanites are to be regarded as entirely Roman Catholics. I think so too, but with this grave difference, that they are Roman Catholics at Oxford instead of at Oscott – Roman Catholics signing the Articles of a Protestant Church and holding offices in its Ministry.' (Oscott was the fine Gothic college built by Pugin for Bishop Wiseman, just outside Birmingham, where Newman was later to preach the famous sermon on *The Second Spring*.)

Earlier in this year of 1841 Newman had written Tract 90, defending the possibility of taking the Articles in a Catholic sense; Arnold felt that this Tract could not be acquitted of a 'very serious moral delinquency'. Since he too had signed a petition to alter the Articles, he defended his own position by saying that subscription was honest when a sympathy was felt with the system, a positive and not a negative attitude to its characteristic points. 'Now the most characteristic points of the English Church are two; that it maintains what is called the Catholic doctrine as opposed to the early heresies, and is also decidedly a reformed Church as opposed to the Papal and priestly system.' Arnold's common-sense view was shared by many; nor did it occur to them why they should accept the Catholic doctrine rather than the *early* heresies, but refuse the Catholic judgment of later deviations. It was just his study of the parties within the Church in the centuries of the great Councils which had led Newman to the position where he began to think out his theory of the development of doctrine and the continuity of tradition, the ultimate authority of the Church. For this, and not a magic transference of power, was what the Apostolic Succession meant to him.

Arnold, however, had made up his mind long before 1841. He continued his letter: 'Undoubtedly I think worse of Roman Catholicism in itself than I did some years ago. But my feelings towards (a Roman Catholic) are quite different from my feelings towards (a Newmanite), because I think the one a fair enemy, the other a treacherous one. The one is a Frenchman in his own uniform, and within his own praesidia; the other is the Frenchman disguised in a red coat, and holding a post within our praesidia, for the purpose of betraying it. I should honour the first and hang the second.'

When he wrote this letter Arnold had accepted the Regius Professorship of Modern History at Oxford. Modern history was then an extra-curricular subject; the appointment was a Crown (political) nomination; and Arnold's qualifications were no worse than most others' – based, no doubt, on his work on Roman history and on the Greek historian Thucydides. He was soon to go up to deliver his Inaugural Lecture and was delighted at the prospect of renewing his bonds with the university; in spite of his readiness to hang the Newmanites, those Frenchmen in red coats, he wrote to his friend Mr Justice Coleridge that he wished to live peaceably with them. 'But courteous personal intercourse, nay, personal esteem and regard, are different things, I think, from assisting to place a man, whose whole mind you consider perverted, in the situation of a teacher.' This was apropos the election of the Professor of Poetry: Isaac Williams, a poetic friend of Keble's, was not elected because he was a Tractarian. He was to remain a Frenchman in a red coat till his dying day.

Typically, Arnold went on to say that he hoped, when he got to Oxford, to find 'that the Newmanites' minds are not wholly perverted; that they have excellences which do not appear at a distance'. And indeed, when he met the arch-Newmanite himself at Oriel on 2nd February 1842 (he had forgotten 'disputing' his BD with him), he found him not the dissimulating hypocrite he expected, but someone with whom, after an evening's talk, he could warmly shake hands. He even wrote to a friend that 'it would not do to meet Newman too often'. It might interfere with his battle against Newmanism.

The Inaugural Lecture had taken place before this meeting, on 2nd December 1841. Arnold could only spare one day and left Rugby by train at 5 a.m. accompanied by his wife, his daughter Jane, Matt, who had now become a scholar of Balliol and his two best pupils, both now young dons at Oxford, Arthur Stanley and Arthur Hugh Clough. Sitting in the train, he corrected Sixth Form essays. The Sheldonian Theatre was packed from top to bottom and ex-pupils were moved to tears at seeing the Doctor in his scarlet robes and hearing that well-known voice in that august building.

The lecture was a tremendous success. It was a defence of the study of history, especially modern history, which Arnold conceived as the biology of a society or nation. And not merely of a nation's government and foreign relations but of its internal state and moral ends. The peculiarity of modern history, as distinct from classical, was the importance of the German race. When the lecture was published Arnold added a long appendix on the relations of Church and State, in theory and practice. The course of eight lectures which followed at the beginning of the next term elaborated the pattern traced by the Inaugural. Arnold spoke humbly of his own ignorance, just as he had to his Sixth Formers, thereby winning their respect.

Now his eldest son was at Oxford, and Tom was to follow. In November 1840 Matt had won the open scholarship to Balliol. 'The news filled me with astonishment,' said his father, who had been continually worrying over Matt's laziness, his apparent incapacity to concentrate and work hard. 'Matt likes general society and flitters about from flower to flower, but is not apt to fix,' Dr Arnold had observed. And then Matt had sailed in and won the coveted scholarship. Balliol was now rising to the intellectual first place at Oxford, taking over from Oriel, which had never recovered from Newman's demotion in 1830.

So there was Matt at Oxford, a tall elegant Matt, nineteen in December 1841, with his coal-black hair, his strong features, full-lipped mouth and blue-grey eyes, Matt the poet and almost, his family thought, Matt the dandy. Tom, a year younger, was expected to go up in 1842; he was tall too, but quiet and stammering, with dark eyes and hair, Cornish in looks like his mother's brother, Trevenen Penrose.

And Jane, the eldest, was engaged to be married to George Cotton, an assistant master whose 'moral thoughtfulness' outweighed, for the Arnolds, his awkwardness and the sad fact that his mother was given to drink. Wordsworth thought him unattractive in the extreme but Jane was in love and it came as a dreadful shock to her when, in May 1842, Cotton broke off the engagement. Jane suffered deep depression, could scarcely eat, and caused her parents much anxiety. Distress for Jane, perhaps his favourite child, who acted as his secretary, may have contributed to Arnold's first collapse, on 17th May 1842. Although he recovered from this attack and went back to work in the school, it was in fact a warning of the end. Arnold seems to have felt it so, though he did not expect the end quite as soon as it came. He wrote a good deal in his diary, praying for grace to become more tender – he was aware of his irritable temper and tendency to hard hitting.

As for the school, it had never been more successful. The trustees had issued a statement of confidence in their unusual headmaster; Queen Adelaide, widow of William IV, had visited Rugby – and Jane sketched her, being shown round by Arnold and his two elder sons in long gowns and mortar boards; Arnold had even been summoned to an audience with young Queen Victoria – his glimpse of court life amused him. And favourite pupils were now out in the world, making their way, writing back to him for advice, coming back to see him whenever they could. His work was bearing fruit, the Rugby community flourished.

After a perfectly normal day on 11th June, a Saturday, which had ended with Sixth Formers coming to supper at 9, Arnold was awakened between 5 and 6 on Sunday morning with a sharp pain across his chest. Mary Arnold got up and dressed, fetched a servant and sent for the doctor – or rather, his son, for the doctor himself was unwell. Arnold's pain increased, but when Tom came in he teased him, saying that he should not be there, for he had recently said he did not like sick rooms. But when Tom sat down at the end of the bed, Arnold said, 'My son, thank God for me – thank God, Tom, for giving me this pain: I have suffered so little pain in my life that I feel it is very good for me: now God has given it to me, and I do so thank Him for it.' But he also presently added, 'How thankful I am that my head is untouched.'

While they waited for the doctor to return with medicines, Mrs Arnold read the exhortation from the Visitation of the Sick, in the Prayer Book, Arnold saying a heartfelt 'yes' at the end of every sentence. Dr Bucknill returned but it was too late for medicines to do any good. Arnold had realized that, like his father, he had been struck down by *angina pectoris*, and before he had been given the dose of laudanum he was seized with the last spasm. The

(45)

room filled up with crying children and servants, but Arnold was nearly unconscious, breathing in gasps, and about eight o'clock he died. It was 12th June, the day before his forty-seventh birthday.

Arnold's sudden death, in the full tide of work and energy, came as a great shock to the school and to the many pupils to whom he had been for fourteen years a figure of inspiration, if also of awe. Proof of the soundness of his work lay not only in the continuing success of Rugby but in the fact that so many of his disciples took up teaching as a vocation and contributed much to the moral and intellectual developments in the educational world in many English-speaking countries.

His personal influence was greatly increased by the biography, with letters, published by Arthur Stanley in 1844, which caught public attention and went into many editions. Mary Arnold saw to the publication of all that remained of his work, and the volumes of sermons continued to sell for years.

When the *Life* came out, Arnold's old friend Keble was inclined to shake his head over it; would it not spread Arnold's wrong-headed ideas about the Church? But Newman did not agree. He thought there was so little system in Arnold's ideas that they could not have much effect; whereas his influence as a man and a headmaster was all for the good.

Arnold's friends got up a fund to assist with the education of his nine children – the youngest, Walter, was only six or seven. Mary removed with her daughters to Fox How, where she was to live out the rest of her long life, and where her sons would always return, to a loved mother in a loved place, from the ends of the earth.

II

Young Arnolds at Oxford and in London

'Mat. Arnold has come up to reside as a scholar at Balliol,' wrote Arthur Hugh Clough on 10th November 1841, to his Rugby friend John Philip Gell, then in Van Diemen's Land (Tasmania); 'and as a report has whispered to me (which as you are a long way off I will venture to send you) has been going out with the Harriers.'

Thus Matt, after astonishing his father by gaining the Balliol scholarship, started his university career, and as he began, so he went on, as Clough was to discover when he took on the job of tutoring him in vacation reading parties. Matt tended to go off fishing.

When Matt came up, he was nearly nineteen and Clough was not quite twenty-three and had hardly got over the misery of missing First-class Honours in Schools that year, and in the autumn the Balliol fellowship he had tried for. Tom Arnold remembered him 'coming up to my father in the front court of the Schoolhouse, standing in front of him with face partly flushed and partly pale, and simply saying, "I have failed."'

It seemed inexplicable to everyone, for not only was Clough brilliantly clever but extremely industrious; it was not from idleness that he failed. In her biography of Clough, Katharine Chorley suggests that the Oxford curriculum of the day offered him no proper intellectual challenge – he came up knowing more than most young men knew at the end of the course. There was no interest in his work to stimulate him and the ideas that did stimulate him were of no use to his work. Although he was the first Balliol scholar to fail to get a First since the beginning of the lists, he was not the first young man of brilliance and industry to fail this test, for Newman had done the same in 1821.

And like Newman, Clough redeemed his Oxford career by winning election to a fellowship at Oriel, at Easter 1842. He was, in fact, one of the last candidates Newman himself assisted in examining, for he had withdrawn to Littlemore and the next year was to give up the charge of St Mary's, and later his fellowship. Dr Arnold, fresh from his success with the lectures on Modern History, was delighted to hear that Clough had won through; it was to be one of the last satisfactions of his life.

Arthur Stanley, who had gained a First in 1837, the year in which Clough had come up to Oxford, had had his own difficulties about a fellowship. At that time, Arnold's attacks on Hampden's opponents had so much annoyed the members of the Senior Common Room at Balliol (Zs, as Froude called the establishment men, not Apostolicals) that Stanley, one of the first of Arnold's protégés, heard his election would be opposed. But, when he turned his thoughts to Oriel, he realized that there too he was unlikely to win a place, for not only were Newman and his friends ensconced there, but Hawkins the Provost, though a friend of Arnold's, was at that time as pained by his radical views as any Z.

Not wishing to become a bone of contention and doubting the outcome if he did, Stanley instead took up an offer from University College – it was a safe bet that he would get in, but it was, he felt, a dull college and the Common Room a cool and rather uninteresting group. He became a fellow there in 1838.

Although he said he did not know Clough intimately, Stanley wrote to a friend in 1841: 'But the little that I do know of him has always made me think and maintain that he is the profoundest man of his years that I ever saw, or that Rugby ever sent forth. His very misfortunes invest him with a kind of sacredness, for, academically speaking, who was ever so unfortunate – so able, so laborious, and yet so unaccountably failing?'

It was to be a cry heard many times from Clough's puzzled friends and admirers. Perhaps the wrong things were expected of him; he was not what Stanley and so many others from Rugby were – a natural Dean, or Headmaster, an academic or administrative Principal in embryo; he was a natural poet and writer. But the trouble was that after his intensive training at Rugby he *expected himself* to do what others expected of him, even while probably knowing in his heart that such a life was not for him. Nor had he Matt's tougher temperament, which was to prove

(48)

equal to two careers running side by side. Like many writers Clough was most at ease as an observer; he did not really *want* to lead, guide, influence, rule others. He did feel a strong obligation to serve his fellow men but not by doing any of the tasks that most obviously lay before him. Possibly he could once have been a happy clergyman, but he had lost the simple faith of his school-days and was too conscientious to take on a position which would entail subscription to the Articles of the Church of England. Even to sign them to take his MA became a major problem.

Clough had come to Oxford at the height of the controversies about the Church, and the Articles were the storm point of the battle. Nowadays people are inclined to wonder why such a fuss should have been made about these Articles of Religion, drawn up at the time of the Reformation conflicts in order to provide a rough standard of orthodoxy for the Church of England after the English government had taken it out of communion with the See of Rome. But it must be remembered that the Articles were still, in the early nineteenth century, a test which blocked the entrance to most professional careers. Non-subscribers might be Dissenters, they might be Roman Catholics, they might be sceptics – no matter; they could not matriculate at Oxford, could not take their degrees, could not proceed to any important position in society, without this indispensable certificate of religious respectability.

It was not merely a matter for intending clergymen, though at that period, when only Heads of Houses and Professors were allowed to be married, almost all the dons were in Holy Orders; and the fellows and tutors were nearly all young men, since they left when they did marry. Newman, who was now forty-odd, was beginning to feel he no longer had a place in the university.

Important as this practical problem was, it was not that which engaged the chief attention in the eighteen-thirties and early forties. The real question was, what authority had this test of belief? It was a series of statements on points of Christian doctrine – those round which the sixteenth-century storms had gathered. To sign them, to subscribe, was to declare that one believed them. But by the nineteenth century many people had come to realize that, on one or another point, they did not believe them. Did the Articles have the authority of the Bible? No: the Bible was of unique authority. (Why? Some were already asking this question but not, as yet, many.) Were the Articles as authoritative as the Creeds? But what, after all, was the authority of the Creeds? Dr Arnold was not the only man who objected to the Athanasian Creed, as much for its abstract formulations as for its damnatory clauses. Yet he seems to have accepted the so-called Apostles' Creed without question.

It was Newman who, goaded by the intervention of Parliament in the affairs of the Church, demanded, in the first brief Tracts, what was the authority on which Christ's ministers must base their mission and answered: 'OUR APOSTOLICAL DESCENT.' Once that question of authority was asked, you were plunged into problems of history, even of the truth of religion. There was no stopping anywhere. And theorize as you might about the nature of the Church, in England you would always come up against these Articles; they were not only the test imposed by society but the trial of conscience: the point at which theory and practice met. Thus, to worry about the credibility of the Articles was not a sign of neurotic obsession with some unimportant side-issue.

At the beginning of the year 1841, the year Clough took his finals, Newman himself had been driven to write Tract 90, just because people were always asking him how he squared his views with the Articles. And Tract 90 caused the most almighty row in the university because Newman's contention, that the Articles could be interpreted consistently with Catholic doctrine, horrified men who had always looked on them as designed to maintain the Reformation in England.

Arthur Stanley, who had himself felt scruples, of an Arnoldian, not a Newmanic provenance, against signing the Articles, had in the end subscribed and received ordination in 1840. He had been abroad for nearly a year and arrived back in May 1841 to find the crisis in full swing. He wrote to a friend, 'I have read No. 90 and almost all its consequences.' (The pamphlets, for or against, which followed in its wake.) 'The result clearly is, that Roman Catholics may become members of the Church and universities of England, which I for one cannot deplore.'

This reaction was very typical of Stanley, but very unlike the reaction of the majority.

By the time Matt Arnold came up in November, the immediate row was over; Newman had long since promised the Bishop of Oxford to put an end to the series of Tracts, if No. 90 remained uncensured. He kept his word: there is no No. 91. But on the episcopal side the bargain did not hold, for Newman was censured in the 'charges' of nearly every bishop during the ensuing year. Since at that time there was no Convocation, these charges were the only method open to the bishops to make known their views; it gradually became apparent that the authority of the Anglican episcopate was overwhelmingly opposed to a Catholic interpretation of the Articles. When he met Arnold in 1842, Newman was already on the way out, and beginning to be aware of it.

Matt went to hear Newman preaching at St Mary's and was to remain always full of admiration for the gentle shrewdness of his mind, so deeply and so widely cultured, catholic in the simplest sense. But Matt arrived at the end of the great Church battle and started more or less where Clough had by then ended – in a state of doubt. Matt, however, seems to have taken doubt fairly cheerfully; he was then much more interested in political, social and literary ideas than in religious ones – what was more, he went out with the Harriers, he took much interest in dress, in the theatre and other worldly things. He seemed to be totally unlike his father, even unlike the other earnest Rugbeians; yet he never repudiated them. He was not really reacting against Arnold's ideals but he was, very determinedly, growing up in his own way.

Tom, who went up to Stanley's 'dull' college, University, in 1842, was much more like the other ex-Rugby young men; in some ways he was closer to Clough, if not in friendship, in likeness. It was not apparent at first, for Tom came up with his religious faith intact and settled down to work hard, getting a First in 1845, whereas careless Matt only scraped a Second. But Tom was to go through a crisis of faith similar to Clough's, though perhaps simpler, since Tom's was a simpler nature, and to leave a definite account of it in the *Equator Letters* he wrote to J. C. Shairp, which were intended to explain to his friends why he was sailing to the Antipodes in 1848.

The *Equator Letters* suffer from Tom's not being a writer by nature; they are stilted and stiff and give no impression of the natural Tom of his real letters. But they do give the facts about his religious experience, set down soon after the crucial years. He undertook the task so that his friend might know 'that in no light or reckless mood, but as the sworn servant of Duty, he left you and his home and England, to seek a dwelling place in the distant South'. And he went on to observe that 'Deeply will it rejoice my heart to communicate to my Brethren some of the experiences of a soul which, great as have been, and are, its weaknesses and shortcomings, has ever sought Truth before all things.' Not claiming any original ideas he determined to avoid the first person and speak 'in the character of an unconcerned observer'. The use of the third person removed his account even further from immediacy but the observer became more concerned as he proceeded.

Tom recorded that he was brought up in the sincere practice of religion, instructed in Creeds and Catechisms but 'not taught to attach an overweight to these, but rather to think, that the state of the Soul and its relations to God and Christ, were the real questions of importance for a Christian'. He did not consciously realize this at the time, 'but it sunk not the less deeply into his mind'.

The day of awakening was not till 'the period of youth was just beginning'. 'Suddenly he seemed to awake as out of a trance; and the sense of the reality of life and the perception of the responsibility which life carries with it, rushed upon him with an almost overwhelming force.' He realized that he had been repeating prayers, joining in services, and even going through the rite of confirmation (and presumably communion) without really knowing what he had been doing. But he turned to an old favourite, Bunyan's *Pilgrim's Progress*, which now 'unfolded its true meaning to him'. Tom describes his conversion: 'He threw himself upon Christ, as the one only Way, Truth and Life; casting upon Him both the burthen of his sins and the care of his salvation.'

It was typical of him that he at once 'endeavoured to apply his Religion to the things of daily life, especially to the restraining of his temper, which was naturally peevish and hasty; and in all ways he sought to live as he believed'.

Tom Arnold was still in this state when he went to Oxford; 'scarcely a doubt troubled the serenity of his faith'. But at Oxford he began to read widely and discovered that 'some of the writers who most delighted him seemed to stand apart from Christianity, and to owe their culture, and even that noble morality which most won upon him, to other sources.' At first this did not much worry him and he even thought of 'devoting his life to the task of showing that Christianity was not irreconcilable with the new light which had come into the world: on the contrary that it lay at the bottom of, and was essentially involved in, all true Philosophy and all pure Art – an audacious project indeed! but what is there that we are not ready to attempt at the age of twenty?'

When he wrote this, Tom was just twenty-four. It was at the end of 1843 that he had his twentieth birthday, the autumn when Newman resigned St Mary's and preached his famous sermon on *The Parting of Friends*, at Littlemore. But Tom, though his rooms in University College were only just across the street from St Mary's, did not trouble to cross it to hear any of the famous sermons. Only once Matt got him to go, for the sake of the experience; but Tom appears to have received no particular impression. Newman did not appeal to him then; he was one of a generation of undergraduates whose minds were moved by a current of scepticism too strong to be held by the banks of a now discredited Anglo-Catholicism.

'It must not be thought that during this period his habitual life was always consistent with his highest moods,' wrote Tom, scrupulously, and shook his head over 'the defilement of the prison house'. In this half-hearted state he first took hold of the idea of going to New Zealand, and it was almost like another conversion. 'He was carried away by a flood of feelings and fancies, which attended him all day long and assumed a thousand beautiful forms to his imagination.'

This was in 1844, but during the winter questions of faith returned to perplex him; in reading books by materialists he came across fatalistic views powerfully expressed. His emotional, personal religion was unable to cope with the intellectual doubts thus raised. 'However it was, he fell into a state of dejection, such as he had never before known, and which, by the mercy of God, has never since returned. Outward nature seemed to harmonize with the gloom of his mind. The spring of that year (1845) was unusually cold; and the blasts of the north-east wind shook the large Oriel window of his room, and made him shiver with cold as he crouched over the fire. A universal doubt shook every prop and pillar on which his moral being had hitherto reposed.'

Anyone who has been through a similar experience, when life appears suddenly meaningless, will recognize the signs, remember the feelings, on reading this suddenly vivid account.

'Something was continually whispering, "What if all thy Religion, all thy aspiring hope, all thy trust in God, be a mere delusion?"' It whispered to him of 'iron laws'. 'What art thou more than a material arrangement, the elements of which might at any moment, by any accident, be dispersed, and thou, without any to care for or pity thee throughout the wide universe, sink into the universal night. Prate not any more of thy God and thy Providence; thou art here *alone*, placed at the mercy of unpersonal and unbending laws, which, whether they preserve or crush thee, the Universe with supremest indifference will roll onward on its way.'

These recurring thoughts, he recorded, 'took away the charm from the human face, the glory from the sky; the beauty from the flowers - all these seemed to be garlands round the victim's neck; designed to cheat it for a time into a little ease and forgetfulness of the cold inexorable necessity that lay beneath.'

Tom added the significant fact that these doubts 'at last passed away of themselves, without his having been able to find any means of facing and overcoming them'. What happened, as he relates in Letter 2, was that 'exhausted by vain attempts to find a sure basis for religious conviction, his thoughts now took a direction outwards, and he began to busy himself with the social and political questions of the day. He said to himself, "Religion is a labyrinth without a clue ... Why then, in Heaven's name, let us leave all that, and let us work at things which we *know*. Let us shorten the hours of labour for the poor: let us purify our cities: let us unfetter our trade – surely we can unite for these objects. As for religion, we must agree to differ; that problem is incapable of solution, and we begin to suspect that it matters little, after all, to what form a man adheres." ' And the 1848 Tom adds, from the height of his then maturity, that he was almost led to acquiesce in the Church's creed, 'from a distrust of his own ability to attain anything higher'.

This was his state of mind when, having taken his First, he left Oxford, refusing to stand for a fellowship, which he would almost certainly have got, because he would not sign the Articles. Academic life was to prove his true vocation, but following Truth led him a long way round before he was able to get back to it.

Tom's refusal to compromise had its effect on Clough, five years his senior and a don at Oriel, feeling uncomfortable as an official member of the Church of England. But it had no effect at all on Matt, who, in his casual way, probably had less belief than either at that date. All three were seeing a lot of each other during those Oxford years, part of a group who remained friends for life, breakfasting with Clough at Oriel, meeting for the debates of their club, 'The Decade', which had been formed to discuss more serious subjects than those debated in the Union. It was with the Decade group that Tom discussed hours of labour, free trade, sewage disposal, the iniquity of religious tests; it was here that he began to form ideas of what human life should be, and he found it was Clough who most often, by his contributions, made sense of the debates for him. From Tom Arnold we can get an idea of the Clough who was regarded as a leader, a man who would go far.

We do not get it from Matt, whose way of talking to Clough was as if he were the elder; he is always pulling Clough along, teasing him, cheering him up and ticking him off. Matt's family, deceived by his dandyism and French airs, seem not to have realized the power of Arnoldian energy in him, so plain to the reader of his early letters to Clough, bursting with likes and dislikes, ideas, indignation and nonsense.

Clough was a keeper of letters; Matt wasn't, and so the correspondence is one-sided for us, and only begins after Matt had gone down, after his ignominious Second, to teach at Rugby till he too secured an Oriel fellowship, in March 1845. But it shows the Matt of Oxford days in all his Mattishness. Impishly, 'with true Xtian simplicity' Matt had filled in the missing word for Tait, the new Headmaster at Rugby (later Archbishop of Canterbury) when he had said that Calvinism devoted 1000s of mankind to be eternally – and paused. 'Damned,' said Matt sweetly.

' – But you are not to suppose that these Druidical Remains, these touches, if I may so speak, of the aboriginal Briton, are found often among the stately Edifices of our Magistracy: nor yet are you not to suppose that it is so late at night that this licentious Pen wanders whither it will. True, I give satisfaction – but to whom? True, I have yet been late on no Morning, but do I come behind in no thing? True, I search the Exercises, but the Spirits? – for which Reason it seems not clear why I should stand at Oriel: for wisdom I have not, nor skilfulness – after the Flesh – no, nor yet Learning: and who will see a delicate Spirit tossed on Earth, opossum like, with the down fresh upon him, from the maternal Pouches of nature, in the grimed and rusty coalheaver, sweating and grunting

> with the Burden of an honour
> Unto which he was not born –

I have other ways to go.'

He had indeed, but he was to go to Oriel first, all the same.

'But, my dear Clough, have you a great Force of Character? That is the true question. For me, I am a reed, a very whoreson bullrush: yet such as I am, I give satisfaction. Which you will find to be nothing – nor yet is a patent Simulation open to all men, nor to all satisfactory. But to be listless when you should be on Fire: to be full of headaches when you should slap your Thigh: to be rolling Paper Balls when you should be weaving Fifty Spirits into one: to be raining when you had been better thundering: to be damped with dull ditchwater, when in one school near you sputters and explodes a fiery tailed Rocket, and in the rest patent Simulators ceaselessly revolve: to be all this and to know it – O my Clough – in this house they find the Lodger in Apricot Marmalade for two meals a day – and yet? – But, my love, the clock reminds me that I have long since sung, "Night comes . . .", and he ended with a burlesque of one of his own poems.

I have quoted at length from this high-spirited effusion because it so splendidly shows the young Matthew Arnold's vitality and delight in comedy; one sees why he fascinated both friends and brothers, even while they shook their heads over his lack of earnestness.

But friends were apt to misunderstand his casual manner – Clough himself did so, later. Matt was not yet twenty-one when he answered a complaint from John Duke Coleridge (son of Arnold's friend John Taylor Coleridge) that his friends felt he lacked interest in them; he called it even then 'an old subject'. 'The accusation as you say, is not true. I laugh too much and they make one's laughter mean too much. However the result is that when one wishes to be serious one cannot but fear a half suspicion on one's friends' parts that one is laughing, and so the difficulty gets worse and worse.'

Matt, who had been taken abroad first by his father, lost no time in going on his own to France as soon as he could. Clough wrote to their mutual friend J. C. Shairp: 'Matt is full of Paris-ianism; theatres in general and Rachel in special: he enters a room with a chanson of Béranger's on his lips – for the sake of French words almost conscious of tune: his carriage shows him in fancy parading the Rue de Rivoli; and his hair is guiltless of English scissors: he breakfasts at 12, and never dines in Hall, and in the week or 8 days rather (for 2 Sundays must be included) he has been to Chapel *once*.'

It was very unlike the serious and anxious Tom, crouching over his fire with the north-east wind whispering doubts in his ear. It was also not entirely like Matt himself, not the whole of him; but it was not till 1849 when his first poems were published that even his own family realized that he *could* be serious. For these were also the days of long rambles over Cumnor and Shotover, gazing out into the mild English landscape of the Thames country, days of romantic dreamings on classical themes: the scene of *The Scholar Gipsy* and later of *Thyrsis*.

Perhaps this is the place to recall Charlotte Brontë's meeting with Matt, though it did not take place till some five years after he had left Oxford and was already engaged to be married. But at twenty-eight he gave the same impression to that shrewd, intense, rather sad little woman, who had won fame by then, but lost all her sisters and the brother who had once been her special intimate but had long since sunk into a ghost of himself, through drink and drugs and illness.

It was Harriet Martineau who took Charlotte Brontë to dine at Fox How on Saturday 21st December 1850. Charlotte wrote to James Taylor of Matthew: 'Striking and prepossessing in appearance, his manner displeases from its seeming foppery. I own it caused me at first to regard him with regretful surprise; the shade of Dr Arnold seemed to me to frown on his young representative. I was told, however, that "Mr Arnold improves upon acquaintance." So it was: ere long a real modesty appeared under his assumed conceit, and some genuine intellectual aspiration, as well as high educational acquirements, displaced superficial affection.' It is amusing to listen to Miss Brontë giving Matthew Arnold grudging marks for intellectual aspiration. She thought the untimely loss of his father most unfortunate for him, but it is possible that dear Papa's influence proved more potent than his presence might have done in Matt's critical period of growth.

Matt, meanwhile, had written gaily off to his fiancée, Fanny Lucy Wightman: 'At seven came Miss Martineau and Miss Brontë (Jane Eyre); talked to Miss Martineau (who blasphemes frightfully) about the prospects of the Church of England, and, wretched man that I am, promised to go and see her cow-keeping miracle tomorrow – I, who hardly know a cow from a sheep.

I talked to Miss Brontë (past thirty and plain, with expressive grey eyes, though) of her curates, of French novels, and her education in a school in Brussels, and sent the lions roaring to their dens at half-past nine and came to talk to you.'

This was Matt after his time in London, but still very much the young Matt, the enthusiast for France, George Sand, and the new republicanism – the last with reservations. After his brief time teaching at Rugby, and when he had, to the surprise of all, gained his Oriel fellowship, he did not stay long in the university but launched into the political and social world of London, as private secretary to Lord Lansdowne. There was not much in the way of salary attached to this post, but there were opportunities for the future. His mother and sisters did not quite approve; surely London life would put the finishing touch to Matt's 'worldliness'?

Meanwhile, Tom came to London too, but under very different circumstances. Refusing to subscribe to the Articles, he was persuaded to enter at Lincoln's Inn, where he read Law for three months, from April 1846. Tom thought it a 'hardening, worldly profession' and already wanted to emigrate, but when he gave it up, Mrs Arnold got him to take a post at the Colonial Office as a précis-writer; he did quite well, but still read everything he could about New Zealand.

It has long been known that a 'disappointment in love' contributed to Tom's desire to emigrate, but it is Professor Bertram who has discovered the details, which he makes known in his introduction to the *New Zealand Letters*. Far from being a girl of lower social status as has been supposed from 'Philip's' affair in Clough's poem, *The Bothie of Tober na Vuolich*, Tom's sweetheart was Henrietta, daughter of Archbishop Whately, Dr Arnold's friend. Whatelys and Arnolds had grown up visiting each other, in Ireland and at Fox How. Tom must have proposed to Etty, as she was always called, soon after he left Oxford. He was refused, as much by Etty's parents as by herself, though she was much under their influence. The reason seems to have been Tom's refusal to accept the Articles and settle down as a clergyman or a lawyer.

In the *Equator Letters*, Tom wrote: 'Take but one step in submission, and all the rest is easy; persuade yourself that your reluctance to subscribe to Articles which you do not believe is a foolish scruple, and then you may take orders and marry, and be happy; satisfy yourself that you may honestly defend an unrighteous cause, and then you may go to the Bar, and become distinguished, and perhaps in the end sway the counsels of state; prove to yourself, by the soundest of arguments of political economy, that you may lawfully keep several hundred men and women and children at work for 12 hours a day in your unwholesome factory, and then you may become wealthy and influential, and erect public baths and patronize artists.'

'All this is open to you,' he continued; 'while if you refuse to tamper in a single point with the integrity of your conscience, isolation awaits you, and unhappy love, and the contempt of men; amidst the general bustle and movement of the world you will be stricken with a kind of impotence, and your arm will seem to be paralysed, and there will be moments when you will almost doubt whether truth indeed exists, or at least, whether it is fitted for men.'

So he wrote in his semi-public confession for his friends, but his family knew about his unhappy love, and he referred to it several times in his letters written on the voyage, two or more years later. He said it had 'inwoven itself in every fibre of [his] being,' and to his mother in June 1848 he could write, 'Since I lost Etty, my heart is much deadened to pain and pleasure and nothing can now so vividly affect me as in time past.' In his loneliness in New Zealand he spoke to his sister Jane of companionship: 'Were there but one – but wishes and complainings are vain; I have done my duty, and it was never promised me that I should be the happier for doing it, but only the better and purer.' He had stuck to his conscience, and lost Etty Whately.

At Oxford Tom had turned from the whispers of universal doubt to the cause of social reform, and when he came to London this was much in his mind. Struggling with his unhappy love, his uncongenial work, living in lodgings in Margaret Street, he tried to do something for those even worse off. 'But when he came up to reside in London,' he wrote in one of the fragmentary *Equator Letters*, 'and almost with the feelings of a Sister of Mercy began to visit the poor, and was thus brought into daily contact with the extremity of human suffering and degradation, and forced to behold our common human nature, prostrate and debased, "not struggling but sunk", all other subjects seemed to fade into insignificance beside this one, all other evils to be as nothing compared with this monstrous and unutterable woe.'

The effect of this was to force him to realize that he could do little to alleviate these horrors; better to try to help to build a better society in a new world, far away from the hideous corruptions of London. 'I hope for nothing from life, either for myself or for others through me,' he wrote to Clough on 16th April 1847, when he had been a year in London. 'Our lot is cast in an evil time; we cannot accept the present and we shall not live to see the future. It is an age of transition; in which the mass are carried hither and thither by chimeras of different kinds, while to the few, who know the worthlessness of the chimeras, and have caught a glimpse of the sublime but distant future, is left nothing but sadness and isolation.'

Referring in the *Equator Letters* to this sense of frustration and uselessness he was able to write, 'Yet in your loneliness you will be visited by consolations which the world knows not of; and you will feel that, if renunciation has separated you from the men of your own generation, it has united you to the great company of just men throughout all past time; nay, that even now there is a little band of Renunciants scattered over the world, of whom you are one, whose you are, and who are yours for ever. . .'

Clough was one of these, though it took him longer than Tom to renounce the bonds of the Articles, and Clough often visited Tom in his lodgings, slept on the couch there once and left a poem behind: *Qui laborat orat*. They went to hear Jenny Lind, for whom Tom had conceived a passionate admiration. Clough wrote to a friend in 1846 that Harriet Martineau was going to mesmerize Tom out of his stammer; she did not succeed in banishing it. 'She smokes regularly and says that it does good to her deafness,' wrote Tom of her; 'this however, I was told by the people she was staying with, is a pure figment of the dear creature's brain.'

During this time in London Tom rediscovered a religious faith, thought it was not in orthodox Christianity. Towards the end of 1846 he came across Southey's *Life of John Wesley* and read it through. It was almost like a second conversion; he felt he must at all costs find God, know him and serve him. Yet it did not lead him to become a Methodist. 'He could not but ask himself,' he wrote in the first of the *Equator Letters*, 'whether the form in which Wesley expressed these great and central truths was really that which the wants of the age demanded, or which he himself, consistently with the logic of his past thoughts, could consistently accept.' He considered Methodism the last genuine development of orthodox Christianity, but he thought that orthodoxy had been challenged intellectually by German criticism and practically by the French Revolution. Could any great man ever again believe in Articles of Religion, or express his 'theory of the universe' in terms of 'ancient formularies'? Tom was so sure he could not that he announced that his new convictions 'led him to renounce orthodoxy and Churchmanship for ever'. He little knew that barely eight years later his pursuit of truth would lead him into the Catholic Church!

Tom burst into a panegyric of his new faith. 'Christ, for 18 centuries adored, but never yet truly known, appeared no more as a stumbling block to faith; he stood up no more to divide History into sacred and profane, to part asunder nations into Christian and Heathen – but whenever and wherever the divine soul of a man had risen against the tyranny of sense, and preached the excellency, the necessity, of an inward and spiritual life, that man appeared as a fellow worker with Christ . . . The History of Man and Nature then appeared like the seamless vesture, whole and undivided, enveloped in eternal beauty . . .'

Tom Arnold was a natural mystic, tormented by the inadequacy of the formulations of Christianity, unadapted as they were from the language of a pre-scientific age, to give an intellectually satisfying basis for the spiritual communion with the source of all being which was so necessary to him. The faith he formulated for himself was to prove too vague and etherealized to be much use to him in the business of daily living, but for the time it satisfied him. He mentions Lamennais and must have read his later works, but it was George Sand who drew from him a reverence which, at this distance of time, cannot but seem slightly comic. 'Thanks be to God and George Sand . . .' he could write, in perfect seriousness, in the third *Equator Letter*, where he suddenly abandoned the third person for the first, impatient at the formality of his earlier approach.

George Sand it was, however, who showed him the Spirit of Love at work in the world. 'With inexpressible joy I read and pondered upon the sacred symbol "Freedom, Equality, Brotherhood." ' George Sand demonstrated the ideals behind the new revolutionary movement of 1848, with which the young Arnolds and their friends eagerly identified themselves.

Matt was already a devotee of George Sand and had called on her on one of his early visits to France. In 1876, when she died, he heard from a friend that she had said of him to Renan that he had given her the impression of 'un Milton, jeune et voyageant'.

But perhaps just because of Matt's enthusiasm, Tom had taken little notice, while he was at Oxford. It was his own unhappy love which led him to find interest in her novel *Jacques*; he says he found 'the divine stoicism of Jacques congenial to his nature, and the fate of his love impressed me with sad forebodings which were but too soon destined to be realized'. So he must have read it before the final veto on his desire to marry Etty Whately.

His sister Jane wrote to him when he was in New Zealand of Etty's engagement to a Mr Wale, and added that she did not think Etty suited to be the wife of a man of original opinions – nor could she be happy with anyone who was not absolutely guided by her father, which Mr Wale, a lawyer, conveniently was. It is a curious development of this history that Etty's daughter, Henrietta Wale, was to marry Tom's eldest son, William Arnold. Willy believed much less than his father had ever believed, but then his Henrietta's father was not Archbishop Whately.

With a conventional career and marriage closed to him by his conscience, Tom Arnold had to decide what to do with his life. Funds had been found to finish the education of Dr Arnold's children, but once grown up, they had to make their own way.

It was through the republican ideals that Tom had learned from his reading of George Sand and others that he came to see himself as part of an unjust society. 'I am one of this rich class; I have *servants* to wait upon me; I am fed and clothed by the labour of the poor and do nothing for them in return. The life I lead is an outrage and a wrong to humanity.' So he came to the great decision: 'I will leave it; I will cast it out from me altogether; I will come to my God; I will cast myself into the lap of Nature; and through their strength and fulness, I shall enter before I die into new and pure relations with Man.'

This was what took him across the world to begin a new life at the antipodes. At first he had wondered whether to try to live among the poor in England, 'whose condition is, on my own showing, contrary to the will of God and the desires of Nature. Shall I clothe myself in rags, forget all I have read and dreamed of the beautiful and true, and become, like them, ignorant and brutish?' That error seemed to him almost worse than to live off their labour. He was resolved at all cost to descend among those who laboured and to labour with them, but if he remained in England there were insuperable obstacles. 'England is now a land for the rich, not for the poor.' He was inextricably involved with the rich, nor was a good natural life possible for the poor. And so the answer was: emigration.

Tom Arnold had found his religious and social vocation – or so he thought.

He made up his mind and he made his preparations carefully and thoroughly. He got a passage on the *John Wickcliffe*, one of two vessels which were carrying an expeditionary force of Free Churchmen to found a community in New Zealand. Writing to Clough from Mount Street on 18th November 1847, Tom remarked, 'I hope I shall like the free church people; how alarmed the dear creatures would be if they knew what a mass of heresy and schism I had got down in the hold. Rousseau! Spinoza!! Hegel!!! Emerson!! Stanley observed that Spinoza and Hegel had probably never crossed the Line before.'

Tom's sisters, Jane and Mary, came to breakfast with him and say goodbye. Mary had married Aldred Twining, who almost at once was stricken by incurable disease. 'Mary looks as if she had suffered much,' Tom wrote to his mother, 'yet she was in tolerably good spirits. I grieve to say there has been a change for the worse in Aldred.' He died in 1848 and Mary, after ten years of active life – she attended lectures in London by Christian socialists – was to marry a clergyman and settle near Loughborough, at Woodhouse, a small estate that seemed like fairy land to her niece and namesake Mary, later Mrs Humphry Ward, who remembered her strong face, like her father's, her inconsistencies and her passionate idealism. Mary, though never well known, ran true to type.

Tom's elder brother Matt and his younger brother Edward came to Gravesend to see him sail, at the end of November. Edward Arnold recorded: 'It was very cold, yet it was a brilliant sunset and the river with all its shipping is always beautiful.' Asked if he felt inclined to change his mind, Tom said no, but he felt most the parting with Matt. 'I saw tears in his eyes when it came to that,' said Edward. Months later, arrived in New Zealand, Tom wrote home: 'Dearest old Matt! when I think of the last look that I had of his tall form on the wharf at Blackwall, it is almost too much for my manhood. Unlike as we are, and perhaps even by reason of that unlikeness, there is not another person in the world to whom it is such an entire satisfaction to me to be with and talk to as Matt.'

It was to be nine years before the brothers met once more.

III

Revolution and Poetry

The February Revolution in Paris of 1848 and Europe's revolutionary year, which culminated in Mazzini's short-lived Roman Republic of 1849, were critical events for the young Arnolds and their friends. It is true that Tom Arnold was on the high seas and heard the news long afterwards; nevertheless his enthusiastic replies to Clough's letters, months out of date, give the exact flavour of revolutionary idealism in his generation.

It was a very different affair from the great Revolution, which had begun nearly sixty years earlier. And Matthew and Tom Arnold had been little boys under ten at the time of the Revolution of 1830, which Dr Arnold had greeted as 'blessed' to the alarm of his Oxford friends, because it had put an end to the reactionary régime of Charles X. After those July days, Louis-Philippe, the Duc d'Orléans, had become King of the French; in 1848 he was an old man, his government had become more conservative, and after a few days of riots but little bloodshed, the Citizen King fled to England and a republic was proclaimed with the poet Lamartine at its head.

What could appeal more strongly to young men with reforming ideals? An exciting uprising of 'the people', splendid speeches about Liberty, Equality and Fraternity, an old king running away and a (comparatively) young poet in charge of the affairs of a great nation – it was just the stuff for youth! And the later arrival on the scene of Louis Napoleon, nephew of the great Napoleon, who very soon transformed the republic into the Second Empire, was even more of a disillusion to the young idealists of 1848 than had been the compromise of the Citizen King in 1830. From the great Revolution onwards France has attempted every kind of constitutional government, and each experiment seems to end with some 'strong man' in control. And naturally what goes on across the Channel affects each generation in England, so near and yet so different.

Clough was still at Oxford, though he was taking steps to leave. 'If it were not for all these blessed revolutions, I should sink into helpless lethargy,' he wrote in March to his friend John Campbell Shairp. The excitement caused by the revolution shows in his letter to Tom Arnold, begun in a desultory way in January and suddenly taken up on February 25th with a rapid description of events in Paris, ending, 'Well, my dear Tom, I fear I must stop, and leave the Revolution to take its chance.' But the next day he was adding more, on the king's abdication, and on Saturday night a postscript, after the evening papers were out, in which he remarked, 'The King is said to be at Eu (packing up the silver forks). The Red Flag is flying at Paris.'

He went on: 'And so my dear Vive la République, Vive le Drapeau Rouge! But I anticipate considerable trouble in getting any constitution into Marching Order. Our friends the Communists will give a little trouble, I think, and perhaps be unreasonably eager to introduce the millennium . . . Good-night.' He scribbled more on Sunday and on Monday recorded triumphantly, 'The Republic lives and thrives.' He gave more news, lists of ministers of the new government, a last few words on Monday evening and posted his bulletin off on its long journey to the antipodes.

Tom Arnold did not receive it till August, but something of his reply is worth quoting, even though Clough was not to receive it till he was in Rome, besieged by the French in 1849. On 13th August 1848, Tom wrote from Wellington, 'I had already heard of the French Revolution, but your letter was not the less interesting. You may imagine with what joy and thankfulness I heard this great, this heart-stirring news. I was even so far moved from my propriety as to write a letter to a newspaper on the subject; a thing which I never did before and probably shall never do again. My first feeling about it was, "a God still lives then! Justice is still the basis of things! I had thought that aspirations after the good and the true, that endeavours to realize them, could only be found in a few individuals, but lo! a whole nation rises as one man, and declares that it will have no more to do with lies and hypocrisies, but that God's will shall be done on earth as it is in Heaven." . . . But after all, by the time this letter reaches you, you in England may be in the midst of a Revolution your-

E

selves, the cockneys guillotining the aristocrats on Bethnal Green and commissioners sent down to Oxford from the National Convention to lay hands on all the plate etc etc; so that I shall cut short my reflexions on an event which may be so stale four months hence.'

When Clough read these words he was listening to the bombardment of Rome by – the French army! So much for Fraternity.

Meanwhile Matthew Arnold was nearer at hand than Tom. In the midst of those exciting February days, writing to Clough about his poems in his usual admonitory way, Matt, from his position as Lord Lansdowne's secretary, was able to send him the latest information. 'Later news than any the newspapers have is, that the National Guard have declared against a Republic and were on the brink of a collision with the people when the express came away . . . Tell Edward, I shall be ready to take flight with him the very moment the French land, and have engaged a Hansom to convey us both from the possible scene of carnage.'

His younger brother Edward was then at Balliol; Matt's reference to an expected invasion was his comment on alarmist reports in London and some remarks of the old Duke of Wellington on the weakness of England's defences.

Heading his letter merely 'Wednesday' Matt wrote again on 1st March to correct his previous stop press news – the National Guard had sided with the people and the king had fled. With Carlyle's *French Revolution* in mind, Matt referred to the upper classes as Gig-owners. 'However, I think Gig-owning has received a severe, tho: please God, a momentary blow: also Gig-owning keeps better than it re-begins. Certainly the present spectacle in France is a fine one: mostly so indeed to the historical swift-kindling man, who is not overhaunted by the pale thought, that, after all man's shiftings of posture, *restat vivere*. Even to such a man, revolutions and bodily illnesses are fine anodynes when he is agent or patient therein: but when he is a spectator only, their kind effect is transitory.'

Although Matt was younger than Clough, temperamentally he was more detached; he was less engaged by the revolution and always inclined to remember that although one must have ideals, *restat vivere* – life must go on.

'My man' – Matt called Lord Lansdowne, jokingly, his man – 'My man remarks that Poets should hold up their heads now that a Poet is at the head of France. More clergyman than Poet, tho:

and a good deal of the cambric handkerchief at that. No Parson Adams.'

Lamartine addressed a manifesto to the French diplomatic agents in Europe, printed in the *Moniteur* on 5th March and copied in the later editions of *The Times* next day. 'You will have seen Lamartine's circular,' Matt wrote to Clough and observed that in England neither the aristocracy nor the people would understand it. He felt that ideas which in England were only understood by a few were in France 'the *atmosphere* of the commonplace man as well as of the Genius. This is the secret of their power; our weakness is that in an age where all tends to the triumph of the logical absolute reason we neither courageously have thrown ourselves into this movement like the French: nor yet have driven our feet into the solid ground of our individuality as spiritual, poetic, profound *persons*. Instead of this we have stood *up* hesitating; seeming to refuse the first line on the ground that the second is our *natural* one – yet not taking this. How long halt ye between two opinions: woe to the modern nation, which will neither be philosophe nor philosopher. Eh? Yours with apologies for longness, M. Arnold.' Then he added: 'Yet it is something for a nation to feel that the only true line is its natural one?'

That 'Eh?' is endearing. Although he was only twenty-five, Matthew Arnold had already found the line in which he was to develop his thought about England and France to the end of his life. France always attracted his intellectual side and made him laugh at Englishness. Yet the force behind that postscript continued to grow too, so that, European though he was in outlook, Matthew Arnold always retained a belief in the usefulness of the English pragmatic sense. *Restat vivere*.

The next day, 7th March, he was writing to his mother, praising Carlyle, whom he came later to distrust, because 'he alone puts aside the din and whirl and brutality which envelop a movement of the masses, to fix his thoughts on its ideal invisible character'. Then he went straight on: 'I was in the great mob in Trafalgar Square yesterday, whereof the papers will instruct you: but they did not seem dangerous, and the police are always, I think, needlessly rough in *manner*. English too often are. It will be *rioting* here only; still the hour of the hereditary peerage and eldest sonship and immense properties has, I am convinced, as Lamartine would say, struck.' Later he remarked, 'But I do not

(67)

think England will be liveable-in just yet. I see a wave of more than American *vulgarity*, moral, intellectual and social, preparing to break over us. In a few years people will understand better why the French are the most civilized of European peoples, when they see how fictitious our manners and civility have been, how little inbred in the race.'

He was right that in England there would only be rioting; in fact there was less than before the Reform Bill of 1832. The great Chartist meeting of 10th April 1848 was not the beginning of an English Revolution but merely the end of one phase of the working-class movement for social justice and political representation. However, the hour of the peerage and immense property had *not* struck – or only the first stroke of a long midnight hour. Nor had it struck much further in France, in spite of the idealist republicans in Paris.

Clough stayed with Matt in London for the weekend of 18th/19th March and they were sufficiently unpolitical to go to the theatre, though not to Macready's season at the Princess's, of which Matt had written vividly a few days before: 'The squalor of the place, the faint earthy orange smell, the dimness of the light, the ghostly ineffectualness of the sub-actors, the self-consciousness of Fanny Kemble, the harshness of Macready, the unconquerable difficulty of the play, altogether gave me a sensation of wretchedness during the performance of *Othello* the other night I am sure you would have shared with me had you been there.' Instead they went to Miss Fortescue's performance of *Sweethearts and Wives* at the Haymarket.

They also discussed Clough's letter of resignation from his tutorship at Oriel. On 24th March Matt wrote: 'I was glad to see you the other day and spiritually to shake hands. Do not let us forsake one another: we have the common quality, now rare, of being unambitious, I think. Some must be contented not to be at the top.'

This was true; but possibly the lack of ambition was due to their both being poets and therefore not able to commit themselves whole-heartedly to another career. As to the revolution, Clough was the more committed, in theory. Matt went straight on: 'I have G. Sand's letter – do you want it? I do not like it so well as the first. From my soul I cannot *understand* this violent praise of the people. I praise a fagot where-of the several twigs are nought: but a *people*?' George Sand, heroine of Matt's Oxford days, had written two *Lettres au Peuple* for 7th and 19th March. Matt might be sure of the superiority of the French intellect, but he reacted to the rhetoric of the intellectuals in a typically English way.

At the beginning of April Matt's youthful and arrogant judgments on America received a jolt when Clough brought Ralph Waldo Emerson to London. Emerson became a real friend to Clough and Matt was not so prejudiced as to fail to recognize his quality. However, the day the two returned to Oxford was the day of the Chartist demonstration, 10th April, and Matt's brief letter was taken up with that. 'The Chartists gave up at once in the greatest fright at seeing the preparations: braggarts as they are, says my man . . . The petition is quietly progressing in cabs, unattended, to Westminster.'

Yet he had told his mother that he was much struck with the ability of the Chartists' speakers. 'However, I should be sorry to live under their government – nor do I intend to – though Nemesis would rejoice at their triumph. The ridiculous terror of people here is beyond belief and yet it is not likely, I fear, to lead to any good results.'

The danger of revolution in England in 1848 was now over. Free from his tutorship at Oriel, Clough left for France on Mayday, and arrived just when the provisional government was breaking up. Yet at first he found the atmosphere heady, writing to Stanley on 14th May, 'I do little else than potter about under the Tuileries Chestnuts and here and there about bridges and streets, *pour savourer la république*. I contemplate with infinite thankfulness the blue blouses, garnished with red, of the *garde mobile*; and emit a perpetual incense of devout rejoicing for the purified state of the Tuileries, into which I find it impossible, meantime, to gain admittance. I growl occasionally at the sight of aristocratic equipages which begin to peep out again, and trust that the National Assembly will in its wisdom forbid the use of livery servants.' Those Gig-owners were already re-beginning, more easily than Matt had supposed possible.

Clough was back in England at the beginning of June, to be greeted by a letter from Matt addressed to 'Citizen Clough, Oriel Lyceum'. In July he was writing to Tom Arnold from Liverpool, where his mother was then living: 'When I last wrote to you the 3 days of February were still echoing. And now the 4 days of June have scarcely ceased to reverberate.' He did not think Lamartine had had a fair chance; he was beginning to wonder if the whole outbreak had not been premature and if the French 'had better have endured a little longer the immorality of L. Philip's government'. He could still add, 'But yet on the whole one accepts the whole thing with gratitude. – It will I think on the whole accelerate change in England; and perhaps, my dear Tom, you may yet live to see some kind of palingenesy effected for your repudiated country.' And then he added, 'Matt was at one time really heated to a very fervid enthusiasm; but he has become sadly cynical again of late. However I think the poetism goes on favourably.'

Matt was indeed cynical. He wrote, sarcastically, to Clough: 'What a nice state of affairs in France. The New Gospel is adjourned for this bout. If one had ever hoped anything from such a set of d—d grimacing liars as their prophets one would be very sick just now.' The tone betrays his own revulsion. The fine words of the revolutionaries had petered out in quarrels; Louis Napoleon got his chance and took it.

The letters between the two friends reverted to their primary common interest in literature. This was the summer in which Clough suddenly wrote *The Bothie of Tober na Vuolich*, the best known of his longer poems and one which Matt did not much like, partly because of its subject matter, which was that of a contemporary novel. It was, in fact, a short novel in English hexameters, and became rather popular with the younger generation of readers.

Perhaps Matt's irritation was increased because this was for him too a summer of poetry and love, which he expressed very differently from Clough. From the Baths of Leuk, in Switzerland, in September, he wrote to his friend: 'Tomorrow I repass the Gemmi and get to Thun: linger for one day for the sake of the blue eyes of one of its inmates: and then proceed by slow stages down the Rhine to Cologne, thence to Amiens and Boulogne and England.' It was to be from Thun, in the next year that he wrote an unusually self-revealing letter to Clough, in a mood of weariness which he did not explain, but which others have since explained for him, trying to discover more of the blue-eyed girl who was the original of the poems to 'Marguerite'.

Most of these poems did not appear in his first volume of 1849, but in that of 1852, the year after his marriage, so that he cannot have felt there was anything in them to hurt or offend his wife. The one poem published in 1849: 'To my friends, who

ridiculed a tender leave taking,' is light-hearted in tone, but in it
the girl makes a reproachful advance which ends in a kiss. In the
later poems, however, we get the impression that though Marguerite was at first eager to resume the affair, she afterwards re-
vealed that there was another, or others, and this seems to have
caused Matt to retreat, and at the same time to care more. The
feelings expressed are complex, but it was not a great love and
they are not great love poems. They are more explorations of
himself than anything, and the most haunting line could have
occurred in one of his poems on the general human predicament:

> A God, a God their severance rul'd;
> And bade betwixt their shores to be
> *The unplumb'd, salt, estranging sea.*

Some of the love poems of the 1852 volume were inspired not
by Marguerite but by Fanny Lucy, the girl Matt was to marry;
most of them express frustration and despair and are the more
real for that. However, they belong to a later phase of his development than the poems printed in 1849, which included *The
Strayed Reveller* – the original title poem. Some, such as *A Modern
Sappho* and *The New Sirens*, may express some of the poet's own
feelings transposed; this may be true even of *The Forsaken
Merman*. Matthew Arnold fiercely defended classicism in the preface he wrote for the book, but his own classical poems are by
no means his best. The descriptive couplets of *Resignation: To
Fausta* (his sister Jane) are more alive, and though he becomes
rather preachy at the end, the section which begins:

> The World in which we live and move
> Outlasts aversion, outlasts love. . .

has something of the value he was to achieve in the best poems of
the 1852 volume: *A Summer Night*, which gives a vivid impression of the torn-in-two feelings of the young, seeing the alterna-
tives of life as 'slave or madman'; and *The Buried Life*, where love
gives a respite to the mind in conflict, releasing unconscious
springs of vitality:

> And then he thinks he knows
> The Hills where his life rose
> And the Sea where it goes.

Finally, in the 1852 volume, there is one of the most haunting of
all his poems, *The Future*, which ends with the famous line:

> Murmurs and scents of the infinite sea.

Matthew Arnold's poetry seems to me to reach its highest peaks when he uses nature to express his thoughts about the mystery of life and man's destiny. Mountains and water – sea, lake, river – are for him the images of deepest power, and the fate, or predicament, of man was always the deepest preoccupation of his mind. In his poetry, one concretizes the other. I suppose the most famous example is that fine poem *Dover Beach*. It is in these poems that Matthew Arnold expressed a certain kind of modern unease with the world as no one else of his time did, in a way which still holds meaning now, more than a hundred years later.

But in 1848, when Clough was laying aside his shorter poems, which he was to publish, with a friend's, in a volume to be called *Ambarvalia*, to write, suddenly and straight off, *The Bothie of Tober na Vuolich*, Matt had hardly yet acquired his stance. He knew what he wanted to do, none better, but he had not yet done it. And then here was Clough, doing something quite different, in a style which Matt did not consider suitable to poetry at all.

The Bothie is the story of a reading party in the Highlands and the love affair, in particular, of a young gentleman from Oxford and the daughter of a Scottish crofter, which rather improbably ends in a decision to marry and emigrate to New Zealand. People said that Tom Arnold was the original of 'Philip' but in his reminiscences he maintained that there was much of Clough himself in the character. Tom had certainly fallen in love before his departure, but it was with the daughter of an Archbishop. But Clough himself felt an attraction for girls not of his own social class; the poem *Natura Naturans*, printed in *Ambarvalia*, describes with charm a transient instance in a railway carriage, with nothing said on either side. About this Tom Arnold wrote to their friend Shairp: 'Some irreverent dogs, upon reading it, would smile, and say they had experienced the same feeling many times. But this does not hinder it from being a beautiful picture of innocent sensations of beings not blasés who have not yet learnt to profane and vulgarize, that which in itself is wonderful and sacred.'

Clough's way of falling in love (apart from passing attractions) was to prove more like that of 'Claude' in *Amours de Voyage*, another novel in verse which he began the next year, during the siege of Rome. Claude, like Clough, finds difficulty in making up his mind about anything, and whenever he does, circumstances prevent the action he takes from reaching fulfilment. Clough's

correspondence with his fiancée, Blanche Smith, reveals so tor-
tuous and self-torturing a way of being in love, yet so uncertain,
as to be most unlike either of the Arnolds, who were both direct,
and Tom headlong, in action.

It is curious that in their poetic natures Clough and Matt seem
to reverse roles. Matt, the ironic wit, almost the fop, observant,
self-admittedly worldly, as a poet was serious, melancholy, ro-
mantically classical, aiming for the high subject, the sense of the
beautiful and concerned for the architecture of verse, for the
whole. He despised the incidental 'fine line'; yet he often produced them himself – lines, more than poems, of his, haunt our
memories. But Clough, the idealist, the impractical academic man,
self-tormenting, self-analysing, anxious and always somehow
unhappy, yet wrote off these busy English hexameters, based on
stress, sketching a whole party of young gentlemen, cigars and
all, the idiomatic conversation, the love affairs of a long vacation,
all in a carefree ironic style. One would expect the London Matt
to write a poem like *The Bothie* and the Oxford Clough to write
The Strayed Reveller. Clough's poetic self is extremely sophisticated, unlike his everyday self. In everyday life it was Matt who
was by far the more sophisticated.

I suppose the existence of the two sides in each accounts for
their friendship, but the fact that they were expressed in opposite
ways accounts for Matt's irritation with Clough for writing *The
Bothie* at all, and his even greater irritation when other people
liked it, as many did. It went against everything Matt was saying in his preface to his own poems, his deepest feelings on the
use of poetry and what it ought to be. 'A great human action of
a thousand years ago,' he wrote, 'is more interesting than a
smaller human action of today, even though upon the representation of this last the most consummate skill may have been
expended, and though it has the advantage of appealing by its
modern language, familiar manners, and contemporary allusions,
to all our transient feelings and interests.'

He wrote to Clough in a tone so critical as to be almost offen-
sive, but Clough does not appear to have taken offence – or to have
taken any notice. He went on writing in his conversational contemporary way, and in spite of his self-deprecation was perfectly
convinced it was the right style for him, as it evidently was.

In November 1848 Matt was writing to Clough. 'I have been in
Oxford the last two days and hearing Sellar and the rest of that

clique who know neither life nor themselves rave about your poem gave me a strong almost bitter feeling with respect to them, the age, the poem, even you. Yes, I said to myself, something tells me I can, if need be, at last dispense with them all, even with him: better that, than be sucked for an hour even into the Time Stream in which they and he plunge and bellow. I became calm in spirit, but uncompromising, almost stern.' However, he went on to give good news of *The Bothie*'s sales and ended up, 'When are you coming up hither love? My man has the gout at Bowood.'

All of these Oxford friends addressed each other as 'love' and 'my dear' indiscriminately; it was a trick, but not a sentimental one.

Tom Arnold's reaction to *The Bothie* was quite different from Matt's; his own enthusiasm took him by surprise. It was not that he identified himself with Philip but that he shared with Clough so many of the feelings and thoughts which went to make up the poem, weaving together the social and political and amorous ideals into an almost religious vocation. Strange as it may seem from its subject matter, the poem was the result of the sense of liberation and hope which the February Revolution had given to Clough, and which equally affected Tom, even at such a distance of time and space.

The time lag was such that it was in March 1849 that Tom was writing from Nelson some of his political feelings, ending with slogans in the Clough style:

> Vive Cavaignac!
> À bas Thiers et Louis Napoléon!
> Viva l'Italia e Mazzini!
> Abasso Carlo Alberto e Pio Nono!
> Vive la Démocratie Fraternelle!
> À bas le privilège.
> Vive l'Art et la Science!
> À bas l'ignorance et l'imposture.

But it was not till September 1849 that he mentioned *The Bothie*, almost a year after it came out, when he was still in Nelson but expecting soon to go to Tasmania to take up his new job of Schools Inspector. Clough's poem had arrived at last in August, along with Matt's book – *A Strayed Reveller and Other Poems*, by 'A' – which had appeared in February. Of the latter Tom merely said, 'I must write to dear old Matt himself. It was very pleasant to recognize old friends . . .' But then he went on: '*The Bothie* greatly surpasses my expectations. With a vein of coarseness cropping out here and there, it is yet on the whole a noble poem, well held together, clear, full of purpose and full of promise. With joy I see the old fellow bestirring himself, "awakening like a strong man out of sleep, and shaking his invincible locks"; and if he remains true and works, I think there is nothing too high and great to be expected of him. I do not think Matt is right in saying that Clough "had no vocation for literature." '

On 24th September 1849 he wrote to Clough himself: 'I cannot quite say I hasten to thank you for the "*Bothie*" and your poems (*Ambarvalia*), for I have now had them more than a month; but believe me, during that time, in my inmost heart, I have thanked and blessed you for them not seldom. *The Bothie* is my especial delight; though I very much like also some of the short poems, particularly "When Israel came out of Egypt"; which I am pleased to think you wrote in my old frowsy lodgings in Margaret Street. But *The Bothie* – tho' the *Spectator* may jeer, and by the bye, I should like to see its remarks – places its author, in the view of thinking men, above a legion of poetasters; presents itself to me indeed rather as an action than a literary composition – an action, I truly think, among the boldest and purest that I have known . . . I feel now as if I could put entire trust, not only in your genius, but in your fortitude; about which alone I had formerly any doubts . . .'

He continued the letter from Wellington about two months later, on 22nd November: 'This is a long interval, but there has been no opportunity of sending the letter in the mean time. *The Bothie* – I am afraid I shall tire you with talking about it, but I cannot help it – has been much read and discussed since I came here . . . At first I thought there was something of coarseness in parts, but I don't know; the more I read it, the less I wish for any even the slightest alteration.'

Clough himself, in a letter written from Liverpool in February 1849, told Tom of his recent discovery than the original name Toper na fuosich contained in Gaelic (so he had heard) some kind of reference to female genital parts – which Clough indicated through a line of Horace – and, thinking of the book lying in the drawing rooms of England, he broke out, 'O Mercy! – it is too ludicrous not to tell someone, but too appallingly awkward to tell anyone on this side of the globe: – in the Gath and Ascalon of the

Antipodes you may talk of it, and laugh at your pleasure.' Argument as to the meaning of the place name has gone on since then, but the poem's title was quickly changed to the intentionally meaningless Tober-na-Vuolich.

Clough was certainly not the poet to *intend* coarseness and Tom's comment on *Natura Naturans*, quoted above, shows that he thought there was less of it in his friend than in the 'irreverent dogs' who laughed at his simplicity. Perhaps he was thinking of such things as the reference to the country girls' legs, when the excited Philip, growing romantic at the sight of a girl lifting potatoes is interrupted by Lindsay:

> Or, – high-kilted perhaps, cried Lindsay, at last successful,
> Lindsay this long time swelling with scorn and pent-up fury,
> Or high-kilted perhaps, as once at Dundee I saw them,
> Petticoats up to the knees, or even, it might be, above them,
> Matching their lily-white legs with the clothes they trod in
>   the wash-tub!

Tom Arnold was like Clough in his romantic approach to nature; he seems less introverted, less inclined to brood on difficulties. The difference of temperament appears in their approaches to marriage, into which Tom was soon to plunge with passionate love, while Clough, the older man, had not yet entered the long labyrinth of his engagement to Blanche Smith.

Clough's letter of February 1849 had begun by announcing that he had accepted what he called 'the Stincomalean position' – that of Principal of University Hall, a residence of the newly established non-denominational University College of London. It was known as Stincomalee because of its supposed devotion to Science. Clough had many misgivings, but he also had a widowed mother partly to support. He was tempted to join Tom, but not very strongly. 'You know too, I am not, my dear Tom, so clear as you are of the rottenness of this poor old ship here – Something I think we rash young men may learn from the failings and discomfiture of our friends in the new Republic – the millennium, as Matt says, won't come this bout.' He felt more tolerant himself, less impatient. 'Whether London will take my hopefulness out of me as it did yours, remains to be seen. Peut-être.'

He went on to affirm that he never questioned Tom's choice; 'but for thy departure I should perhaps still be lingering undecided in the courts of conformity . . . but quit the country for ever, is not, so far as I can tell, my vocation.' And on 24th

(76)

February he added to his letter in a mood of disillusion: 'Today my dear brother republican, is the glorious anniversary of the great revolution of '48, whereof what shall we now say? Put not your trust in republics nor in any constitution of man. God be praised for the downfall of Louis Philippe. – This with a faint feeble echo of that loud last year's scream of *à bas Guizot* seems to be the sum total. Or are we to salute the rising sun with *Vive l'Empereur* and the green liveries! President for life I think they will make him, and then begin to tire of him. Meanwhile the Great Powers are to restore the Pope! and crush the renascent (*alite lugubri*) Roman Republic; of which Joseph Mazzini has just been declared a citizen.'

Back from revolutions to poetry: 'At last our own Matt's book. Read mine first, my child, if our volumes go forth together. Otherwise you won't read mine, *Ambarvalia* at any rate, at all. I have been pressing them to my bosom for the last 48 hours – no 36 I believe.' A sly little correction!

Tom had received this letter when he wrote his own, giving his feelings about *The Bothie*, but before his reply reached his friend, Clough had gone to Rome, and came in for the siege by the French army which Louis Napoleon had sent to help restore the Pope. This cynical attack by one republic on another influenced Clough; he was less involved with the cause of republicanism, but felt more on behalf of the Roman people.

'This, my dear Tom,' he wrote on 3rd June 1849, 'is being written while the guns are going off – there – there – there! For these blackguard French are attacking us again – May the Lord scatter and confound them . . .' On 18th June he added to his letter; they had had a fortnight of gunnery. 'But we've been bombarded, my dear, think of that: several shells have fallen even on this side of the river: and I actually saw two grenades burst in the air! Lots of killed and wounded too, of course – French, please God, however, as well as Romans. But it is funny to see how much like any other city a besieged city looks: – unto this has come our grand Lib. Eg. and Frat. revolution!'

There he broke off and the letter was not finished till the end of October in London, when Clough added to it an early version of his most famous poem: *Say not the struggle naught availeth*.

But he began a letter to Matt soon after he broke off the one to Tom. 'Dear Matt, why the d—l I should write to you he only knows who implanted the spirit of disinterested attention in the heart of a spaniel.' He hoped he might get out of Rome in July. 'Our orbits therefore early in August might perhaps cross, and we two undeviating stars salute each other once again amid the infinite spaces – Not that I particularly desire or in any way urge such an event – but I advertise you that I hope to be in the Geneva country about that time, reposing in the bosom of nature from the fatigues of Art and the turmoil of War!!!!'

The letter could not be sent and at the beginning of July he added the final scenes of the siege: 'On Saturday evening the Assembly resolved to give in: Mazzini & Co. resigned; and a deputation went off to Oudinot . . . Today they say the French will enter. Altogether I incline to think the Roman populace *has* shown a good deal of "apathy" – they didn't care about the bombs much, but they didn't care to fight *very* hard, either . . .' After signing his initials he added, 'I shall just stay to see these black-guards behave and then cut north.'

In fact, as he later told Tom, he went first to Naples, which he greatly enjoyed, and then home by Switzerland. 'I am full of ad-miration for Mazzini . . . But on the whole, "Farewell Politics, utterly. – What can I do!" ' This was a quotation from his own new poem, *Amours de Voyage*, begun under siege.

Although he went through Thun he missed Matt who was not there till September. It was Matt who was suffering from Amours de Voyage – this was the second summer he had gone to Thun for the sake of Marguerite's blue eyes. In the long letter he wrote to Clough on 23rd September 1849, he said nothing of this love affair, though the fact of its having gone sour in some way per-haps drove him to express more than usual of his brooding thoughts – gathered, as usual, round his central preoccupation of poetry.

'With me it is curious at present: I am getting to feel more independent and unaffectible as to all intellectual and poetical performance the impatience at being faussé in which drove me some time since so strongly into myself, and more snuffing after a moral atmosphere to respire in than ever before in my life. Marvel not that I say unto you, ye must be born again. While I will not talk much of these things, yet the considering of them has led me constantly to you, the only living one almost that I know of

The children of the second birth
Whom the world could not tame –

(78)

for my dear Tom has not sufficient besonnenheit [prudence] for it to be any *rest* to think of him any more than it is a *rest* to think of mystics and such cattle – not that Tom is in any sense cattle or even a mystic but he has not a "still considerate mind".

'What I must tell you is that I have never yet succeeded in any one great occasion in consciously mastering myself: I can go thro the imaginary process of mastering myself and see the whole affair as it would then stand, but at the critical point I am too apt to hoist up the mainsail to the wind and let her drive. However as I get more awake to this it will I hope mend for I find with me a clear almost palpable intuition (damn the logical senses of the word) is necessary before I get into prayer: unlike many people who set to work at their duty self-denial etc like furies in the dark hoping to be gradually illuminated as they persist in this course. Who also perhaps may be sheep but not of my fold whose one natural craving is not for profound thoughts, mighty spiritual workings etc etc but a distinct seeing of my way as far as my own nature is concerned: which I believe to be the reason why the mathematics were ever foolishness to me.'

It is a feeling about religious experience which was to become common during the later part of the century, and after.

'I am here in a curious and not altogether comfortable state,' Matt continued: 'however, tomorrow I carry my aching head to the mountains and to my cousin the Bhunlis Alp.' He quoted some lines of his own, from the poem *Parting* (published in 1852) which end 'Ye torrents, I come!' and went on, 'Yes, I come, but in three or four days I shall be back here and then I must try how soon I can ferociously turn towards England.'

Suddenly he burst out, 'My dear Clough these are damned times – everything is against one – the height to which knowledge is come, the spread of luxury, our physical enervation, the absence of great *natures*, the unavoidable contact with millions of small ones, newspapers, cities, light profligate friends, moral despera-does like Carlyle, our own selves and the sickening consciousness of our difficulties: but for God's sake let us neither be fanatics nor yet chalf [sic] blown by the wind . . .'

Matt was within a few months of his twenty-seventh birthday when he wrote this and it provides a sample of what was maturing in that curious mind of his, so fastidious and yet so energetic and concentrated. But the old high spirits had by no means dis-appeared; he wrote an amusing scrap to Clough from Rugby in

November. 'I said a lovely poem to that fool Shairp today which he was incapable of taking in. He is losing his hair.' He mentioned the offer to Tom of the Inspectorship in Van Diemen's Land: 'I shouldn't wonder if he took it. I think I shall emigrate. Why the devil don't you.'

He did not emigrate, and Clough, though he was to spend a spell in America, homed back to England, midcentury smoky England, 'unpoetical' as Matt found it; even Tom returned at last from Tasmania. But all of them were uneasy in their own country and their own time, acutely aware of the miseries of the poor, the sudden hideous growth of the industrial towns, the way in which money was coming to dominate society more and more, the debasement of so many standards in that time of rapid change – far more fundamental change then than now, for all that is said of the technological revolution today. For our situation is simply an accelerated and intensified version of what began then.

For the young men of the Arnolds' generation it was the transition from an agrarian, trading, traditional England to a vast commercial imperialism haunted by religious and moral uncertainties. For young liberals the situation was particularly obscure, since the revolutions came and failed to bring the people any nearer to the natural good life, the life of honest work and art, with a religion that both supported and expressed the meaning of living. And poetry was no longer something you just did if you felt like it, but was becoming something you had to think about and justify, separate from the rest of life, not part of it, and nothing to do with earning your living.

'Farewell Politics, utterly.' The Revolutions had ended in fiasco. *Restat vivere.*

IV

At the Antipodes

I

On Sunday 19th March 1848, Tom Arnold got his first sight of New Zealand, just before 6 in the evening. It was of Stewart Island, the southernmost part of the country. 'The land was high and bold,' he wrote in his journal letter to his mother, noting that 'the peculiar feeling comes across one of having seen it all before.' He was to have a similar feeling when he met his future wife; those who have experienced something like it will know how strange it is.

After the excitement of arrival there succeeded an intolerably prolonged stay in Otago harbour, and Tom did not arrive in Wellington until 23rd May. Almost at once he met Bishop Selwyn, who took him to a levée at Government House and introduced him to Mr Eyre, the Lieutenant Governor. Although he was not dressed for the occasion Tom felt quite up to it when he noticed the *gaucherie* of the colonials who made their bows to the Governor. For all his radical views he naturally gravitated to people of a social background similar to his own. He was lucky in meeting a congenial friend in the person of Alfred Domett (Browning's 'Waring') who had come as a settler to Nelson in 1842 and had recently been appointed Colonial Secretary for New Munster, the southern part of New Zealand. Domett was a poet and an original character, who later became Prime Minister of New Zealand.

Tom Arnold lost no time in going to see the two sections of land which his father had bought in enthusiasm for colonial expansion. They were about a hundred acres each and situated in Makara valley, about eight miles due west of Wellington. It was uncleared virgin forest and unfortunately the two plots were on opposite sides of the valley. He was advised by the agent of the

New Zealand company to exchange one for a better tract front-
ing a good road, and believing that the trustees in England could
make no objection, he wrote to them and set to work on the new
plot on the Porirua Road. He lodged with a Kentish couple, the
Barrows, who had children and grandchildren with them, and
paid the men to fell trees, clearing five acres on which he proposed to build a two-roomed hut.

But already, by the end of June, Domett had made him a
proposal which attracted him very much. There was £8000
available to found a college at Nelson, and what better Principal
for it than the son of Dr Arnold of Rugby? On Sunday 25th June
1848 Tom told his mother of this offer, adding that he had already
been wondering how he could make best use of his abilities for the
good of the people around him. 'For I am well enough aware that
I have no particular genius for farming, and that I am better fitted
to teach little boys English History than to invent improved
methods of cultivation or breed fat cattle.' When he discovered
that he would be 'left unfettered in matter of opinions' he was all
enthusiasm for Nelson College, and his first thought was of
Clough.

The next day he was writing to him: 'Though I have not hitherto had time to write to you, I have often thought of your jolly
old countenance, and longed for a sight of it; especially when
walking alone in the forests or among the hills of this beautiful
country . . .' The college would not become a practical proposition
for about a year, but 'do you not think, my dear Clough, that you
could make up your mind to come out and join in a work which
seems to promise so well, and which would require no unworthy
compromises to embrace it? Fancy if Shairp and you and I were
working together here, living in the light of a common faith, and
united by the affection which we already bear one another, – do
you not think we might make a glorious onslaught on the great
kingdom of Darkness, and do somewhat towards speeding the
coming of that day, when Kingcraft and Priestcraft shall be among
the things that were, and Love shall bind up the wounds of this
bruised and suffering Humanity. Perhaps I speak too wildly, but
at any rate it is my fixed belief that until Education is taken out of
the hands of the priests, little will be done.'

Curiously enough, he was shortly afterwards offered the head-
ship of another college, planned for Porirua by Bishop Selwyn.
Tom was writing a letter to his sister Fan, fourteen when he left

(82)

England, and remarked: 'After this Edward Whately may well say that we Arnolds are born with silver spoons in our mouths.' But there could be no question as to which appointment he would prefer. 'For to be obliged to teach Anglo-Catholicism to unhappy juveniles would infallibly make me sick, which would be highly undecorous in the Head of a College, would it not, my Skrat? Head of a College! to think that I, the Radical, the – etc etc. – should ever come to be classed in the same category with those dear old respectable Conservative pudding-headed worthies of the Hebdomadal board! I could laugh till I cried at the ludi-crousness of the thought.'

Meanwhile he had started teaching the Barrow grandchildren in the evenings. 'The lesson book was full of the most stupid prosy reading-lessons that can be imagined, all about morality and the pleasures of virtue and so forth.' So he used Words-worth's *Lyrical Ballads* instead. 'It answered very well, and what is more, the old people, who cannot read themselves, listened to the verses as they were puzzled out, with the most fixed attention, and thought "Lucy Gray" in particular, "as pretty a sad story" as they had ever heard.'

Tom was astonished at the superstitions of these simple people. 'In an age of materialism and steam, here are people who firmly believe that a fiery serpent, as big round as a man's leg, once appeared in an iron furnace at Tunbridge a few years ago, and that it was just going to spring out and destroy everyone in the place, only fortunately the fire was immediately put out and the serpent vanished.' But he thought some of their ghost stories poetical, and their faith in the unseen world a relief, for 'real life wears such a harsh and forbidding aspect for the English poor, that one must rejoice if some belief or other, though it be but a superstitious one, remains to poeticize and ennoble their daily life'.

He had now heard about the revolution in France, but his en-thusiasm for that did not lessen his hopes for Nelson College, which he saw as 'an institution like Iona in the middle ages', as he wrote to Clough, 'which might one day spread the light of Religion and Letters over these barbarous colonies and through-out the great archipelago of the Pacific, where hitherto only the white man's avarice or lust or his imbecile Theology have pene-trated.'

He finished this letter at the end of September by mentioning that the Governor had offered him the post of private secretary till the college scheme was begun. Tom thought he might accept this, as it would enable him to see much of the country. 'At least I shall be able to be of some use to Grey, whom I really like. I might certainly rusticate in the bush as a free and independent citizen, until the College was ready, but the fact is that house-keeping in the bush without a wife is next door to an impossibility.' In point of fact he ultimately refused the job and in his memoirs, written long afterwards, said he had determined to have nothing to do with the Colonial Government so long as it was carried on by nominees and not by representative assemblies. Democratic ideals must be upheld.

But nor did he stay, wifeless, in the bush. In September he heard from his uncle on behalf of the Arnold trustees in England that they would not agree to the change of sections. So he had cleared his five acres for someone else! The original section was inferior and difficult of access; and he had spent nearly all his money. He decided to go to Nelson.

He travelled in an unconventional way, for he was offered a passage across the straits between the two islands in a ten-ton sailing cutter belonging to Frederick Weld, son of a famous Catholic family of Chidiock in Dorset, and a settler who was to become Prime Minister of New Zaeland in 1864. On meeting him again in February 1849 Tom wrote to his mother: 'The young Catholic aristocrat is looking quite handsome, with his blue eyes and long curling hair.' In his memoirs he also recalled Weld's 'lithe well-knit figure and resolute look'.

Tom stayed several days with Weld at Flaxbourne, his isolated sheep station, shooting teal, and reading a history of philosophy by the Jesuit professor Freudenfelt, which struck him as better than anything of the kind he had come across at Oxford. He also came in for an earthquake. His bed was shaken from side to side, he told his mother on 10th October 1848, 'Every plank in the house creaked and rattled, the bottles and glasses in the next room kept up a sort of infernal dance, and most of them fell. When the shock was past there came a few spasmodic heavings, like long drawn breaths, and then all was still.' Slight shocks went on for several days and he had a curious experience on a hill where Weld had taken him to see the view. 'We were sitting down on the top, when a smart shock came, and we distinctly saw the whole top of the mountain heave to and fro.'

He eventually arrived in Nelson, where he found the climate intoxicating and the fruit luxuriant. But it was only when he had decided to return to Wellington in search of work that a deputation of *pères de famille* came to ask him to start a school for boys in Nelson. Tom told them he would undertake it if they could muster twenty boys and a rent-free house; then he returned to Wellington.

There, in January 1849, he found all the home letters written in August and September, which brought tears to his eyes as he read them. He continued to be lonely in this busy colonial life, so different from his radical visions in London. But the references to his lost Etty had died away from his own letters; instead there were mentions of other young women whom he met socially. He had already heard of Etty's engagement to a Mr Wale, a lawyer living in London – Jane Arnold had sent him the news in June 1848.

Tom now heard to his satisfaction from the family men in Nelson and decided to return there, describing in his letter home on 7th February, the 'merry bachelor party' they had had before he left. 'There was a great deal of singing, and they made me take a considerable part of it; indeed, I am, though rather against my will, one of the established nightingales of the place. This does not say much, you will think, for the state of musical knowledge in Wellington, and indeed it does not. However there are one or two songs I can sing with a kind of go, "verve" as the French call it, that has a certain effect. I have learnt to sing the Marseillaise . . .' In his memoirs Tom recalled that he once sang 'The Shan Van Vocht' at a party of young Irish officers in Wellington and remembered that a senior officer had remarked that twenty-five years ago 'that young man would have got himself into trouble by singing that song'.

By March he was back in Nelson, established in a small white wooden house, with a respectable housekeeper, and boys arriving on the 26th. Boarders were to pay £35 a year. 'From the smallness of the sum,' he wrote to his mother, 'you will perhaps think I am going to treat them à la Squeers; but it is not so very small when you take into consideration the cheapness of everything here. I should go on swimmingly if I had a wife. But where is that necessary of life to be procured? The charming Emma Sutton is married by this time, I suppose; besides, she would probably think colonial life a decided bore. However, I mean for the present to take your advice, dearest mother, and be patient; it does not do to plunge into marriage with the eyes shut.'

Wise words, but in a year's time he was to do something very like that.

Meanwhile he unpacked his books and hung up a picture of Jenny Lind who, he felt, seemed to watch over him and guard him from 'low thoughts and unmanly despondency. I look into her deep deep eyes, and it seems as if something of her purity and nobleness passed, for a time at least, into my heart also.'

Those low despondent thoughts returned however, as it became clear that the boys were unruly and the fathers did not pay the bills. He had time for private study, but the difficulty of getting books was extreme. He did not attempt to din Latin and Greek into his pupils' heads but told his mother that he meant to make French his *cheval de bataille*, 'as being the most easy and direct road to an acquaintance with modern literature and modern thought as they exist in other countries besides our own' – a very Arnoldian plan. But the College plan had run into difficulties and he was uncertain whether he would stay in New Zealand, even asking Clough to look out for jobs for *him* – 'that's a good old Stupo'. His stammering, he said, was all but gone.

However, he moved to a new, larger house in town, though it was still in an unfinished state, like his current letter to his mother, when on 20th August he concluded it in great excitement, telling of an offer he had received from the Governor of Van Diemen's Land (Tasmania) of the Inspectorship of Schools there, with a salary of £400 a year and travelling expenses. 'You may imagine my feelings. How good is God; how he watches over the children of the righteous ... Shakespeare says, "What's in a name?"; but our father's name has been to us, not only a source of proud and gentle memories, but actually and literally better and more profitable than houses and land.'

He got rid of the lease of the house in Nelson with relief. Though Mrs Arnold might like to think of him 'with his boys about him' as another Thomas Arnold, it did not really suit Tom and he found the time long before he could get a boat, first back to Wellington by a slow coaster, and then to Australia in the brigantine *William Alfred*, which after much pitching and tossing against adverse winds, landed him at Sydney on 17th December 1849. He stayed there over Christmas and then embarked for Tasmania in a steamer. Gales and storms pursued him and it was with relief that he arrived at last, on 13th January 1850, at Launceston.

'Mountains again!' he wrote to his sister Jane. 'Those dear old friends, the sight of which is always a comfort to me.'

2

Tom pushed on for Hobart Town by coach the next day and on 17th January he was picking up his letter to Jane. 'Since I arrived here, my dearest, I have been in such a constant bustle, that hitherto I have not been able to continue my letter. Last Monday at 4 o'clock I left Launceston on top of the mail; we arrived at 7 in the evening.' He stayed one night at the Ship Inn but after that with his cousin John Buckland, son of Dr Arnold's sister Frances. Buckland, ex-Rugby and ex-Oxford, was twenty-five and had come out in 1846 as head of the newly founded Hutchins School, a position he was to hold until his death in 1874.

By letter, Tom had been welcomed by Charles Stanley, a brother of Arthur's and private secretary to the Governor, but he had suddenly died, and one of Tom's first calls was on the young widow, who had just come in from a drive and was lying on a sofa with her bonnet on. 'Tears are never far distant from the eyes of an exile,' wrote Tom; 'and had it not been for the fear of agitating her, I could have wept like a child to see that pale wan face, and to mark the twitch of agony which sometimes came over her features when speaking of her Charles . . .'

However, for Tom a new life was beginning and he was very soon installed in office. The Governor, Sir William Denison, was 'rather short, but strongly built and with the solid compact brow, and intelligent but unimaginative eye, which you so often see in men of science. He has a straightforward manner of delivering himself, which I like.' This was a first impression; later Tom was to come into conflict with him over educational policy. Denison supported the transportation of criminals from England, and resisted any movement towards representative government.

Tom was handed over to James Bicheno, the Colonial Secretary, 'an immensely fat jolly looking old man, rather a bon vivant I believe, but with literary tastes.' Mr Bicheno immediately invited Tom to a large party, so that work and social life began simultaneously.

Soon after his arrival Tom had a bout of jaundice but recovered quickly and began his first tour of inspection. The population of Tasmania was not more than about 70,000; in his memoirs Tom lamented that the aboriginal people were already a dying race, there were few in the schools and he noted that the last old woman died in 1876. The schools were founded by the various churches but were granted one penny a day per child by the government. Tom Arnold found this system unsatisfactory and was instrumental in altering it. In 1853 a fixed salary was introduced for the teachers and various administrative reforms made, as a result of a commission of four, driven round in a wagonette, Tom records, by a genial Archdeacon.

Tom began work in January 1850 and early in March he met Julia Sorell. Let Tom himself describe the occasion, as he did in his memoirs at the end of his long life. 'I was at a small party at a Mrs Poynter's in Davey Street. On a sofa sat a beautiful girl in a black silk dress, with a white lace berthe and red bows on the skirt of the dress. My friend Clarke presently introduced me to her. I remember that as we talked a strange feeling came over me of having met her before – of having always known her – as if neither the tone nor the drift of her words were unexpected.'

They met early in March and by the end of that same month they were engaged and Tom was writing to her on the 28th as 'My own dearest Julia'. It was a sudden and passionate falling in love of two people unlike in almost every way.

In a letter of the following November to his sister Mary, Tom wrote: 'K. [Jane] wants a description of Julia; so here is an extract from a letter to Clough, written a long time ago but never sent.' It is strange that he did not simply write a new description, since by then he had been married five months, but perhaps he felt that an early impression might present a clearer portrait. 'She has the most singular profile, the forehead high and straight, the nose prominent but thin and most delicately formed, the lips very slightly parted; the chin rather receding and inclined to be double. Her eyes are brown; not large, but full of life and fire; her hair is nearly black. Her hand is small and very pretty, and she gives the most frank and engaging shake of the hand that you can imagine.'

Their daughter Mary, afterwards the novelist Mrs Humphry

Ward, also describes her mother as having small hands and feet and delicate features; she called her vivacity and overflowing energy 'French', believing the Sorell family to have been French Huguenots. They may have been, or have come originally from Spain, but they were certainly settled in England from the late seventeenth century and had a long connexion with the British Army.

Julia had a curious background. Her grandfather, Lt.-Col. William Sorell (1775–1848) had been forced to leave the army in consequence of having abandoned his own wife and six children to live with the wife of a brother officer, when he was stationed at the Cape. In 1816 he was appointed Lieutenant Governor of Van Diemen's Land, arriving there the next year and installing Mrs Kent at Government House. He had a second family by her and was an easy-going and popular Governor till his recall and retirement in 1823. Meanwhile his eldest legitimate son, William (1800–60), who had been assisting his mother in England, came out late in 1823 and was provided for by an appointment as Registrar of the supreme court in Hobart Town, fortunately confirmed by the next Governor in the following year.

This William Sorell settled down to a respectable life but he married the daughter of a man as 'wild' as his father, though in a different way. Captain Anthony Fenn Kemp had travelled in his youth in France and in the United States, becoming an ardent republican before he arrived in New South Wales in 1795 at the age of twenty-two. Settling at Mount Vernon in Van Diemen's Land, he became 'a thorn in the side of several governors' as Tom recorded in his memoirs. Kemp enjoyed opposition, fathered eighteen children and died in his ninety-fifth year in 1868 – so he was very much alive when his grand-daughter married Tom Arnold.

His daughter, Elizabeth Julia, who married William, son of Governor Sorell, bore her husband three daughters and two sons. She took the three girls to Brussels, where Governor Sorell had retired, to finish their education, but almost at once went off with an army officer and was never seen by her husband again. Julia and her sisters were sent back to Hobart Town, where Julia soon became the belle of the garrison society.

Born in 1826, she was about twenty-four when Tom Arnold met her, and he was then a few months past his twenty-sixth birthday. Julia Sorell had already been twice engaged, first to

Chester Eardley Wilmot, son of a former Governor, and then to an army officer called Elliott, not further identified, who was holding the field when Tom Arnold arrived on the scene. Besides these engagements there had been a good deal of gossip about Julia, in connexion with Eardley Wilmot's father, the Governor, and with Captain A. C. L. Fitzroy, the son of a Governor of New South Wales. There is no doubt that Julia had a passionate and wilful nature, but she must also have had great charm; she retained the affection of her intellectual daughter Mary, who was also devoted to her father. Julia herself seems to have had little intellectual power; there are no references to reading or opinions of hers, such as occur in connexion with Matt's wife – an equally pretty feminine person who was yet able to share her husband's interests as Julia never shared Tom's. She was full of energy and feeling and loved a social life, but the thought of the intelligent women of the Arnold family filled her with alarm.

Nevertheless she fell in love with Tom, tall, dark and earnest, yet able to enjoy life with all the Arnold exuberance. His republicanism could not have worried the grand-daughter of Anthony Fenn Kemp, 'who had conversed with Washington' and at that time Tom had such a dislike of Anglo-Catholicism that it never occurred to her that he would become a Roman Catholic. Her prejudice against Romanism was so intense that one wonders if there was some special reason for it, some experience in Brussels, where her mother had deserted them, perhaps. It was not as if she were particularly religious, though it was she who made Tom have their first children baptized, a rite he then considered pointless.

Tom's letters to Julia after their engagement give an impression of a man sure of her love, yet aware of those other men with whom her name had been linked. In the very first he referred to Captain Fitzroy, whose holiday in Van Diemen's Land in 1849 was the occasion of the flirtation. (He was to die, unmarried, of wounds received at Sevastopol in 1855). Tom wrote: 'You know the Fitzroys, dearest, do you not? I remember hearing a story which rather amused me – though I daresay it was not true – that at the time of Captain Fitzroy's last visit, after he had gone away, you said, in fun of course, that you felt quite ashamed of yourself for having gone on with him in the way you had, and that you should go down into the country and rusticate there for some months as a punishment; which you accordingly did. But the good people of Hobart Town are such capital hands at improving and embellishing, that I dare say you will not recognize in the above much of what you actually said.'

Then he went on at once, 'Darling Julia, I want you to write to Fox How. I wonder I did not think of mentioning it before. Something of this sort will do; "My dear Mrs Arnold", (I suppose it will not do to say "Mother" until the knot is actually tied) "I am going to marry your son Tom; he is a sad scamp but I hope to make something of him, etc." Or suppose it is to one of my sisters, "My dear Jane, your brother Tom has had the impudence to make love to me; what am I to do with him?" But seriously, darling, I wish you would write a little note to my mother, and send it to me, that I may enclose it in my next letter to Fox How. You cannot think how much pleasure it would give them all at home. What a proud and happy day it will be for me, if God in his mercy permits it, when I bring you to that dear old house, embosomed among the mountains, where, till I knew you, all my affections were centred, and introduce you to that dear home circle, of which you will henceforth form one.'

Defeated by the country posts he added to his letter next day, which was Good Friday. 'My own Julia, you cannot think how unspeakably happy your love makes me. The first thing in the morning, and the last at night, comes that sweet thought, my Julia is mine, and I am hers. I am prouder than if I was king of the world. And even as to ambition and the love of fame, "that last infirmity of noble minds," what is there that a man need despair of effecting, who was sustained by the love of a being like you – Goodbye, my own dearest love. How I hate the word goodbye! "Au revoir" has a pleasanter sound . . . It would be so very inconvenient, dearest, to come down to the officers' ball, that I am sure you would not wish me to do it. Ever, my own Julia, yours most fondly and affectionately, T. Arnold.'

The mention of ambition is interesting, since it had not occurred before; Tom Arnold was the least ambitious of men. He was an idealist, but not by nature an activist. Years later he was to tell his daughter that Julia should have been linked to someone more worthy of *her* ambition, and probably from the start the ambitions were hers. If so, they were to be bitterly frustrated by that very strength of will and conscience which must have distinguished Tom among her officer admirers.

Julia had evidently taken fright at the idea of the clever and virtuous Arnolds, for in his next letter Tom wrote: 'You need not be afraid, my dear Julia, of my family's being too good; they are much like other people, and when we are all at home, there is nothing but joking and fun from morning to night; but I suppose they fall into a serious vein when they are writing out to such a distance. I am sure they will love you, and I think you will love them.'

Tom's courtship, though brief and successful, had not been without its difficulties. The next day he was recalling how Dr Bedford, the clergyman who had baptized Julia and was to marry them, had been 'quizzing' her at a party, though she had not then told Tom *all* he had said. 'O my own Julia, I shall never forget how beautiful and captivating you were that night; nor what a rage I was in at finding you had gone home without me. After all, it was chiefly my own fault, for leaving my place by your side, where I was as happy as a prince, in order to ask Mrs Chapman to dawdle through an insufferable quadrille. But the truth is, I did not know then that you had broken off your engagement with Elliott, and I therefore thought it was hardly fair to you to remain by your side quite as much as my heart prompted me. My prudence was of little use, however; for I could not help looking at you every instant, and envying every one to whom you vouchsafed a word or a smile; so much so that some young lady, Miss Swan, I think, declared that she would never dance opposite Mr Arnold again, for instead of looking towards his "vis-à-vis" his eyes were always turned towards – you can guess who.'

On the end of that letter he added a note, insisting that she should not stay away from parties because he could not be there.

They were married in St David's cathedral, Hobart Town, on 13th June 1850, chosen because it had been Dr Arnold's birthday. On the 18th, Tom wrote his mother a long description of the wedding, which began, 'My dearest Mother, it is but a few days since I sent my last letter, and yet how much has happened since then. I am now sitting in the dining room of our new house, with a cheerful wood fire blazing in the hearth, and my own wife is sitting by me, hemming a silk handkerchief.' Then all the details of the great day were told – how Mr Bicheno lent his carriage, who was there, what was worn. 'Susy and Fan will perhaps like to know what I had on, so I will indulge their weak minds. I had on a blue frock coat, white waistcoat with lappels, light grey doeskin trowsers, and a tie of brown and white silk, tied in large bows.'

In the church, 'Julia looked pale, and was more moved than I expected her to be. She was dressed as follows: I tell you from her own mouth. She wore a white hook muslin dress over white muslin, high to the throat, with two deep flounces; a white lace mantle, white chip bonnet with a small feather and white lace veil; and white satin shoes. She also wore a massive Indian gold chain round her neck . . . I omitted to say that Julia's "brides" were composed of orange blossom and jasmine. There you have it all; whether from these data you will be able to form any sort of notion of the actual appearance of my beloved bride, I know not; but I know that in my eyes a thing so beautiful has rarely been seen.'

Dr Bedford, he said, had the good sense to leave out a good part of the service. 'There was something very delightful in taking Julia's hand and plighting my troth to her for life and till death.' When they returned to her father's house, 'she burst into a fit of tears, not altogether, she says, tears of sorrow,' but recovered upstairs and the wedding breakfast went off well. Still using Mr Bicheno's carriage they then drove straight to their new home, 'and here we have been ever since,' he ended, 'as happy in each other and in our lot as it is given to mortals to be.'

This letter lay unfinished for several weeks, but when Tom picked it up on 14th July, it was to say that their affection was not over with their 'honey moon'. They went for walks in the bush and Tom carved their initials on a log where they sat. After that he had to go off on an inspection tour to Ross, and returned with a bad attack of mumps. On 21st July Julia added a note in the corner, 'Dear Tom is at this moment groaning with pain, Dr Bedford [brother of the clergyman and MD, not DD] has just ordered him leeches which I am in hopes will relieve him. He is a dear patient invalid.' They sent some wedding cake, all the long way back to England.

3

Tom's was not the only marriage in the Arnold family that year. On 29th September he began a letter to his mother complaining that he had had no mail from England since April, when Jane had been ill, but now had heard from a friend that a nephew of Sir Fowell Buxton was to marry Miss Arnold. Tom immediately wondered if this marriage had taken place on the same day as his own, since it was that great occasion 'Papa's birthday'.

In fact, Jane Arnold married William Edward Forster in August 1850. She was within a year of thirty and it was a long time since her early, broken, engagement. Forster was a woollen manufacturer, well off, sprung of a Quaker family but himself becoming a member of the Church of England. He took up a political career and was destined for high office; Jane was an excellent wife for him and it turned out a happy and successful partnership, marred only by childlessness, which was, in a sense, remedied nine years later when they adopted the orphan children of Jane's brother William, the third Arnold to marry in 1850.

On 2nd October 1850 William was writing to Tom in his ebullient way, 'Today, my Thomas, I sit, a married man in the Bengal army, writing to a brother, it may be a married man, in Van Diemen's Land.' Willy was only twenty-two; his bride, Fanny Hodgson, who was four years his senior, was the daughter of General Hodgson, the discoverer of the sources of the Ganges and at that time Surveyor-General of India. They had met at Christmas 1849, when William gaily wrote: 'Miss Hodgson was rather pretty and talked pleasantly – but alas! I did not fall in Love: India has I fear changed my Nature.' However, by 16th February he was engaged, and began reading with Fanny a hymn of Keble's and a sermon of his father's, and told his mother that he hoped 'to do this great Thing, as he did, in the name of Jesus Christ'. The four-year gap impressed him as being exactly the same as that between his father and mother. Fanny herself wrote to her aunt, 'Though I acknowledge his manners are boyish, his mind is not so,' and said he was supposed to be more like his father than any of the four sons. They were married early in April 1850.

William Arnold, like his brothers, had been sent to Oxford, but could not settle there. He went up to Christ Chruch first on Christmas Eve 1846, having breakfasted in Matt's rooms, and spent about a year there. He had once intended to take Orders, but the Articles became an obstacle almost at once. Edward Oakfield, the hero of his novel *Oakfield*, said he had 'a vague feeling he was going to the devil there', and his creator may have felt the same. At Rugby he had been a great player of the school game and had helped to codify its rules; he was tall, with a shock of dark hair a hasty temper and impetuous nature.

He became a cadet in the 58th Regiment of Native Infantry, as
the old East India Company corps was now called, and sailed early
in 1848, spending his last month in London with Matt, which
gave him, he said, 'a very tender Feeling towards the rich old
villain'. Once in India, he did not get on very well with his fellow
officers, whose language at the mess he considered revolting,
even after what he had heard at public school and university.
As early as May 1848 he was writing to his mother, 'I must find
some soul, man woman or child to care for, or I shall burst.'

He nursed a dying friend and was soon helping at a school of
thirty boys, but he was restless and unsettled till he met Fanny
Hodgson at the Lahore Residency. Lady Lawrence wrote to Mrs
Arnold, 'Her calm self-possessed and stable character is just what
you would choose to mate with the more excitable nature of your
son.' She also spoke of her 'quiet good sense, thoughtfulness for
others and unmistakeable *reality*'. Tom Arnold, who happened
to have met a Mr Woodcock of the Indian Civil Service, had heard
that Fanny was 'a good and amiable young woman but by no
means pretty, rather the contrary', and told his sister Mary that
Woodcock thought Willy 'had done a foolish thing in marrying
so young'. But Tom thought that 'considering Willy's peculiar
character, he has done well in marrying. May God's blessing go
with him.'

William and Fanny certainly were happy together, and next
year he was offered a civil appointment by Sir Henry Lawrence,
as Assistant Commissioner at Amritsar in the Punjab, much more
suited to his abilities. That same year his first child, Edward
Penrose, like his nearest brother, was born in August, a couple of
months younger than Tom's first child, Mary, the future novelist.
Willy was to be a loving and boisterous father, as Dr Arnold had
been, but in 1852 he was severely ill with dysentery and the
following year came home, with wife and baby, on sick leave.
At Cairo they unexpectedly met Arthur Stanley, who rushed
down from his hotel room in the middle of shaving, to greet this
returning member of the Arnold family. Willy's next two children, Florence and Hugh Oakeley, were to be born in England,
during this long leave. But by the time Tom came home, in 1856,
William had left again for India, so the two brothers, who had
kept in constant touch from their far flung posts, never met again.

In the autumn of 1850 it was Matt's turn to get engaged, news
which surprised his brothers. Willy wrote to Tom that Matt was

'the very last man in the world whom I can fancy happily married, – or rather, happy in matrimony'. But then he went on to tease Tom: 'After all, Master Tom, it is not the very exact finale which we should have expected to your Republicanism of the last three or four years, to find you a respectable married man, holding a permanent appointment!'

Tom had not altogether lost his republicanism, or at least his radicalism, but marriage and a government job had certainly made a difference. In his memoirs he describes a meeting with 'Frost the Chartist', exiled for his share in the Newport riots of 1839, and now keeping a school. 'The old man did his work conscientiously and wrapped himself in a kind of dignified reserve, behind which there lay the impenetrable obstinacy of a Welsh Reformer. It is needless to say that I treated him with entire respect.'

His feelings about the ordinary criminals deported from England were quite different. 'The hateful red flag is flying from the signal staff,' he wrote to his mother on 3rd October 1850, 'showing that another ship of male convicts is coming in.' He asked her to imagine what she would feel if twenty villainous men were established in her valley every year, 'and you will be able to realize in some degree the horror and disgust which those feel, who are bound to this unhappy country by ties which they cannot break, who see free emigration entirely stopped and its place supplied by the deportation of the felonry of England to their shores'. The ticket-of-leave system he thought the worst possible, as the convicts, given relative freedom and unable to find work at once, often returned to their lawless ways in the new country.

Tom himself had just had experience of this, which he proceeded to relate. After dining out with friends he was driving Julia home when, 'as we came to a rather lonely part of the road, near a large tumbledown house now unoccupied, we observed a man sauntering along the footpath, who, as the gig drew near, sidled off into the road. He looked hard at the gig as we passed; a moment after Julia looked back; and cried out, "Tom, he is running after us." I looked back; and sure enough, the rascal was running after us as hard as he could and was within three or four yards of the gig. I whipped the old horse into a gallop and soon left the fellow at a distance, poor Julia however was very much frightened, and was sobbing hysterically all the way home.'

One cannot help feeling that, however frightened, none of the Arnold women would have sobbed hysterically all the way home.

Julia could be a delightful companion, however; on a visit to friends, who had made Tom sing one evening under the weeping willows, the next morning, out on the hillside, 'Julia was like a young colt, the bright sunshine, the fragrant air of the bush, elated her spirits, and we played together like two children.'

In these early days Tom often took Julia with him on his school visiting. In a November letter to his sister Mary he described how an old man who kept a village school had showed him a book called *Life's Last Hours*, 'in which, amongst other deathbed scenes, the particulars of dearest papa's death are given'. When he found Tom was the son mentioned, the old man brought out an engraving of the Schoolhouse at Rugby, pasted on a hexagonal wooden plaque. 'I took this out to show Julia, who was sitting in the gig outside,' wrote Tom. The schoolmaster insisted on giving him both book and picture. Thus did Dr Arnold's image and influence spread to all kinds of schools in distant parts of the world.

Tom was writing to his old friend Clough, after a long interval, in September 1851, 'Tell me what you think of Matt's wife, if you have seen her. It is very difficult to fancy the "Emperor" married! I have a daughter three months old; is that very easy to realize? A delicate featured little thing, with grey eyes and plenty of brown hair.'

The eyes were to turn darker later. Mary was born in June 1851 and began to take notice of people early.

The beginning of the letter suggests that Tom was feeling starved of intellectual communication with congenial friends. 'How little do I know of all that that capacious head of yours is scheming and imagining; yet how certain I feel, that whatever be the particular objects of its activity, truth is ever its polestar, and moral nobleness its guide. And I too, dear soul-friend, am less changed than you might imagine. Some intellectual weapons, which in old days I may have essayed to wield with what little strength I had, may now be rusted for lack of use; that is, alas! only too possible for a man situated as I am, with so few to exchange thoughts with; but the great hope within the grand effort of will – the great beacon lights of life – remain what they were, and point in the same direction as of old.'

But they were not to point for long in quite the same direction.

In the fragmentary *Equator Letters* which Tom Arnold wrote to his friend J. C. Shairp while he was sailing to New Zealand in 1848, he ended the last with his answer to an objection which he felt would naturally present itself to the reader: 'How strange and sad that the son should depart thus widely from the father's faith, and seek to undo the father's work!' Tom's reaction was intense. 'Oh, if it were so indeed, it would be truly sad; a sadder and more unnatural sight could not be witnessed upon earth. But it is my comfort to believe that at the bottom it is not so, but the very contrary. If thou, my father, from thy place of rest, couldst still behold the scenes of thy pilgrimage and look into thy son's inmost heart, do I not believe that thou wouldst bless me, and bless also the work which I have chosen? Is not thy spirit with me? Do I not, like thee, hate injustice and falsehood with a perfect hatred, like thee await and hope for the establishment of that "glorious Church", that divine Society, which shall unite men together in a common faith and in mutual love? . . . The form, the outward vesture of thy faith – it is only this which I cannot accept.'

From this heartfelt conviction that his own kind of belief in God and service to man were not in real opposition to his father's more traditional Christian faith, it is clear that Tom Arnold had never lost his sense of the primacy of religious truth. And as the years went on and he became responsible for a growing family – a boy, christened William, was born about fifteen months after Mary and there were to be eight children in all – he was driven to think more deeply about the roots of his faith. His republicanism had always been more of a way of life than a political opinion; now that he was not really living it, and could see small chance of its ever being lived as he had conceived it in his idealistic youth, he began to realize the shapelessness of life without a central orientation. It was not surprising that he should turn once more to the Christian religion, but it did surprise his family and friends that he turned to Catholicism.

This was because, to most of them, the Catholic Church was just another human institution, a form of Christianity warped by its very age, stained by dreadful episodes of crime and oppression, dominated by popular superstition and with the message of the Gospel overlaid, if not distorted, by a system of theology evolved in a pre-scientific age, and carried on by priestly customs and laws which seemed far removed from the freedom of the disciples of Jesus of Nazareth. It looked thus, certainly, to that very English and independent-minded family of Thomas Arnold's.

The Church is all that, but it is also the way in which belief in Christ has been carried through nearly two thousand years of history – thought through, lived through, by countless millions of human beings linked together in faith since the first group met in an upper room in Jerusalem. The Church is the community, the communion, of mankind in Christ, the witness to him, both to what he is and to what he has done and is doing. All other forms of Christianity (I speak historically) have come from this matrix, and without its being they would not have been.

Tom Arnold's conversion was to this Church: the living witness to Christ. He was drawn to it just *because*, following his father's liberal principles, he had lost what he called 'the form, the outward vesture' of his father's faith: that is, its intellectual (theological) and social (ecclesiastical) structure. And having lost that, he found himself losing more and more of the foundations of his personal faith. Once a person is mentally outside all Christian societies, it is very likely that if he comes to see what Christianity is, he will turn to the most ancient, most coherent and autonomous existing body to learn the traditional teaching. Tom Arnold's generation was perhaps the first in England from which men could come to the Catholic Church from this angle – the post-Christian angle, the point of view of those who have discarded Christianity as untrue, in their youth, and discover it again in maturity. Before this, in England, it was highly unlikely that such persons should become *Catholics*. But the Catholic revival in the Church of England had made Catholicism visible once more to Englishmen.

And so it was to John Henry Newman, the acknowledged leader of this movement, that Tom Arnold wrote a long account of the state of his mind, which he sent off in the early spring of 1855, though his moment of crisis had come the preceding autumn, on a Sunday in October. Tom was then close upon his thirty-first birthday. When introducing himself to Newman, after mentioning his father, he said: 'My excuse for writing to you is that your writings have exercised a great influence over my mind.' How many people wrote to Newman for that reason! Yet at Oxford this son of Dr Arnold had not come under Newman's spell; he was travelling then in the opposite direction – towards unbelief.

It was since the experience in October that he had read Newman, certainly the early *Tracts for the Times*, now some twenty years old, the essay on the *Development of Christian Doctrine*, *The Idea of a University*, and perhaps other works. In 1855 Newman had been ten years a Catholic and was fifty-four years old.

Tom continued: 'I will try to make this intelligible in as few words as possible. My Protestantism, which was always of the liberal sort and disavowed the principle of authority, developed itself during my residence at Oxford into a state of absolute doubt and uncertainty about the very facts of Christianity. After leaving Oxford I went up to London and there, to my deep shame be it spoken, finding a state of doubt intolerable, I plunged into the abyss of unbelief. You know the nature of the illusion which leads a man to this fearful state far better than I can tell you: – there is a page in your lectures on the University system where you describe the fancied illumination and enlargement of mind, which a man experiences after abandoning himself to unbelief, which, when I read, it seemed as if you had looked into my very heart and given a clear outline to feelings and thoughts which I had in my mind, but never thoroughly mastered.' Again, this was a common experience among Newman's hearers and readers.

Then Tom described his emigration and present situation and went on: 'Up to last October I remained in the same way of thinking, unable to pray, without peace and without God in the world. In various ways I fell into grievous sin and philosophy proved no preservative against it. At last, by God's mercy, a meditation into which I fell on my unhappy and degenerate state was made the means – a text from St Peter suddenly suggested itself to my memory – through the violent contrast which I found to exist between the teaching of the apostle and the state of my own soul, of leading me to inquire again, to pray again, and to receive again, most unworthy as I was, the precious gift of faith in Christ.

'This, however, is not all. You who have said that a man who has once comprehended and admitted the theological definition of God, cannot logically rest until he has admitted the whole system of Catholicism, will not wonder if, after having admitted Christianity to be an assemblage of real, indubitable historical facts, I gradually came to see that the foundation of the one-Catholic Church was one of the facts, and that she is the only safe and sufficient witness, across time and space, to the reality of those facts and to the mode of their occurrence. These convictions, the meditations of each day only tend to strengthen, and I ardently long for the hour of making my formal submission to the Catholic Church. It is here, however, that my perplexities begin, and it is to you who can understand and enter into all such, and to whose writings I feel most deeply indebted, that I venture to come for a resolution of them.

'First – could you advise me as to the time of making such a submission? My dear wife, who is without any positive religious convictions (in a great measure, alas! through my fault) has imbibed the strongest prejudices against Catholicism and I see no prospect, humanly speaking, of her altering her mind. My mother and sisters, all in England, are sincerely Protestant, and I cannot doubt that my conversion will be a serious blow to them. And it is impossible for a son to owe more to a mother in the way of tender respect and consideration than I do to mine. I could with difficulty bring myself to take any important step without her having at least full *knowledge* of it beforehand.'

His second question concerned the 'lawfulness' of continuing in his job, which at that time seemed possible, and if he could not, what were the chances of his obtaining employment in England 'at some Catholic seminary or college'. With a final request for his letter to be taken in confidence, he concluded it: 'Believe me to remain in hope, sincerely yours, T. Arnold', and sent it off on the long voyage home.

In his autobiography, written at the end of his life, after mentioning the episode of the text from St Peter, he added, 'But who was this Peter? What was his general teaching? Who were his helpers and successors?' In other words, what was the authority on which he was to commit himself to belief in Christ? This was why he read the famous Tracts, for they dealt with this very question of the historical basis for the authority of the Church as witness to Christ.

In this reading Tom was struck by 'the account by an eye-witness of the valiant death of the martyrs at Lyons in 177; the story of the death of Polycarp, also by an eyewitness [Polycarp, the old bishop who in his youth had known St John], the epistles of Ignatius [the martyr], so Pauline in spirit, yet betraying the natural development of the Christian organization in the direction of a rigid episcopacy, of which only the germs appear in the Pauline epistles, the epistle to Diognetus and the Muratorian fragments – all these bore, I thought, consenting testimony to the essential and necessary oneness of the Christian revelation. The unity of the Christian system from the first, and the care with which that unity was preserved, seemed to me undeniable.'

Then, having discovered the early Church of the martyrs, Tom suddenly, almost accidentally, discovered the later Church of the saints. At a country inn he came across the volumes of the *Lives of the Saints*, and opening one at random fell upon St Brigit of Sweden. 'This saint,' he wrote in his memoir, 'who was aunt or cousin to the reigning king of Sweden, was married and had eight children; nevertheless she lived a most holy and self-denying life, adhering to and obeying the Catholic Church as strictly as St Ignatius or St Irenaeus, and revering the popes of her day, whom, under very difficult circumstances, she aided to the utmost of her power.' Tom's interest in St Brigit was increased when he found that her feast day fell on 8th October, that very day in October when St Peter's words had come to him like a revelation and a command.

A religious conversion is always a very personal thing; it reveals much of Tom Arnold's character that it was for him the human facts of the martyrs and the saints which opened the way into the ancient but ever-growing community of the Church. He was by nature and training a scholar, but also the sort of man who must always translate ideals into action. He was not speculative, not one whose thinking was abstracted from everyday life; he still had that kind of simplicity and industry which had gained him a First at Oxford while Matt, with all his brilliance and imagination, had won only a Second. Tom saw the *idea* of the Church – the communion of witness – but also the historical *fact* of its life in these ordinary people who had become the holy ones, the whole, the perfected, the true lovers and followers of Christ. He was converted to the Church – the active community.

Newman received Tom Arnold's letter in July; on the 2nd July he wrote from Dublin to Lord Dunraven: 'The same post which brought your letter this morning, brought one from the other end of the earth, showing the working of God's grace in a way so wonderful, that it is distressing to have it all to oneself and not to be at liberty to mention it.' He wrote back to Tom at once, a letter which reached Tasmania by 1st October, but which has not survived.

On 18th October Tom replied to Newman: 'Pray accept my

best and warmest thanks for your kind and most comforting letter, which reached me on the first of this month, having come with wonderful despatch, since not six months had elapsed since I sent mine.' The usual interval was eight months, and because he had not expected an answer so soon, Tom had, in June, promised a lady (not named) that he would take no action for six months and read Anglican books on the subject of the Church. He was, he said, 'very desirous not to be self-willed in the matter, a vice from which I have suffered so much already'.

But dutifully reading St Vincent of Lerins, on the rule that we must hold to whatever has always and everywhere and by all been received, he remarked that he did not see how this could be twisted into an apologia for Anglicanism. His mind was quite made up and before he finished his letter he was able to report that 'the lady' had released him from his promise. But it was not so easy to deal with Julia.

'My dear wife, as I told you before, has a violent prejudice against the very name of Catholic,' Tom wrote now. 'I fear it was not right, but in order to calm, if possible, her excited feelings, and allay the extreme irritation into which she was thrown by the knowledge of my state of mind, I promised her that I would not without her consent join the Catholic Church until I had seen my mother in England, or unless I were *in articulo mortis*. I am now therefore in a state of great perplexity. I do not give up the hope that her eyes may one day be opened but at present she seems resolutely bent on shutting up every avenue by which conviction might reach her soul. I think my best course will be to ask for short leave so as to go home, see my mother, and return again, in which case I might be received at home. But I think I had better see Bishop Willson and ask his advice.

'My poor wife has written you a letter, which I suppose will reach you; if it should, forgive, I entreat you, its unjust and half frantic language and pray for the unhappy writer. An evil spirit, I verily believe, at times possesses her and she does not know what she does or says. When I think of my own and others' sins and sorrows, it seems as if life ought to be one continual act of prayer.'

That Tom did not exaggerate the violence of Julia's expression of her feelings is attested by similar excuses in letters of her daughter Mary, years later. All the same, Mary declared that love was the basis of her character; she insisted that Julia felt a passionate affection for Tom till the end of her life, but could never reconcile herself to what he had done. Perhaps these passionate emotions could only have been controlled by an equally strong reasoning power, but this Julia Sorell never had. She seems to have been all feeling, to have had little educational training, and few, if any, intellectual interests. Nor was she particularly practical in the ordinary affairs of life, as the future was sadly to disclose. She loved Tom fiercely without understanding him at all; she could fall into a frenzy against him, though their daughter scarcely ever refers to him without mentioning his gentleness. And, as Tom seemed to realize from the start, she was never to change. She hated everything to do with Catholicism; what he, whom she loved, felt about it made no difference at all. They were to endure more than thirty years of this contradictory marriage.

In the end Tom decided he must settle the thing where he was. Well over a year after his first experience of conviction he was received into the Catholic Church by Bishop Willson on 18th January 1856, the feast of St Peter's Chair at Rome – symbol of the final authority of his apostolic successor, the Pope. On 26th May, St Philip Neri's day (founder of Newman's religious community, the Congregation of the Oratory), Tom wrote to Newman: 'Since then, though I have had my share of trouble, especially of a domestic nature, yet every day, I may almost say, has deepened the fervour of my allegiance to our holy Mother [the Church] and increased my joy and thankfulness to God and inward astonishment that he has been pleased to lead me, in every respect so unworthy, into such a heavenly resting place.' And he quoted the words of Jacob, when he woke from his vision of the ladder of angels, which are used in the mass for the dedications of church buildings: 'How terrible is this place: this is no other but the house of God and the gate of heaven.'

He went on to tell Newman of his practical difficulties. Bishop Willson, whom he called 'a good old man', advised him not to resign his job but to await events. Although his superiors had no wish to sack him, his conversion caused so much hostility that his position eventually became untenable. The organ of the Conservatives, *The Hobart Town Courier*, attacked him in a bitter and contemptuous leading article. In that small colonial society it was impossible to escape notice and it was clear that the majority would not tolerate a Roman Catholic as Inspector of Schools. In consultation with his superiors it was decided that he should go home on long leave at half pay, with the understanding that he should not return.

The Arnolds had recently been living rent free in the Normal School, originally planned as a training college for teachers, but not used as such because it was found cheaper to get already-trained teachers from England. For the last few months they moved into lodgings, and little Mary, now five years old, was sent to a friend, Mrs Reibey.

On 12th July 1856 they sailed for England in the *William Brown*, a small vessel of 400 tons, infested with rats. Tom recalled one falling off a beam on to his bed and another chewing off the ends of his wash-leather braces; small Mary was to remember those rats all her life and the uncomfortable sea-water baths taken in barrels on deck. The Arnolds were the only passengers, but they were quite a party, for as well as their own three children, they had under their care four more, cousins of Julia's from India, who were being sent home to school. And Julia herself was pregnant.

Apart from the rats the journey was uneventful and they never once saw land till they reached England, arriving at St Catherine's dock, London, on 17th October 1856.

Mary wrote in her book *A Writer's Recollections*, 'I can remember being lifted, weak and miserable with toothache, in my father's arms to catch the first sight of English shores as we neared the mouth of the Thames; and then the dismal inn by the docks where we first took shelter. The dreary room where we children slept the first night, its dingy ugliness and its barred windows, still come back to me as a vision of horror. Next day, like angels of rescue, came an aunt and uncle, who took us off to other and cheerful quarters.'

That was, as her father recorded, 'the finest of old hostelries', *The Four Swans* in Bishopsgate. The aunt was Dr Arnold's eldest daughter Jane, the uncle her husband William Forster. In a few days Tom Arnold and his little family were racing north to Westmorland, home to Fox How.

V

Poet as School Inspector

I

Matthew Arnold's life would have been very different had he not married Frances Lucy Wightman, not only because a happy marriage, as his turned out to be, alters the complexion of any life, but because, in order to marry, he took the job of Inspector of Schools, which he was to hold for over thirty years. He became one of the professional salaried class which was increasing all through the nineteenth century in numbers and importance, and provided a livelihood for men who could not or would not go into the Church, the law or the services – till then the only occupations for gentlemen apart from politics and leisure.

Matthew Arnold was surely the first poet to make his living as a School Inspector, an office only recently invented, as the State began to take an interest in education. Most schools had been started by religious bodies, principally the Church of England, which would only allow inspection by ordained clergymen, so that Matt's duty would be confined to those run by Dissenters. They were elementary, or primary, schools, but the Inspector had to examine the teachers as well as the pupils. The work would be demanding and not at all the sort of thing Matt and his friends were accustomed to do; it was not like being private secretary to Lord Lansdowne, nor even like the work undertaken by higher civil servants. Yet, as a new profession, it had not been labelled as unsuitable for gentlemen with Oxford degrees. Lord Lansdowne, as President of the Council, could offer the post, and the son of Dr Arnold could accept it, without any question of loss of status. Matt took up the appointment without much enthusiasm for education but with a great deal for Fanny Lucy, on 14th April 1851. They were married in June that year.

Matt had known her over a year and had been engaged since

the previous autumn, when they were writing to each other daily, but although he seems to have fallen very much in love almost as soon as he met her, things had not gone easily, chiefly because her father, Judge Wightman, appears to have discouraged a suitor who had so little to offer. He carried off his daughter on a tour abroad in 1850; Matt, not allowed to accompany them, contrived to be in France first and watched their boat come in. He longed to walk with Fanny Lucy on *Calais Sands* – the title of a poem he wrote then but did not publish till 1867.

> I must not seek to grasp thy hand,
> To woo thy smile, to seek thine eye;
> But I may stand far off, and gaze,
> And watch thee pass unconscious by,
>
> And spell thy looks, and guess thy thoughts,
> Mixt with the idlers on the pier. –
> Ah, might I always rest unseen,
> So might I have thee always near!
>
> To-morrow hurry through the fields
> Of Flanders to the storied Rhine!
> To-night those soft-fringed eyes shall close
> Beneath one roof, my queen! with mine.

Other poems written during this time of rejection were later published under the sequence-title of *Faded Leaves* – later still, this was dropped, and the poems appeared under their separate titles. The feeling expressed is more despairing than the event warranted – but it shows the strength and depth of this love. Fanny Lucy, like Marguerite, had a mocking smile, an arch look, but her eyes were nearer grey than blue:

> Eyes too expressive to be blue,
> Too lovely to be grey.

She was small, she had brown hair; she was musical, a lively sociable girl, interested in politics, and in spite of Matt's poetic gloom, she was in love with him, which was probably what settled the affair in the end.

Like his brother Tom, Matt could think of nothing else when he was in love; but, typical of himself alone, he concealed the seriousness of his feelings.

Arthur Clough was writing to Tom on 23rd July 1850, and remarked that 'Matt comes to Switzrld in a month; after your sister's wedding. He is himself deep in a flirtation with Miss Wightman, daughter of the Judge. It is thought it will come to something, for he has actually been to Church to meet her.' The next day he heard of Tom's engagement and added a postscript to congratulate him, wryly remarking, 'I myself begin to think I shall be a last rose of summer, werry faded.'

Since Fanny Lucy outlived Matthew and herself edited the letters she sent to G. W. E. Russell for the volumes of correspondence, and since she was a modest person, she must remain a little shadowy to posterity, though in fact she seems to have been someone of character, good sense and humour. In spite of the gloomy poems of *Longing* and *Too Late*, and the rather fierce *Separation*, in which the lover wishes to forget either nothing or all:

> *Who*, let me say, *is this Stranger regards me,*
> *With the grey eyes and the lovely brown hair?*

– in spite of all that, the engagement was made, and Matt was writing confident letters to Fanny Lucy long before Christmas, and long before he had got any job to satisfy the Judge's paternal solicitude.

On 16th March 1851, Clough was again writing, rather plaintively, to Tom Arnold: 'My dear Tom, you have never written to me – since God knows when – not since you first were engaged to be married; which now undoubtedly, though not having heard it from you, I half do doubt it, you are . . . I am not; nor even engaged; though "the good they fall around us" and the bad too, Matt included (I do not mean among the latter – necessarily).'

He signed this letter but left it lying till 16th May, when he made excuses about his embarrassment in finding words to introduce himself to Tom's wife and added, 'For to a certain extent even at this distance old friends have to make their graceful withdrawal – so it seems to me with Matt at any rate, on this side the water; and I consider Miss Wightman as a sort of natural enemy – how can it be otherwise – shall I any longer breakfast with Matt twice a week? Miss Wightman, you will like to know, is small with aquiline nose and very pleasing eyes, fair in complexion – I have only seen her however in her bonnet – I think she will suit well enough – she seems amiable – has seen lots of company and can't be stupid –'

On the very end of the letter he added, on 14th June, a postscript: 'When shall I send this? I don't know why I keep it. However, it will now convey to you that Matt is married . . . Nobody cried; Matt was admirably drest, and perfectly at his ease – it rained, but we did well enough – they went off before the breakfast – where old Croker sat *cum Judice* – She seems, as Matt calls her, a charming companion – *Vale*.'

Curiously enough, this letter must have crossed with one from Tom dated in September, where he had said, 'Tell me what you think of Matt's wife, if you have seen her. It is difficult to fancy the "Emperor" married!'

Their brother William had also expressed the opinion that Matt was one of the very last men in the world whom he could fancy happily married.

They were all wrong. Tom's daughter Mary quoted her uncle William's letter in her *Recollections* but speaks warmly of 'the dear and gracious little lady whom we grandchildren knew as Aunt Fanny Lucy' – she means Dr Arnold's grandchildren. She also quoted from a letter of Arthur Stanley's to Tom, about Matt. 'He is also, – I must say so, though perhaps I have no right to say so – greatly improved by his marriage – retaining all the genius and nobleness of mind which you remember with all the lesser faults pruned and softened down.'

Matt was twenty-eight when he married, and whatever his sorrows about Marguerite he was more deeply in love with Fanny Lucy and the love was to endure, maturing but not diminishing, so that even his beloved foreign travel lost its savour when she could not accompany him and years later he could write, on the anniversary of their wedding, that it seemed like yesterday.

About eighteen months after their marriage, when they already had their first child, the much loved delicate 'little Tom', Matt received a letter from Clough, then in America, complaining of his neglect and coldness. Matt replied at once in a long letter, hastily written, dated 12th February 1853, in which he tried to put things straight. Here I quote only what is relevant to his marriage.

'I remember your being annoyed once or twice, and that I was vexed with myself; but at that time I was absorbed in my speculations and plans and agitations respecting Fanny Lucy, and was as egoistic and anti-social as possible. People in the condition in which I then was always are. I thought I had said this, and explained one or two pieces of apparent carelessness in this way:

and that you had quite understood it. So entirely indeed am I convinced that being in love generally unfits a man for the society of his friends, that I remember often smiling to myself at my own selfishness in half compelling you several times to meet me in the last few months before you left England, and thinking that it was only I who could make such unreasonable demands or find pleasure in meeting and being with a person, for the mere sake of meeting and being with them, without regarding whether they would be absent or preoccupied or not.'

This last comment was inspired by the fact that it was then Clough who was in love, engaged to Blanche Smith, and going to America to earn money enough to marry. But Clough and Matt were, as has already been suggested, unlike in temperament: Clough, ironic and direct in verse, was in living relationships complex and uncertain, even suspicious; while Matt, whose verse was introspective and melancholy, was straightforward with other people, humorous and unworried.

Towards the end of his letter Matt wrote: 'There – but now we will have done with this: we are each very near to the other – write and tell me that you feel this: as to my behaviour in London I have told you the simple truth: it is I fear too simple than that (excuse the idiom) you with your *raffinements* should believe and appreciate it.'

It seems unlikely that Matt ever wrote to Fanny Lucy the sort of letters Clough wrote to Blanche, analysing every feeling and thought, so that one is quite surprised that they did eventually marry and have a family of children; Clough became in many ways happier, but poetry fell by the wayside. And he was never to be happy in the way Matt was; there was in Clough a strain of melancholy too deep to be exorcized either by love or work.

The few letters Matt wrote to Fanny Lucy during his engagement that were printed, run on from day to day in very good spirits, tell her what he was doing and thinking, and so he continued to write, whenever they were separated, all through the rest of his life. And this evidently suited Fanny Lucy.

Sir William Wightman, her father, a judge of the Queen's Bench, had been born in 1784 and in 1819 he married the daughter of James Baird of Lasswade near Edinburgh. The Judge became very much part of Matt's life – rather, Matt became part of his, as for seven years the young couple had no home of their own, shifting lodgings all the time and spending weeks, including every Christmas but the first, at the Judge's house in Eaton Place. Until Wightman's death in 1863 Matthew frequently acted as his Marshal when on circuit, earning some much needed extra money thereby and usually managing to combine it with inspecting some schools. After the initial suspicions had been overcome, the Judge evidently came to like his son-in-law and Matt became quite fond of him; he was a good-humoured energetic man who continued working till he died in harness in his eightieth year. Nobody seems to have said much about Lady Wightman, but she was there too, part of the establishment at Eaton Place, during these hard-working years.

At first Fanny Lucy travelled with her husband, but when the children began to arrive the expense and upheaval became too great and she stayed generally in London or its environs, where he returned as to base. Hence the many vivid letters describing his work and peregrinations. By 15th October 1851 he was already becoming more interested in his job, writing from the Oldham Road Lancasterian School, Manchester: 'I think I shall get interested in the schools after a little time; their effects on the children are so immense, and their future effects in civilising the next generation of the lower classes, who, as things are going, will have most of the political power of the country in their hands, may be so important.' But at this time he was still not regarding it as a lifework, but dreaming of 'retiring to Italy on £200 a year'. The dream of getting away from it all was to recur, but in fact he never gave up the struggle.

And struggle it certainly was. On 2nd December 1851 he wrote to Fanny Lucy, 'I have had a hard day. Thirty pupil teachers to examine in an inconvenient room, and nothing to eat except a biscuit, which a charitable lady gave me.' He was then in Birmingham and wrote enthusiastically of it. 'The schools are mostly in the hands of very intelligent wealthy Unitarians, who abound here, and belong to the class of what we call ladies and gentlemen. This is next to Liverpool the finest of the manu-facturing towns: the situation is high and good, the principal street capital, the shops good, cabs splendid and the Music Hall unequalled by any Greek building in England that I have seen.'

Newman was writing very similar views on Birmingham's healthy situation to his friends, and on the future political power of the working class; at this time he was living in the back-streets, with a chapel made out of a gin distillery, to which hordes of half-heathen factory children came 'like herrings in season' to learn the Catholic faith from this Oxford convert with his band of enthusiastic young priests. But it was Tom, not Matt, who was soon to meet Newman; and Tom never did like the climate of Birmingham.

Matt's children began to arrive, almost as frequent as Tom's; the first, born 6th July 1852, was a boy and proudly christened Thomas, but for most of his short life was known as 'little Tom'. Always delicate, he suffered from circulatory trouble due to a heart condition. This was not recognized at first and even in November 1854 Matt could write to his friend Wyndham Slade, 'the big baby pulls his brother over and over'. This second son was then about a year old; he was Trevenen William, known as Budge, born 15th October 1853.

In the summer holidays they usually went up to Fox How, to visit old Mrs Arnold, fish and walk on the hills. Matthew remarked once to his wife how happy it had made him that Fanny Lucy took to his family and they to her; it was indeed a permanent source of happiness that each liked the other's relations.

But the work continued grinding. From Battersea he wrote to his wife in December 1852: 'This certainly has been one of the most uncomfortable weeks I ever spent. Battersea is so far off, the roads so execrable, the rain so incessant. I cannot bear to take my cab from London over Battersea Bridge as it seems absurd to pay 8d for the sake of the half mile on the other side; but that half mile is one continued slough, as there is not a yard of flagging, I believe, in all Battersea.' His friends of a few years back would hardly have recognized their exquisite Matt, tramping through the mud to save 8d.

In February of the next year, 1853, he was inspecting schools in the eastern counties and found that the 'school managers who have held out till now against the government plan ask me on my father's account to come and inspect them, and to refuse is hard'. In consequence he had to fit in even more difficult cross-country railway journeys. 'At the station I had just time to eat a bun and book for St Ives.' On this expedition he saw Cambridge for the first time and remarked, 'It seems so strange to be in a place of colleges that is not Oxford.' But he was taken round by one of the Gell family, an old Rugbeian and a fellow of Christ's College who had Dr Arnold's picture hanging in his room. The two things Matt most wanted to see were Newton's statue and King's College

Chapel. On 2nd March he told Fanny Lucy: 'I want you sadly to go about with me; everything would be just doubly interesting.'

She must have felt his meals were shockingly irregular and inadequate. That March he wrote from Sudbury, in Suffolk, 'I got here a little before two, had a sandwich and then went to the school. I don't know why, but I certainly find inspecting peculiarly oppressive just now; but I must tackle to, as it would not do to let this feeling get too strong. All this afternoon I have been haunted by a vision of living with you at Berne, on a diplomatic appointment, and how different that would be from this incessant grind in schools; but I could laugh at myself too, for the way in which I went on drawing out our life in my mind. At five I took a short walk, got back to dinner at a quarter to six, dined, and started the pupil teachers.'

He was often invited to dine with brewers, coal merchants and others, mostly Dissenters. At Sudbury he was 'most hospitably entertained by a Quaker', and described the walls in the hall of the house as lined with a vast collection of stuffed birds, 'which gives it a ghastly effect enough'.

'I did not arrive here till just after two, as the train was late,' he wrote on 8th March to his wife, 'went to the school and found there were three of them. About four o'clock I found myself so exhausted, having eaten nothing since breakfast, that I sent out for a bun and ate it before the astonished school.'

No wonder that two days later he was writing from Ipswich Western School at 5 p.m. 'I am too utterly tired out to write. It certainly was nicer when you came with me, though so dreadfully expensive; but it was the only thing that could make this life anything but a positive purgatory.'

Though it continued so for years Matt presently became adept at seizing occasions for visits on his journeys. On 17th October 1854 he wrote from Oxford to Fanny Lucy: 'I am just back from Witney; as cold and uncomfortable a life I have had since I left you as one could desire. My bedroom here is fust and frowsiness itself and last night I could not sleep.' But he was to dine in Oriel.

They also took brief holidays, often at Dover, and slipped across the Channel to spend a few days in France, or Belgium. Matt's itinerant life certainly gave him a wide knowledge of his own country, though it is less apparent in his writing than his acquaintance with Europe, partly because it was one of his aims to open up a European view to his insular fellow-countrymen.

Matthew Arnold was certainly pondering on modern society and culture as he beat his way up and down England on the new railways, in his own thirties and the century's fifties. On that visit to Oxford in October 1854 he wrote to his wife from Balliol, amazed that it could be thirteen years since he was wandering about the quadrangle as a freshman, and telling her how he had 'got up alone into one of the little coombs that papa was so fond of and which I had in my mind in the "Gipsy Scholar", and felt the peculiar sentiment of this country and neighbourhood as deeply as ever'. But then he made some comments on the university which show the way his mind was working.

'But I am much struck with the apathy and *poorness* of the people here, as they now strike me, and their petty pottering habits compared with the students of Paris or Germany or even of London. Animation and interest and power of work seem so sadly wanting in them. And I think this is so, and the place, in losing Newman and his followers, has lost its religious movement, which after all kept it from stagnating, and has not yet, so far as I can see, got anything better. However, we must hope that the coming changes, and perhaps the infusion of Dissenters' sons of that muscular, hard-working *unblasé* middle class – for it is this, in spite of its abominable disagreeableness – may brace the flaccid sinews of Oxford a little.'

The changes he referred to were the first reforms of the university, allowing the entrance of others than members of the Church of England, but probably he also had in mind the shifting of political power as the franchise was extended, and the ever-increasing importance of industrial and commercial interests in England. The eighteen-fifties were a time of transition, of change in all fields, apparent even in such things as the printing of newspapers; the second half of the nineteenth century is in many ways more unlike the first than the first part is unlike the end of the eighteenth century. And this is true of other times too; a noticeable change of feeling often does seem to occur round about the middle of a century, rather than at the turn of it.

Matthew Arnold was sensitive to this time of transition. His fame as a writer was to come in the next decades but the experience which made him was that of the midcentury. In the forties he was a young man growing up in a world of unrest and revolutions; in the fifties he was a married man in his prime, with a young family and a demanding job which took him all over England.

On 27th February 1855 he wrote to his mother from Birmingham, amazed at reading his father's plans for the education of his children, which she had sent him, on discovering them – amazed that they should have been conceived at a time 'when to many men their children are still little more than playthings'. Perhaps that was what his own children were to him. 'It is no use telling you of little Tom's fascinations by letter, when you have Mary with you, upon whom they have been exercised.' Mary, his sister, widowed so young, had been staying with them, and Matt said how much they missed her; he would have liked Mary one six months of the year and Fan the other. But Mary was to make a second marriage, though Fan remained at home with her mother all her life.

It was in the next year, 1856, that little Tom's heart trouble was diagnosed; henceforth it was to be a constant anxiety, but except in times of particular crisis, did not throw a blight over their family life. Tom was very intelligent and very musical. In June 1855 when he was only three, Matt had written to his sister Jane (known as K.): 'Tom put his finger to his mouth as a sign to listen. "Papa, do you hear the mavis singing?" ' It was the first line of one of his songs. His father remarked that he was 'so singularly winning and *unexpected* in all he says and does'.

In the May of 1857 Matt sent K a typical piece of family dialogue to amuse her. 'The day I read your letter I said to Budge [his second son, aged two and a half], as I was dressing for dinner, "Budge, you must go and see your aunt Forster." "No," says Budge, "*do* let me 'top with papa.' " So I turn to Tom, and when I remind him of the Noah's Ark, Tom says he will go and stop with you "for two days." Upon which Budge begins to howl, and running up to Tom, who is sitting on the camp bed in my dressing room, entreats him not to go away from him. "Why not, Budge?" says Tom. "Because I do love you so, Tiddy Tom," says Budge. "Oh," says Tom, waving his hand with a melancholly air, "this is *false*, Budge, this is all *false*." You should have seen the sweet little melancholy face of the rogue as he said this.' And later he added 'Diddy gets very pretty, but he is fretful.'

Diddy was the third son, Richard Penrose, born 14th November 1855.

Matthew's affectionate interest in his children is perhaps less dedicatedly dominating than Dr Arnold's in his, though it is partly a matter of period. Arnold's generation felt entirely responsible for the characters of their children; Matthew's felt a fascination for them as children – hence the enormous popularity of paintings of children, which to a later generation still appeared idealized and sentimentalized.

Matthew was not only a kind father; he was kind to the children he examined, those thousands of nameless children inspected during his long thirty-four years travelling round the schools of England. This is not guesswork; on 14th December 1867, writing to his mother, Matt told her how he had accidentally seen a letter from a head teacher defending his school against a severe report from Mr Arnold. 'He finished by saying he had not a word against the inspector, whom he would rather have had than any other he had come in contact with, "as he was always gentle and patient with the children." The great thing is *humanity*, after all,' commented Matt, with pardonable satisfaction.

So the years went on, and all the time, while he went through the grind of inspection, or the work of a marshal on circuit, while he moved from lodging to lodging, missed his wife and was amused by his little boys, while he snatched holidays at Fox How or Dover, or in Belgium, Matthew Arnold continued to think about poetry.

In May 1857 he was elected Professor of Poetry at Oxford.

2

The most vivid account of the election to the Chair of Poetry comes from Matt's own letter to his brother Tom, who was then at Newman's university in Ireland, which is quoted by Mrs Humphry Ward in her *Recollections*. 'You dear old boy,' Matt wrote, 'I love your congratulations although I see and hear so little of you, and alas! *can* see and hear but so little of you. I was supported by people of all opinions, the great bond of union being, I believe, the affectionate interest felt in papa's memory.'

There had been, as there usually is, an opposing candidate, the Reverend J. E. Bode. Matt later discovered that Keble, whom he had expected to prefer Bode, had voted for his godson after all. Matt himself was in London at the time, busy, as he told his brother, 'selecting waggons for Tom and Trev, with horses of precisely the same colour, not one of which should have a hair more in his tail than the other – and a musical cart for

Diddy.' But all the same he awaited news of the result eagerly. At Eaton Place, 'a little after six o'clock we were joined by the Judge in the highest state of joyful excitement with the news of my majority of 85, which had been telegraphed to him from Oxford after he started and had been given to him at Paddington Station'.

The Professorship was then merely a university, not a national, distinction; it only brought in £130 a year, but did not entail residence. The duties were to look over the compositions for the Newdigate Prize and to deliver three Latin lectures on ancient poetry during the year. Matthew immediately determined to lecture in English, setting a precedent which has been followed ever since; and though he did speak of the classics his inaugural lecture was entitled 'The Modern Element in Literature'.

This lecture, delivered on 14th November 1857, was not published till 1869, and then only in *Macmillan's Magazine*, for he never included it in any collection of his essays. Nevertheless, the necessity for thinking it out and delivering it was an event of great moment in Matthew Arnold's life, for it led him to express in public ideas on literature and society which have perhaps had a greater influence than his poetry. To be made the Professor of Poetry at Oxford was the incentive for *Essays in Criticism* and *Culture and Anarchy*. It gave Matthew Arnold the occasion, and the position of authority, from which to speak.

It has often been said that Matthew Arnold was a poet in his youth and a critic in middle age, as if he had changed professions in mid-career. But he had always been a poet who thought much about poetry and its relation to society and in his criticism he remained a maker, not merely an external observer. As far as posterity is concerned, it was a wise transference of his attention, for few indeed are the poets who write as well in middle age as in youth. Poetry is so much an art of youth that by the age of forty either the poet or the poetry is dead. There are exceptions; the old Yeats is one. Old Browning's poetry, and old Tennyson's, however, seem more expendable than Matthew Arnold's essays. The last collection of his poems was published in 1867 when he was forty-five, but its 'new' additions had mostly been written several years earlier. It shows strength of mind to 'retire' at that point, for the volume contains some of his best work, including *Dover Beach*.

It was soon after becoming Professor of Poetry that Matt took a house in Chester Square, in London, at last settling down in his own home. 'It will be something to unpack one's portmanteau for the first time since I was married, now nearly 7 years ago,' he wrote on 9th February 1858 to an old friend. In this summer Matt for the first time went abroad without his wife and wrote to her from Vevey on 28th August: 'It seems absurd to tell you, now that I have come without you, how I long for you, but so it is. I have not yet once, for a moment, felt as I generally feel abroad; for the first time in my life I feel willing to go back at any moment and do not mind what happens to shorten the journey.'

He was with his Balliol friend Walrond, who walked too fast for Matt's taste, for he liked to look about him. They did some climbing and Matt passed round his pot of cold cream to the whole party to save them from sunburn, but every place reminded him of Fanny Lucy, even the inns – 'we passed the dirty Couronne where you were alarmed by the great spider' – and one of his letters ends, 'Kiss my darling little boys for me.'

He got back to England in September in time for a little more holiday with the family at Dover, and told his sister Jane of an expedition in the Judge's carriage to see St Radegund's abbey, a beautiful ruin with fragments of stone lying in the grass, and how Budge (then about four) looking round 'with the greatest contempt, exclaimed at last these words – "what a nasty, *beastly* place this is!"' Matthew was delighted at the comic effect of this piece of cultural criticism.

They were still settling into their London house, bookcases being fixed in position and pictures hung. Matthew wrote to his sister Fan on 4th November 1858, 'At Colnaghi's yesterday I got a print of papa (as Jane declares I gave her mine, which I doubt) which Colnaghi is to frame; it will hang by itself in the dining room over the mantelpiece.' Matt was thinking much about his father at this time; *Rugby Chapel* was written in 1857 and there are many references to him in the letters which show how his eldest son, so unlike him in many ways, yet agreed in some of his views – political, especially. So Dr Arnold came to preside at 2, Chester Square.

What would he have made of his grandson's religious views, as recorded by Matthew in a letter to his sister Jane? On 21st January 1859 he wrote of a conversation between the boys and their new governess, Mrs Querini. 'From my little study I can hear all that passes. She said to Budge this morning, "Who do you love best of anybody in the world?" "Nobody at all," says Budge. "Yes," says Mrs Querini, "you love your papa and mamma." "Well," says Budge. "But," goes on Mrs Querini, "you are to love God more than anyone; even than your papa and mamma." "No, I shan't," says Budge. Jolly little heathen!'

Apart from this amused comment Matt made no criticism of the governess for presenting God as someone in competition with human loves. It was common form, and one reason why so many people grew up secretly hating God. St John's view that if men do not love their brothers whom they have seen, they cannot love the God they have not seen, is psychologically far more profound.

At the beginning of the year 1859 Matthew Arnold was chosen as Foreign Assistant Commissioner to the Commission on Education, for France and French-speaking countries – Belgium, Switzerland and Piedmont – to report on the elementary education there. Writing to Fan on 18th January he said, 'I cannot tell you how much I like the errand, and above all to have the French district.'

By April 1859 he was in Paris, at the start of his official tour, when the final act of his brother William's tragedy took place, unknown to him till too late, at Gibraltar. William's fatal choice had been made during his long leave in England, where he had written several articles for *Fraser's Magazine* and contributed to *The Times* and the *Economist*. Two more children, Florence and Hugh Oakeley, were born while he was in England, and he even travelled on the Continent with the Forsters. He worked for a time on the staff of the *Economist* and thought of applying for the editorship, when John Lawrence, then Chief Commissioner for the Punjab, wrote in the summer of 1855 asking him to be the Director of Public Instruction there, where he would virtually create the department. William Arnold accepted the post.

It was to the India of the Mutiny that he returned, though not, fortunately, to any active part in that tragedy. 'In the midst of it all,' he could write, 'the happiness of our domestic life has been almost perfect.' He built a house in the hills at Dharmsala, and called it, nostalgically, Rydal Lodge, where he spent all the time he could with his 'four little Dogs' as he called his children, remembering his own father's pet name for his brood. A governess recalled, 'He used to take you all four in his arms at once and run with you up and down – then putting you on the ground again he would make you stand in a row and when he said, one, two, three, away – off you started to try who would get first to the old Dhoolie (covered litter) which stood at the end of the Verandah; and if his little Okey was disappointed at not being able to run as fast as Eddie, he was hoisted on to Papa's shoulder, where he soon forgot his sorrow.' His wife Fanny wrote to Mrs Arnold, 'I daresay you know that Willy, by noticing the children more than most Papas do, does manage to spoil them a little.'

At the end of 1857 poor Fanny was ill with diarrhoea on and off for three months, and had to give up nursing her youngest child, Frances Egerton. On 20th February 1858 Willy left her and the children at Kanga, in the hills, with a German missionary and his wife, and on 24th March she died before he could get back to her, of a 'failure of the red corpuscles'. It was a great shock, and owing to the long voyages, he kept receiving letters from home addressed to 'Willy and Fanny' for months afterwards.

William Arnold continued his work, though he was far from well himself. He had founded well over a thousand vernacular schools in the Punjab, and most of the teachers were Mohammedans. His last battle in India was on behalf of religious freedom, writing against the proposed introduction of the Bible as a school book, in an official memorandum of some length. The situation of mission schools, he argued, was different from these, which were financed in part with Hindu and Moslem money, the Government being in the position of trustee. It had been suggested that the Bible should be read 'as literature' which Willy, who read it every day, thought dishonest. He pointed out that in England any similar measure would be regarded as 'the height of intolerance in a free country, but that we may still allow ourselves the indulgence of a little quiet persecution in India'. That has a very Arnoldian ring!

So has his final summing up of the case: 'I believe that the admission of the Bible as a class book in Government schools while the religious books of the natives of India are excluded would be a measure unjust, impolitic, and utterly opposed to the spirit of true Christianity.'

Although Lawrence did not agree, Arnold's view won the day.

In January 1859 William sent his four children off with their governess by ship for England, and later set off himself by the shorter overland route, forced to take sick leave again. By the time he reached Cairo he was worse, with fever and pains in the

Doctor Thomas Arnold aged forty-three, when he had been Headmaster of Rugby for over ten years. Portrait by Thomas Phillips.

Fox How, the home Dr Arnold built at Ambleside in the Lake District. On his death in 1842, his widow retired here for the rest of her days.

Matthew Arnold photographed at the age of thirty-eight, three years after his accession to the Chair of Poetry at Oxford.

Thomas Arnold the younger, aged twenty-four, three years before his marriage in New Zealand to Julia Sorrell. A daguerreotype.

Sketches of childhood at Fox How by Doctor Arnold's eldest daughter Jane. The top one shows four Arnold children playing with a boat made by their father. The bottom one shows too many children on one plank by the lakeside: it gave way, to their mother's rather than their own consternation.

Arthur Hugh Clough, the poet and close friend of Matthew Arnold, a year before his death at forty-two. A drawing in chalk by S. Rowse.

Mary Augusta (Mrs Humphry) Ward, eldest daughter of Thomas Arnold the younger, aged thirty-eight, a year after the great success of her novel *Robert Elsmere*. Portrait by Julian Story.

chest and side. 'I wish I knew the French for Bowels', he wrote in a letter to Fox How, appealing for a Brother or Brother-in-law to come and help. As soon as his call came, Walter, the youngest, the naval brother, left England for Alexandria, but fate so disposed things that as his ship sailed into Alexandria, another sailed out, bearing his sick brother towards Liverpool, under the care of a Captain Hamond, a distant relative of W. E. Forster's.

Willy wrote to his wife's sister, 'Could I indeed feel assured, as in word people affect to be, of being reunited to her, I should not fear Death: but I cannot believe that in their secret hearts people feel this assurance. The awful Doubt of what lies beyond must surely overpower the confidence of the most energetic believer.' So actively religious by nature, Willy remained all his life attacked by such deep uncertainties as this; and they were very common among men of his own generation and education.

As they came to Gibraltar he was so ill that he was put ashore there on his thirty-first birthday, 7th April 1859, and shortly afterwards fell into a coma, dying the next day.

On April 14th Matthew wrote home from Paris: 'What can one do, my dearest mother, except bow one's head and be silent? My poor dear Willy! If he had but known of my being here and had telegraphed to me from Malta, I might have reached him at Gibraltar in time. And no one else could. I like to imagine, even now that it is so entirely vain, the arriving at Gibraltar, the standing by his bedside, the taking his poor hand – I, whom he would hardly perhaps have expected to see there – I, of whom he thought so far more than I deserved, and who showed him, poor boy, so far less tenderness than he deserved. How strange it seems that he should have overlived his first terrible illness when his wife was alive to nurse him and he had but one child to suffer by his loss, to die now alone, with only a chance acquaintance to attend him, and leave these four poor little orphans, to whom no tenderness can ever quite replace a father and a mother! And then that he should have overlived the misery of his poor wife's death to struggle through a year's loneliness, and then die too. Poor Fanny! She at Dharmsala, and he by the Rock of Gibraltar. God bless you. What I *can* be to you, and to all of them, I will be.'

But it was Jane and William Forster who became second parents to the children, adopting them as their own, so that they took the name of Forster as well as Arnold. Oakeley followed his adopted father into politics and was to become a Minister of War; he married one of the daughters of Nevil Story Maskelyne of Basset Down in Wiltshire and their descendants are the Arnold-Forsters of Salthrop House, near Swindon.

Tom's eldest daughter Mary, then about eight, was at school in Ambleside, kept by Annie Clough, Arthur's sister, who afterwards became the first Principal of Newnham College, Cambridge. Mary wrote in her recollections: 'I remember well my first meeting with the Indian children, and how I wondered at their fair skins and golden hair and frail ethereal look.'

Matthew, in Brittany, wrote *Stanzas composed at Carnac* and later *A Southern Night*, in memory of William and Frances Arnold. On 8th May he was writing to his mother: 'I thought of Willy the other day at Carnac while I looked over the perfectly still and bright Atlantic by Quiberon Bay, and saw the sails pass in the distance where he would have passed had he lived to come home.'

Willy would never return to Fox How – which he had underlined four times in his last letter – but life, its work and interest, claimed his brother Matthew. In the same letter he said to his Cornish mother, 'I could not but think of you in Brittany with Cranics and Trevenecs all about me, and the peasantry with their expressive, rather mournful faces, long noses and dark eyes, reminding me perpetually of dear Tom, and uncle Trevenen, and utterly unlike the French. And I had the climate of England, gray skies and cool air, and the gray rock of the north too, and the clear rushing water . . .'

His letters home were full of political comment. He thought the Orleanists went only skin deep into the nation, 'the Legitimists not so much as that; they are utterly insignificant. The clergy is very strong and, on the whole, favourable to the present régime' – Louis Napoleon's Second Empire. And in May, writing to his wife from Bordeaux, Matt observed: 'The Revolution has cleared out the feudal ages from the minds of the country people to an extent incredible with us.' He was impressed with 'the profoundly democratic spirit which exists among the lower orders, even among the Breton peasants'.

All the time he was visiting schools, but he had chosen his time badly, as they soon began to close for the long summer holidays. Fanny Lucy crossed the Channel to join him and in June they were in Holland, of which Matt wrote unkindly that 'you

live in a constant smell of ooze, hot ooze when in the sun, cold
ooze when you go under the trees'. He could be equally rude
about Belgium. France was always his heart's other home, even
though he often guessed wrong about the French. From Stras-
bourg he wrote to Fan, after a French victory, that they would
always beat 'any number of Germans who come into the field
against them. They will never be beaten by any nation but the
English, for to every other nation they are, in efficiency and intelligence, decidedly superior.' Yet hardly more than ten years
later, in 1870, the Germans were to defeat the French.

By August they were back at Dover with the family, and Matt
got out a pamphlet on 'England and the Italian Question'. Beloved little Tom was well, whistling all day long. Matt told K:
'You know he is too weak to sing, so he solaces his musical taste
by perpetual whistling, when he is well, like a little bullfinch,
poor little darling; but directly he is ill, his pipe stops.' Matt
made one more brief visit to Paris that month, telling his mother:
'This is my last appearance abroad as *"Monsieur le Professeur
Docteur Arnold, Directeur-Général de Toutes les écoles de la
Grande Bretagne,"* as my French friends will have it that I am.'

He was having a splendid time, dining with Sainte-Beuve and
being shown the love letters between Alfred de Musset and George
Sand, of whom Sainte-Beuve said, *'Tout le mal qu'ils ont dit l'un de
l'autre est vrai.'* But Matt told Fanny Lucy that he thought de
Musset's letters were 'those of a *gentleman* of the very first water'.
He was not now so keen to see George Sand again, once his idol.
M. de Circourt had called her 'a fat old Muse'.

And so he came back to London. 'I am rheumatic and full of
pains,' he told Fan, 'coming back after five months of dry air
into this variable climate.' His pamphlet-writing, he felt, had
brought him nearer to his father, for he thought that was Dr
Arnold's strongest literary strain. 'It is the one literary side on
which I feel myself in close contact with him, and that is a
great pleasure. Even the positive style of statement I inherit.'
This was quite true, though in polemic Matthew was less fierce
than his father. Some people found him quite fierce enough –
Newman's brother Francis, for instance, whose idiosyncratic
translation of Homer Matt was to tear to shreds with his mockery
in the lectures of 1860–1.

Anyway, he was back, writing his report for the commission,
and drilling, in November, twice a week in the Queen's West-

minster Rifle Volunteers. 'I like the drilling very much,' he told Fan, 'it braces one's muscles and does one a world of good.' He did not think the volunteer system was 'arming the people' and if it was 'throwing more power into the hands of the middle and upper class' yet he hoped their consciences were sufficiently developed for this to do no harm. He had to admit that 'the bad feature of the proceedings is the hideous English toadyism with which lords and great people are invested with the commands in the corps they join, quite without respect to any consideration of their efficiency. This proceeds from our national bane – the immense vulgar-mindedness, and, so far, the real inferiority of the English middle classes.'

And so the stage was already set for Matthew Arnold's witty attacks on Philistinism, soon to become so well known, cause so much laughter, and make not one atom of difference to English society, which has gone on being Philistine and vulgar-minded ever since.

VI

The Idea of a
Catholic University

When Tom Arnold came back from Tasmania in the autumn of 1856 there was a family reunion at Fox How – of Dr Arnold's nine children only one was absent, William, who had gone back to India. Tom was never to see him again; their last meeting had been before his own departure in 1847.

Tom had to find work quickly to support his family, and he lost no time in writing to Newman, on 23rd October, to ask about his chances of employment, 'if possible in the service of the Church'. He added, 'But my expectations are not lofty; to do some plain useful work and to live in obedience is what I most desire, so only that by my work I can support my family.'

He was forced to report of his wife that she seemed 'to feel as much repugnance as ever to Catholicity; at the same time, mixing in English society is likely to have a generally softening and beneficial effect on her mind and temper; – indeed I trust it has begun to have that effect already'. Perhaps he was thinking of the influence of his sincerely Protestant mother and sisters, who, he told Newman, 'behaved most kindly and affectionately with regard to my change of religion'.

Newman answered from Dublin, whither he had gone on Friday 24th, apologizing for addressing Tom by the familiar 'Arnold' (omitting the 'Mr'), and suggested he should undertake the job of Professor of English Literature in the Catholic University he was starting in Dublin, and of which he was now Rector. 'I am not at all disposed to take offence at your calling me "Arnold"; on the contrary it is a real pleasure to me,' Tom replied, on 28th October. 'The professorship of English, if attainable, would tempt me exceedingly, but I should not do right in accepting it, for I have a certain degree of impediment in speaking which, unless it should please God to remove it, which I sometimes hope, would interfere with my doing the duty properly. But it would not interfere, and indeed never has interfered, with my taking private pupils the least in the world.'

He suggested coming over to Ireland to see Newman and in fact, by 4th November, as Newman reported to his Oratorian colleague Stanislas Flanagan, then in Birmingham, he was already 'installed in Mr Flannery's house as *pro tempore* Tutor – also he is Professor of English Literature vice McCarthy resigned'. Newman regarded Dr Arnold's son as an acquisition to his teaching staff.

The temporary position was to be confirmed later but on 15th December, back at Fox How, Tom wrote to Newman that he did not think settling in Ireland would 'throw back his wife's conversion'. The difficulty was in the social life, since Dr Arnold's friend Richard Whately was now the Anglican Archbishop of Dublin, and had so much dislike of conversions to Catholicism that he had walked past Newman in the street – Newman who had been his protégé as a junior fellow of Oriel some thirty-odd years earlier, at about the time Tom Arnold was born. Tom's wife, however, as he now remarked, 'had never yet seen any of the Whatelys, and as they do not mean to keep up their former intimacy with me, they could not very well be intimate with her, as long as we live together. I have just seen a letter from Whately to my mother, written not a fortnight ago, in which after saying that he has no objection at all to make against those who have been "brought up in the system" he declares that he cannot excuse or think well of those who like myself have been educated in full Protestant light and then have fallen away.'

Tom decided that for his part he would like to resume the Professorship on a permanent basis. 'I do really believe that I shall get my hesitation more and more under control: – I was making progress, I think, before I left Dublin. Still one easily deceives oneself on such matters and therefore I leave it entirely to you.' He added that as his wife had just been confined he would not be able to go up to London during the vacation to see the persons Newman had suggested to him.

The child born at Fox How in December 1856 was Arthur, called presumably after Clough, the fourth baby and third son of Tom and Julia Arnold.

The family moved over to Dublin in the next year, 1857, and in spite of the difficulty over the Whatelys, Julia was not deprived of social life. Harriet Martineau had given Tom an introduction to Lord Carlisle (better known as the Lord Morpeth of the Reform agitation) and the Arnolds received an invitation to St Patrick's ball that March. In his memoirs Tom recalled with amusement that 'the exertions of the good-natured Lord Carlisle, as with red and glowing face, – the George round his neck and the garter binding his knee – he laboured through the crowded country dance, "hands across, down the middle, etc etc" were exceedingly praiseworthy and also slightly comic. As he passed us he said with a laugh, "Hot work, Mrs Arnold! Was it as bad as this in Tasmania?" '

As things turned out, Newman had found Tom Arnold's métier for him, since English Literature became his special field and undergraduates the type of pupil he found most congenial. The Catholic university was still so small and struggling that he had to supplement his salary by coaching work and spent much of his time compiling a manual of English literature which was to continue in use for many years after its publication.

Tom threw himself into the university life and wrote learned articles for Newman's bi-annual magazine *Atlantis* – so called because Newman was hoping to make his university one for English-speaking Catholics, not just for the Irish. Of Newman himself Tom wrote in his autobiography, 'the air of deep abstraction with which he used to glide along the streets of Oxford was now in great measure exchanged for the look of preoccupation and anxiety about temporal affairs, which the features of a man to whom business was neither habitual nor congenial would naturally assume under the new circumstances; but otherwise he seemed quite as vigorous and little older than when I had last seen him in Oxford' – which was over ten years earlier.

Evidently aware of the criticisms of Newman's conduct of the university current in the last part of the nineteenth century, Tom in his memoir paid tribute not only to his intellectual power but to his practical achievements and expressed the wish that the letters of his Catholic period should be published, since they would be found so exceedingly useful to educated Catholics. None in fact appeared until those included by Wilfrid Ward in his biography of Newman, which came out in 1911, when the so-called crisis of Modernism was still reverberating in the Church. Newman's balance and moderation were certainly needed even more then than during the domination of the Ultramontanes – the champions of papal power – of his own day.

As it happened, Tom Arnold's first year in the university was virtually Newman's last. He was coming to the end of his patience, unable to get the support he needed from the Irish bishops, his letters to Archbishop Cullen left unanswered while he was, unknown to himself, unfavourably reported on to Rome, and unable to get from the British government a charter for the granting of degrees. The ultramontane Cullen was shocked at the liberal education Newman was trying to introduce and the freedom he allowed the young men who were boarding in his house. Newman did not know of the derogatory reports to Rome, but he felt the effects of the suspicions he aroused among the Irish clergy; the educated Catholic laity were solidly behind him, but at that time they were very few.

Newman resigned his Rectorship in 1858 and returned to England, feeling that his first responsibility was for his religious community of the Oratory, which he had founded ten years earlier for the benefit of his younger disciples who had become priests like himself. The Oratory, originally started by Filippo Neri, a Florentine who lived in Rome all through the tumultuous sixteenth century, was a loosely knit organization whose members did not take vows but lived together according to a simple rule of life. Each house was intended to be an autonomous self-governing body, a small elective republic, ideally suited to the needs of the times and of the young university men, used to English habits of freedom and individual initiative. But Newman's foundation was given an unfortunate twist when he was joined by Frederick Faber, another convert, who arrived with a train of youthful enthusiasts whom he had directed, as Father Wilfrid, for several years already.

Faber's emotionalism, his flamboyant style, love of Italianate devotions and peculiar brand of submissive wilfulness, not only irked Newman but prevented his building the balanced and sensible Oratory he had intended. Even when Faber hived off to London, things did not improve, for dissensions developed between the two houses and such a collision occurred that Newman determined to break the connexion with the London house. In nearly every way Newman came off the worst from this encounter and his reputation fell while Faber's rose among Catholics carried away by the popular papalism of the day. This disastrous domestic episode occurred while Newman was struggling to start the university in Dublin, and one of his reasons for leaving in 1858 was his conviction that if his own small Oratory in Birmingham was not to collapse entirely, he must live permanently in the community.

Tom Arnold was not then fully aware of these domestic difficulties of Newman's, which he kept as much as possible to himself, but he saw and sympathized with his troubles over the university though, perhaps because he had so recently joined it, he remained for some time more hopeful of its future. On 1st March 1858 he was writing to Newman about his paper on Alcibiades for the *Atlantis*, reporting on the scheme of evening lectures to be run for the young men of Dublin, and glad to hear the good news of a long lease for the university house and ground. 'Sullivan is already chuckling over the pleasing prospect of a "Botanical Garden" to be carved out of part of it. What a satisfactory man Sullivan is to work with. So much good sense and ability, joined to the large local experience in which we Englishmen are so badly to seek.'

William Kirby Sullivan, about the same age as Tom, was Newman's Professor of Chemistry; he had studied in Liebig's laboratory in Germany. He was a Young Irelander, like others of Newman's friends in Ireland. Newman wrote of him to his friend Monsell: 'Sullivan is a rough man, but clever, and, to me, engaging, from his honesty and sharpness.' He stayed with the university till 1873 when he became President of the Queen's College, Cork. He was naturally a man congenial to Tom Arnold and they both contributed to *Atlantis* and later to Acton's *Home and Foreign Review*.

Newman was planning to found a school for boys on the lines of the English public schools, since the convert families were finding inadequate provision for the education of their sons in the small Catholic community of England. Until this period of double influx, from the upper-class converts and the starving Irish immigrants, the few aristocratic Catholics had employed tutors or sent their sons abroad to study, while schools were attached to the seminaries where 'lay-boys' could reach a certain standard along with those intending to be priests. Anxious to secure good masters for his projected school Newman offered Arnold £300 a year to come.

On 1st May 1858, Tom replied: 'It is true my professorship

is much less; still it leaves much more of my time free, which I can use to some advantage, however small it be.' Then, too, he had just furnished a house and a removal would be to his loss. Above all he was still hoping that 'the university *may* come to something after all; if we all put our shoulders to the wheel, that it is a *carrière ouverte* and that it is worth submitting to much privation, even on the mere chance that our hopes may one day be realized. Whereas I see no *future*, no likelihood of promotion, in any sense, if I were to engage in the school, even though it were to succeed as thoroughly as I wish it may.'

All the same, a fortnight later, he was writing to ask the chances of an increase of pay in his present job, as he had heard that another Professor had got one. 'Individually I believe I could live on as little as most men, but my family has to be provided for and it is a hard matter to do it.'

The family increased by two more while Tom was in Ireland; Lucy was born in Leinster Square and Francis after a move to Kenilworth Square. There were now six children to provide for out of that small salary, and what could be made from private pupils.

At the end of October 1858 Newman came over to Dublin for what he intended to be a final visit. On 3rd November he gave a lecture to the faculty of Philosophy and Letters. Tom wrote to him on the 6th: 'I was very sorry that I could obtain no more than one or two glimpses of you while you were in Dublin. But if you had been divided into twenty individualities you could not have satisfied the eager desires of all who wished for an interview or interviews with you, so I must console myself with thinking that I did not fare worse than others. I must tell you how greatly I enjoyed your lecture to our faculty. It threw a broad illumination over a field of thought which I myself have often essayed to enter, so that independently of its general merits it had a peculiar interest for me. I do hope you will print it at the same time as the lecture to the medical faculty.'

He went on to explain why he had not signed the petition got up by Professor Ornsby to persuade Newman not to resign. Tom felt that Newman must know his own mind and would not have made it up except with deliberation. He agreed with Newman that what was most needed was an active resident Vice-Rector. It was because he had not succeeded in persuading the authorities to appoint one that Newman decided to stick to his decision to resign.

Meanwhile the school plan was progressing, and Newman, who feared that Tom's university job was about to collapse under him, tried to persuade him to come and join the staff, offering £300 a year and £50 for the expense of moving. 'Your work would be little more than *musa musae – amo, amavi* – And say, six hours a day, no duty to boys out of school.'

'It is rather afflicting to find the ground thus sinking from under one, but God's will be done,' Tom replied on 3rd December. '. . . I must therefore be prepared to give up duties which I had begun to hope might turn one day to some fruit for my fellow men and for the great cause of Catholicity. So be it, then: – the school at Birmingham would certainly have many attractions for me.' But in the event it proved possible for him to stay on in Dublin and he did not then accept Newman's offer.

But he kept in touch with Newman over university affairs and in January 1859 told him of an interview he had had with Lord Stanley, on the question of its being granted a charter for the conferring of degrees. Tom urged this on the score of preventing the university from 'falling into the hands of the extreme or Celtic party and being converted into a machinery for promoting disunion and alienation'. He added, 'To an English statesman I think this might be considered a good line of argument, but the Young Irelanders of course would not thank me if they knew I had taken up such a line.' Lord Stanley had said it was a thing for the whole cabinet to decide and Tom feared that if it had to be argued by counsel before the Privy Council the delays would be immense, for 'when the lawyers get hold of a thing, they are loath to let it go'.

However, he must have been more optimistic when he went to see Newman, for the latter reported to his friend Sergeant Bellasis, 'He has been here for a few hours and seems to like us – but he does not like to give up the university till the university gives up him; and he thinks we shall get a Charter, of which indeed there is a very fair chance.' Writing the same day to Ornsby, Newman said, 'I cannot quarrel with his zeal for the University in wishing to stay. I wish we had more such zealous people.'

But Newman naturally knew more of the reasons for the precarious state of the university than Arnold, and a month later he was writing of its general prospects to Ornsby, on 14th February 1859, lamenting the shortsighted policy of the hierarchy. 'Yet how the Holy See can be satisfied with a mere College at Dublin as a means of keeping out mixed education from Cork, Belfast etc I can't *conceive* . . . It is giving up the battle – and it is not that *we* fail, but the Catholic cause in the educated classes, and the word of the Pope, fails.' He even wondered if negotiations were going on at Rome with the English government. But meanwhile he knew that Archbishop Cullen proposed to cut down on the professorships and he mentioned Arnold's as one likely to be cut. 'The Divinity Professors would go, and of course Preachers etc. The Medical Professors will be reduced in salary. Perhaps they will *destroy* the Science School – Yet after all it will be most difficult to turn a University into a College, putting aside all I have said above about *principle.*'

The university, however, continued to limp along and Arnold retained his position there.

As it happened, Tom Arnold had come into the Church at a difficult time for a liberal-minded man, when the Temporal Power of the Pope was becoming a flashpoint of controversy, as Pius IX was gradually squeezed out of his Papal States by the rising tide of Italian nationalism. On his election in 1846 the Pope had a liberal reputation himself, but the revolutions of 1848 and the Roman Republic of 1849, had put an end to that; for the rest of his long reign he entrenched himself in secular conservatism and a peculiar brand of sentimental religious autocracy which he was persuaded was the answer to the rebellious and questioning spirit of the age.

People who had other ideas as to how to meet the doubts and disbeliefs of the new era were suspected of disloyalty not merely to the Pope but to the Church, closely identified by its supreme pontiff with himself. During the later fifties Newman found himself in this unenviable situation, partly because he was blamed for the rupture with Faber, whose popular papalism was favoured by Rome, partly because he was associated with the magazine owned by Sir John Acton, then a young, but already learned, student of history with strong views on political and religious freedom. In 1859, after the English bishops had threatened to suppress the *Rambler*, Newman accepted the editorship in an attempt to save it; he did so, but only at the cost of his own reputation at Rome, and was forced to retire after two numbers. Aware that he was no longer *persona grata* with the authorities, Newman felt unable to undertake any new writing to meet the problems of the day; sometimes he put off friends who begged him to do so by saying it was not easy to write anything to the purpose in the present situation.

In November 1859 Tom wrote to him: 'I am astonished at what you say about not writing to the purpose. If you do not write to the purpose I should like to know who among the Catholics of the three kingdoms does so. Your writings form the one *locus standi* which enables a thinking English Catholic, amidst the torrent of argument, satire, scoff, banter, lofty compassion and honest disapproval, which the strong free-spoken race to which we belong is for ever heaping in these days upon the Catholic Church, still to feel that his cause is not in all respects intellectually over matched, that there is a view of things, which has not yet ever been seriously grappled with by the Protestant and infidel side, much less *answered*: hence that, since no great truth ever fails to fight its way at last, there is hope in the future, in spite of the perplexities and discouragements of the present.'

He went on to give his own feelings on the way Catholics should behave in the contemporary situation, which show the width and balance of his own mind.

'We should heartily work with our fellowmen and learn from them all the political wisdom which they have to teach us, so in literature and philosophy, we must first do complete justice to all that non-Catholic genius has produced of true or beautiful, first assimilate and benefit by all that, before even dreaming of a "Catholic literature" which shall have so wide a sweep as to embrace and reconcile all truth and beauty heretofore disclosed. But after all I am only saying what you have said a thousand times better in your book on the *Idea of a University*, together with reservations and caveats which I in my haste have forgotten. My general meaning is that I do not like sectarianism and yet fear I see a strong tendency towards it among our English and Irish Catholics of the present day. The sectarian spirit gives a present strength and compactness indeed, but it is at the expense of the future, because it is essentially *unjust* and injustice does not thrive for ever even in this world. It is because what you write is so utterly free from that spirit, that some minds may especially value it; other qualities may chiefly recommend it to others, but this quality is that which makes it accord so well with the feelings of a certain class of minds which have a pure and high ambition for the Church of God while conscious of possessing powers too feeble and limited to do her much service themselves in the field of thought.'

A hundred years later the Catholic Church in England is at last struggling to free itself of what Tom Arnold called the sectarian spirit; at the time he wrote the atmosphere was unfortunately growing narrower and more constricted, the attitude to the world beyond the Church more suspicious, frightened and denunciatory. If Newman, an exceptional man and a genius, suffered painfully from the effect of this intellectual and moral constriction, it was no wonder that men such as Tom Arnold found it unsettling to his faith in the Church.

On 20th July 1860, he wrote to Newman to thank him for answering some religious difficulties, which, he said, had now receded into the background, while the certainty of faith vindicated itself more and more. 'Next to greater care and regularity in frequenting the sacraments, I think the chief cause of this alteration of mood is the habit, which continually grows on me, of preferring the *Lives of the Saints*, especially modern saints, to all other reading. I cannot find the true hero – the true sage – such as even the natural mind represents these characters to itself – anywhere else depicted. People speak of Wordsworth as a *sage* – but he was so only in *words*; I who knew him well remember that in the daily walk of life, he was far from having that calmness, that mastery over self and outward things, which are involved in the idea that the word conveys.'

This, the first sign of the recurrence of religious uncertainty, and the recourse to the sacraments and the lives of saints, reflects the pattern of Tom Arnold's inner life. He does not mention what his difficulties were, but they must have been connected with doubts on the infallibility of the Church, since this was the point upon which his conversion, and his later lapse, turned. The behaviour of the ecclesiastical leaders of his day did not help.

In this letter he also asked Newman if it was lawful to be present at the family prayers at Fox How which till now he had always been when on holiday there – 'though without joining in them'. An Irish confessor had told him it was forbidden in Ireland, but that discipline might be different in England. Let us hope that Newman was able to encourage him to continue the practice.

So far from being sent away, Arnold received an increase of salary, and moved to Kingstown, where he wrote articles and letters about the university for the *Weekly Register*, an English Catholic newspaper. Newman admired his pertinacity but felt saddened at the waste of his talents. He wrote to Ornsby on 8th November 1861, 'You can't tell how much it distresses me to think of yourself and him and other zealous men labouring so heartily with so little encouragement and so badly paid. How *he* stays I cannot comprehend . . . I believe they have increased his salary – but it seems wonderful to me with his connexions that he does not get something better. I say to myself, here are men losing their best years for nothing!'

It was not surprising therefore that when, at the end of that year, Newman found himself faced with the wholesale resignation of the staff at his new school, his first thought was of Arnold. Newman at that time was in poor health and suffered from prolonged nervous strain under the knowledge that he was being severely criticized in London and Rome and from worry about the school affairs, which had been taken out of his hands into those of Nicholas Darnell, one of the Fathers of his Oratory, who was perhaps too ambitious to imitate the public schools of the day.

Darnell and the three lay masters threatened to resign, no doubt expecting that Newman would give in, but instead he rose to the challenge, accepted their resignation, took over the school himself and began at once to look for substitutes, determined not to be a day late with the new term, due to begin on 24th January 1862.

Newman was to be President, and Fr Ambrose St John headmaster; the latter was sent over to Dublin to secure Arnold if he possibly could. Tom, who was over in London, called at Birmingham, and Newman wrote to the University Rector; the details of salary, Arnold's lectures in Dublin, and the removal of his household were settled in a few weeks. Newman offered the Arnolds, rent free, a house in Vicarage Road, which opened off the Hagley Road, almost opposite the Oratory. This time, Arnold accepted.

Tom himself arrived in Birmingham on 21st January and term began as planned. As Newman said to Ornsby, on 31st January, 'In our sudden and frightful difficulty Arnold's name did wonders for us.'

Thus did Tom Arnold find himself once more a schoolmaster, following in his famous father's footsteps – though his mother, writing to friends, could hardly bear to think of Dr Arnold's grandsons brought up as Catholics, under the eye of Newman.

As for Julia Arnold, she would never allow her daughters to meet Newman. In the custom of the day the daughters followed their mother's religion, the sons their father's. Willy was put into the Oratory School at once, Theodore and, briefly, Arthur, followed him there. Mary remained with Miss Clough at school in Ambleside, only spending some holidays in Edgbaston, and only seeing Newman in the distance, walking along the road. Mary stared at Newman with suspicion, for her mother had given her the impression that all their troubles were due to him.

There was a new baby at 7 Vicarage Road: Julia, known as Judy, born in December 1862, and destined to marry T. H. Huxley's son Leonard and become the mother of Julian and Aldous Huxley. She was the seventh child, over ten years younger than her sister Mary.

Dublin, and the Catholic University for which Tom Arnold had given so much of his energy and zeal for the last five years, receded. When he came to Birmingham he was thirty-eight and immediately threw himself into the work of the school, if not with such enthusiasm, at least with conscientious determination to do his best.

VII

Culture and Criticism

On 26th January 1861, Matthew Arnold gave the last of his three lectures *On Translating Homer* to a full audience and later told his sister Jane that he was cheered – 'which is very uncommon at Oxford'. The lectures were published as a book the same year and elicited a good many retorts, including an attack in the *Saturday Review* for 26th July: 'Homeric Translators and Critics'. A few days later Matt wrote to his mother: 'When I first read a thing of this kind I am annoyed; then I think how certainly in two or three days the effect of it upon me will have wholly passed off; then I begin to think of the openings it gives for observations in answer, and from that moment, when a free activity of the spirit is restored, my gaiety and good spirits return, and the article is simply an object of interest to me.'

Later in the letter he told her he planned a fourth lecture in the autumn, 'and then I shall try to set things straight, at the same time soothing [F. W.] Newman's feelings – which I am really sorry to have hurt – as much as I can without giving up any truth of criticism'.

These two comments reflect the atmosphere of all Matthew Arnold's criticism: it was a battle from start to finish, and he enjoyed the fight, managed to keep his temper and his sense of humour, but never gave an inch of ground. It was perhaps somewhat insensitive not to realize that clever attacks would hurt people's feelings, but he was deceived by his own good will, knowing that he intended no malice. Francis Newman, John Henry's youngest brother, who had lost his faith laboriously in a series of books from the late eighteen-forties onwards, and was Professor of Latin at University College, London, had no sense of humour at all and he had worked very hard on his peculiar translation of Homer, which appeared in 1856. Naturally his feelings were hurt, and in the spirit of the time he had immediately gone into print with: *Homeric Translation in theory and practice: A Reply to Matthew Arnold*. Arnold's reply to the Reply was typically entitled *On Translating Homer: Last Words*. He always thought he had the last word.

In these lectures on translating Homer Matthew Arnold was able to say a good deal about poetry, but the essays which made up his first book of criticism reflect his interest in European literature. They appeared first in the magazines which ruled the literary scene in those days, principally *Fraser's* and the *Cornhill*, during the years 1862 to 1864. *Maurice de Guérin* appeared in *Fraser's* at the turn of the year 1862–3, *Eugénie de Guérin* in the *Cornhill* for June 1863; *Heinrich Heine* (one of the Oxford lectures) in the *Cornhill* for August the same year, and so on. Alexander Macmillan published the book early in 1865 and when they were looking for a title he suggested *Orpheus*.

Matt wrote to him on 2nd August 1864: 'I must not call the volume "Orpheus" or I shall certainly be torn to pieces for presumption by the Thracian women of the periodical press.' It was he who hit on 'Essays *in* Criticism' which kept, as he wished, the sense of 'attempt'. In February 1865 he was writing to Macmillan, 'Pray do not, in advertising my book, put the newspaper panegyrics at the bottom. I have an inexpressible dislike to it.'

These essays gave less reason than usual to the Thracian women of the periodical press to tear him to pieces and he got quite a panegyric in the *Saturday Review*, from R. H. Hutton (editor of the *Spectator*) who found a 'striking resemblance' between 'two of the finest living writers of English prose' – the other was J. H. Newman, still fresh from the triumphs of his *Apologia pro Vita Sua*. Macmillan thought this comparison 'somewhat fanciful – though of course as put by him, not a little gratifying'.

The essay on *The Function of Criticism at the Present Time* provoked James Fitzjames Stephens to write in the *Saturday Review* on 'Mr Matthew Arnold and his Countrymen'. Matthew brooded on this with mischievous delight for some time and finally wrote *My Countrymen* for the *Cornhill* in February 1866; he later published it, with the amusing Arminius letters, in 1871, under the title *Friendship's Garland*. This satire, using invented personages and annotating their supposed works with pseudo-learned footnotes, is the funniest of Matthew Arnold's books, and makes his points with barbed wit.

Criticism had never been entirely literary with Matthew Arnold; it was his comments on society, moral and political, which caught the attention of his contemporaries and provoked the controversies which ran on through the decade and were to take a religious turn in the seventies.

By 1867 Arnold had been ten years professor of poetry at Oxford and although a move was made for him to stand again, he declined. His last lecture was delivered on 7th June and appeared in the *Cornhill* for July. It was called 'Culture and its Enemies'. This drew the enemies all right, if not of Culture at least of its prophet, as Matt was christened by Henry Sidgwick in *Macmillan's Magazine*. Macmillan himself wrote, hoping Matt would like the article: 'Of course he does not agree with you, but he is full of admiration in general. I am sure these discussions do great good and the country owes you much.' All the same, when the time came for a book, it was George Smith, of Smith, Elder, who published it.

Arnold's replies to his critics appeared first as a series of five articles on *Anarchy and Authority* in the *Cornhill*, beginning in August 1868, and were published next year under the title of *Culture and Anarchy*. When the time came for a second edition in 1875, he deleted some of the personal references, and thought he had much improved it, as he told Smith, 'by throwing it into chapters with headings supplied by phrases in the book which have become famous: "Sweetness and Light" "Hebraism and Hellenism" etc.'

'Sweetness and Light' which Arnold takes to epitomize the human perfection aimed at in culture, he borrowed from Swift's *Battle of the Books* where the Bee (the ancients) is judged favourably against the Spider (the moderns) because it fills its hives with honey and wax: sweetness and light. Although Arnold was most concerned with the *light*, the illumination of the mind, his critics tended to seize on the *sweetness*, and jeer at him as a dilettante. He was amused at this, and chaffs Frederic Harrison, one of the younger and more vigorous of his critics, for 'his almost stern moral impatience, to behold, as he says, "Death, Sin, cruelty stalk among us, filling their maws with innocence and youth", and me, in the midst of the general tribulation, handing out my pouncet-box.'

But his purpose in advocating culture, as throwing light on the social scene and preventing action from being merely random and ill regulated, was entirely serious, and culture, to him, was so far from being dilettantism that all its knowledge and art must be directed by 'reason and the will of God' to the perfecting of all men. But as his way of showing this was to ridicule the insufficiency of his countrymen's notions of liberty ('Doing as one likes'), mocking typical members of the various classes and even the British Constitution, it was no wonder that he annoyed some of his contemporaries. He called the upper classes 'the Barbarians', the middle, industrial class 'the Philistines' and the rest 'the Populace'. Criticism of them all was unsparing, however amusing.

Arnold's idea of Hebraism and Hellenism was a deeper one and became a starting point for his religious criticism; and although his attacks on the Puritan ethos of the Philistine middle class were severe, he by no means opted entirely for Hellenism. Hebraism represented moral action and the will to live, 'the will of God'. Matthew was the son of his father, and righteousness was, as he was to say of St Paul, 'what set him in motion'. But in the England of passionate religious Puritanism he saw the necessity for the cooling air of reason, the balance of intellect and imagination epitomized by the civilization of ancient Athens.

'I think "*Barbarians*" will stick,' Matthew wrote to his mother in February 1868; 'but as a very charming Barbarianess, Lady Portsmouth, expresses a great desire to make my acquaintance, I daresay the race will bear no malice.' It was one of the ironies of life that as he became famous, Matt was taken up by the rich and noble, some of whom became real friends; he visited them, went shooting and fishing, his favourite sport, with them. No doubt this made his liberal critics more suspicious than ever. Arnold declared himself a liberal, 'but a cautious one'; he had no use for what he still called Jacobinism – doctrinaire violence in politics. 'Sweetness and light, I call that, Mr Arnold, eh?' said Disraeli to him at a dinner party in 1869. Everyone caught up his phrases.

As early as 1863 he was telling his mother: 'Flu (his wife) told you of my seeing myself placarded all over London as having written on Marcus Aurelius, and having walked up Regent Street behind a man with a board on his back announcing the same interesting piece of news.' He was meeting all sorts of people; back in June he had dined with Monckton Milnes 'and met all the advanced liberals in religion and politics and a Cingalese in full costume; so that, having lunched with the Rothschilds, I seemed to be passing my day among Jews, Turks, infidels and heretics. But the philosophers were fearful! G. Lewes, Herbert Spencer, a sort of pseudo-Shelley called Swinburne, and so on. Froude, however, was there, and Browning and Ruskin; the latter and I had some talk, but I should never like him . . .'

He did like Lady de Rothschild, however, who became a real friend, to his wife and daughters as well as to himself.

The year before, going to a party, they found Thackeray there, 'who was very amusing, kissing his hand to Flu, and calling me a monster, but adding that "he had told all to her father".' Thackeray asked them to dine, but they were engaged elsewhere. Matt later complained that he had to eat and drink more than he wished to, though he obviously enjoyed the social side of all this entertainment.

But the prophet of culture was also the school inspector, and the arduous travelling life went on and on, with the Judge's circuits thrown in. Judge Wightman liked riding and took three horses round with him; he and Matt often rode from one place to another. Matt wrote to Fanny Lucy from court rooms up and down the country, and missed her company. By 1861 they had five children and she was rarely able to visit with him, except at Fox How, though in London they were often out together.

On 20th March 1861 Matt wrote to his mother from Lewes in Sussex: 'The new baby, or gorilla as I call her, is a fiend at night. She nearly wore poor Mrs Young out and I look forward to the sea to make her a little less restless.' They took a house in Brighton and the weather had turned hot when Matt wrote again in June: 'Dear little Tom has entirely recovered under the heat, which relieves his poor oppressed circulation of all struggle and difficulty. A very little cough in the early morning is all that is left of his illness. Budge and Dicky are in splendid force and in their brown holland suits look the most comfortably dressed children in Brighton. Lucy in her white frock looks as cool and as pretty a little object as you can imagine.' It was so hot that Matt preferred to 'crawl about with Tom in his wheel chair to riding'.

In December of that year came the Prince Consort's sudden death and after commenting on the consternation it had caused, Matt told his mother that 'Flu overheard Dicky telling Lucy he had gone to heaven. Upon which Lucy answered, "Should I like Heaven, *Wichard* dear?" "Oh yes, darling," says Dicky, "so much! there's *tookey* there, and toy shops and such *beautiful* dollies!" Fan will be much amused with the first place given by Dick to croquet, even in Heaven.'

Croquet was all the rage and Matt himself played it. In October 1863, he quoted to his mother a Westminster Reviewer who had said, ' "Though confident, Mr Arnold is never self-willed; though bold, he is never paradoxical." Tell Fan to remember this in future when she is playing croquet with me. I also keep it as a weapon against K. who said to me that I was becoming as dogmatic as Ruskin. I told her the difference was that Ruskin was "dogmatic and *wrong*," and here is this charming reviewer who comes to confirm me.'

But life was not all gaiety and hard work. After the death of his brother William in 1859, the saddest loss at the beginning of this decade was of Clough, the friend of his youth, who died in Florence on 13th November 1861. Overworked, suffering from periods of depression, Clough had gone travelling abroad. His wife Blanche was having another baby in August, but before September was over she was hurrying out to Italy to meet him. Lassitude and severe head pains ended with some kind of stroke and in that beautiful city he died, and was buried in the Protestant cemetery. Blanche came back with a death mask and a cast of his long-fingered hand.

The sadness of Clough's death was not in his comparative youth (he was nearly forty-three) but in the feeling of defeat, the failing of vitality, which preceded it; indeed, death may have come as a release, for one cannot help wondering if he would not have suffered a complete mental breakdown had he lived longer. It was for Clough, rather than for Matt, that these were 'damned times'.

Matt wrote to his mother on 20th November: 'First of all you will expect me to say something about poor Clough. That is a loss I shall feel more and more as time goes on, for he is one of the few people who ever made a deep impression upon me ... People were beginning to say about Clough that he would never do anything now, and, in short, to pass him over. I foresee that there will now be a change, and attention will be fixed on what there was of extraordinary promise and interest in him when he was young, and of unique and imposing even as he grew older without fulfilling people's expectations. I have been asked to write a Memoir of him for the *Daily News*, but that I cannot do. I could not write about him in a newspaper now, nor can, I think, at length in a review; but I shall some day in some way or other, relieve myself of what I think about him.'

What he did, in the end, was to write *Thyrsis*, perhaps his most famous poem during his lifetime. The poem was a slow growth, for in spite of his straightforward nature, he was not a quick reactor. Feelings, as well as ideas, took their time to mature in him. *Thyrsis* was first printed in the April number of *Macmillan's Magazine* in 1866, and included in an edition of his poems which came out the following year. Like Shelley's *Adonais* it perhaps says more of the poet than his subject, though Matt knew Clough far better than Shelley ever knew Keats. Even at the time some of Clough's friends thought it gave a defective idea of him; Matt maintained that, though it might not be the whole, yet it represented a real aspect of his personality. But although they often met when both were married and living in London, their friendship in later years was much less close. It was of their youth that Matt was thinking when he wrote *Thyrsis*, and the Cumnor country, where he had loved to wander.

Clough was dead; Clough was to belong always to the first half of the century, with its revolutions, its social ferment, its romantic hopes and disillusions. But Matt, full of inexhaustible Arnold energy, was just entering into his full powers, just feeling the strength of his mind, as the later Victorian age swung massively forward, the age of empire and trade and science, and also the time of the deepest doubting as to the nature of man, the truth of religion, the existence of God.

VIII

Sliding out of
Catholicism

Tom Arnold stayed barely three years at the Oratory School in Birmingham, but it was a turning point in his life, for this was the time when he lost faith in the Church, though he did not admit it till he had left the place. When he wrote about this change of mind in *Passages in a Wandering Life*, it was long after his return to the fold, and his account is therefore distanced by time and alteration of views. He even blamed a great deal on the climate of Edgbaston, which he found trying, especially the north-west wind 'which blew perseveringly for a great part of spring and early summer, and not only was exceedingly cold but brought smoke and abominable vapours from the neighbouring "Black Country" over the unhappy suburb'. The harsh climate and ill-drained house no doubt contributed to a series of illnesses which further debilitated and depressed him.

But there were alleviations. In the August of 1863 they had 'three happy holiday weeks' at Solihull, then regarded as 'a pretty town ten miles from Birmingham'. The boys played in the park and fished in the Blyth. In September Tom paid a visit to Aldenham Park near Bridgnorth, the seat of Lord Acton, then still proprietor and part-editor of the *Home and Foreign Review*, the quarterly successor to the old *Rambler*, and certainly the only periodical conducted by Catholics which was read and respected by the educated public in England. Acton's erudition, his political liberalism, and the journalistic powers of his co-editor, the clever and witty Richard Simpson, made its name as a magazine of solid worth, printing articles on historical and topical subjects, with a long review section, often used for discussing controversial questions which could not be treated directly without offending Cardinal Wiseman and the new English Catholic hierarchy, orientated as they were to the ultramontanism then prevalent at Rome. The periodical staggered from crisis to crisis till Acton finally brought it to an end in March 1864, convinced by the Brief addressed by Pope Pius IX to the Congress of Catholic scholars held at Munich in December 1863, that it was no longer possible to publish as he wished without appearing to be in direct opposition to papal policy.

Before the sad event of this closure, Tom Arnold had contributed several articles, among them 'The Colonization of Northumbria,' 'The Formation of the English Counties', 'Hayti' and 'Albania'. The first two show his interest in the field of Anglo-Saxon studies, then only just opening up academically. Although he was teaching classics at school, his chief interest was still English literature.

At the end of September in 1863 Tom got a severe attack of lumbago and was hardly through that before he went down, early in December, with scarlet fever, then a dangerous illness which carried off many Victorians, young and old. The children were sent off to Fox How, the servant to hospital, and Tom recorded how 'in that bitter winter my wife rose on several mornings before dawn, lighted the kitchen fire and met all the household calls of the day'. She also nursed her husband who, on 20th December, suffered what he called 'a sharp but transitory attack of rheumatic fever', of the same kind as he had endured at Hobart Town in 1852. His recovery was slow, but towards the end of January 1864 they went to Clifton, in lodgings near the Suspension Bridge (begun by Brunel but only finished that year) where Tom soon felt a new man, astonished at the difference made by the situation, 120 miles south of Birmingham and 300 feet less above the sea. He was soon 'diving down the narrow streets of Bristol in search of bits of mediaeval architecture'. He wrote an article on Bristol churches which appeared in *Fraser's Magazine*. His wife Julia made some good friends in Clifton and was happy there.

But alas, in May, Tom went down with measles, unpleasant, if not dangerous, for adults. In July they at last succeeded in moving from the unloved ill-drained house in Vicarage Road to Harborne, then 'a breezy village two miles south-west of Birmingham'. And in August Tom was able to spend some time in Llandudno with Matthew and his family.

Matt wrote to his mother on 7th August 1864 that yesterday he had 'started with dear old Tom for the interior of the country, being sick of lodging houses and seaside'. They went about five miles by rail on the Llanrwst road and then walked to Llyn Eigiau. 'You can imagine how I liked having dear old Tom with me, and how he enjoys it.' Matthew thought he had persuaded Tom to bring his family to join them later that month, but on the 20th he told his mother that they were going instead to Clifton, a decision which irritated Matthew, especially as Fanny Lucy had been indefatigably looking for lodgings for them in Llandudno. He had looked forward to more of Tom's companionship on the walks they both loved. To his sister Fan Matt was writing, 'The poetry of the Celtic race and its names of places quite overpowers me, and it will be long before Tom forgets the line, "Hear from the grave, great Taliessin, hear!" from Gray's *Bard*, of which I gave him the benefit some hundred times a day on our excursions.'

Presumably when he had moved house in the suburbs of Birmingham, Tom Arnold had intended to stay at the Oratory School, but he was soon taking the steps which led to his leaving it. He had no quarrel with Newman himself, whom he describes at the time of recreation after dinner at the Oratory, as 'always cheerful, and if not talkative, *abordable* and ready to talk'. That he was so is remarkable, for these had been very difficult years for Newman, whose sixties coincided with those of the century. He had lived through one exhausting crisis between the two houses he had founded and another within his own, over the school; he had become involved with the *Rambler*'s affairs, disastrously for himself, since it helped to increase the suspicions against him of unorthodoxy and disloyalty to the Pope. All this continued pressure brought him near to a nervous breakdown; rumours even went round that he was losing his mind and not fit to say Mass.

However, in the spring of 1864 came Newman's great triumph of the *Apologia pro Vita Sua*, his answer to the attacks of Charles Kingsley. It came out in parts through April to June and proved an instant and lasting success with the unpredictable English public. Newman's reputation rose almost overnight; it had never been so high, and with the general public it was never to decline, though his popularity with Protestants and sceptics did him no good with the narrow-minded leaders of his own church. Newman became a national, and soon an international figure, whose opinion was sought by many; he recovered his health and entered on a new period of activity and influence.

But this unexpected triumph of Newman's came in the very year when Tom Arnold was beginning to drift away from the Church. In his memoirs he recorded his feeling that his own liberalism alienated him from Newman, instancing the fact that he intended to give, as an extra prize to a boy, the translation of Ignaz Doellinger's book, *The Churches and the Church*, which had just appeared, and which, he says, Newman would not allow the boy to receive. Writing of this so long after – about thirty-five years later – Tom allows that the Oratorians may have been better aware than himself where these liberal religious views were leading: Doellinger became a famous opponent of Papal Infallibility and never accepted the conciliar decree on the subject. What Tom Arnold does not seem to realize was Newman's own involvement in these crucial issues.

Newman had a great respect for Doellinger's scholarship, deplored his falling into excommunication after the Council of 1870, and when he himself had been made a Cardinal by Leo XIII in 1879, was only prevented by illness from calling on him on the way home from Rome. Newman had a deep understanding of the complexities of church history, but perhaps it was not possible for a contemporary to appreciate his delicate position as we, a century later, can discover it through study of his letters and later writings. Newman remained inflexibly opposed to what has since been characterized as the reductionist approach to religious belief and doctrine; the 'nothing but' of rationalism applied to subjects which, like poetry and music, are not indeed irrational, but go beyond reason. This rationalizing reductionism Newman called 'liberalism in religion' which still causes some people to imagine that he was defending intellectual obscurantism and political oppression. Since the Ultramontanes of the day often did just this, it sometimes seemed to Catholics concerned for the cause of freedom that Newman had not the courage to stand up for it. In such times of crisis it is always difficult for priests who are also writers to remain loyal both to the body of the Church and to the principles which they believe should animate it. Newman often felt his only action could be silence; and so he suffered the usual fate of the moderate, to be suspected by both sides as a traitor.

Tom Arnold, whose mind was simpler and less experienced

than Newman's, did not fully comprehend the issues. He describes, though briefly, how 'the misgiving which had long slumbered in my mind, that no clear certainty could be obtained as to anything outside the fields of science, again assailed me'. This was the great difficulty to the intellectual Victorian and one that Newman had brooded over for years and was trying to meet in his *Essay in Aid of a Grammar of Assent*, published in March 1870 when the first Vatican Council was already in session at Rome. If Tom Arnold had discussed the question with Newman while he had the opportunity, he might have received decisive assistance; and yet, in matters of faith, who can tell? Newman himself was well aware of the multitude of factors which go to make up a religious conviction.

In any case, Tom was not close enough to Newman to reveal his state of mind while he was still uncertain. Instead, there are a series of notes about his salary, of which he said nothing in his memoirs. Nevertheless at the time the fact that Newman could not increase his salary or promise that it would receive increase, was a decisive factor in Tom's determination to leave Edgbaston. Schoolwork was not really his métier; he was a natural academic, and it was no wonder that around the age of forty he became restive, seeing no future for himself in Birmingham, hating the place, and with a wife who still hated everything to do with Catholicism so much that she would not allow her daughter to meet even Newman himself.

There was some misunderstanding about Tom's resignation, whether it was to take place and when, and the exchange of notes was cool, but Newman paid the full year's salary, though in fact Tom was absent a good deal of it through illness, and, after the new year of 1865, expected to leave at any time. By April he was in lodgings in Oxford and looking out for pupils, for he intended to make a living by coaching. Newman wrote there to ask if the report was true that he had given up Catholicism but did not wish it to be known at the Oratory till he had left. Tom replied on 24th April: 'The report about me which you mention is false and you have my authority to contradict it. But I fear I must pain you by saying that I cannot guarantee where, or in what form of opinions, the course of thought may eventually land me.'

On 2nd May he was writing again to thank Newman for the salary cheque. 'It cannot but be most gratifying to me that my connexion with the Oratory should be terminated in such a manner; and though I certainly am conscious of having tried to do my duty, I never could have, and never did, expect that what I did should be met in such a generous spirit, so much more than met, I may indeed say.'

A month later, on 4th June, Newman wrote again, having heard that Tom had told W. G. Palgrave that he had given up the doctrine of the infallibility of the Church. 'Do not suppose that I write these lines to trouble you with controversy, or to exact an answer – but I cannot bear to let you go from the one fountain of grace and spiritual strength, without saying a word, not of farewell, for well it cannot be so to direct your course, but to express my deep sorrowfulness at hearing the news. I will not believe that you have not found strength and comfort in Masses and Sacraments, and I do not think you will find the like else-where. Nor shall I easily be led to believe that the time will not come when you will acknowledge this yourself, and will return to the Fold which you are leaving. Meanwhile, as you have for some weeks been in my prayers with reference to these sad waverings of faith, so shall you be still.'

It was 13th June before Tom replied from Oxford, apologizing for the delay: 'In this bustling term it is difficult to find time to write. The kindness of your letter struck me very much and I feel I do not in the least deserve that any of your kind thoughts should be wasted upon me. As I look back, to whatever part of my past life I turn my eyes, shame and confusion of face are the result of my reflexions. No party or school has ever been the better for my adhesion, and probably never will. One portion of my career has always balanced and neutralized some other, and the worst of it is that I cannot even feel that wherever my weight has been applied for the time being, it has been of any perceptible use; my stroke has been both weak and intermittent. A certain general honesty of purpose is all I can urge on my own side: and that is not much. As to the subject of your letter – yes, it is true that I can no longer believe in a permanent and living infallibility in the Church. I tried hard to believe it for a long time, in spite of the objections that constantly presented them-selves, but at last I broke down. And in connexion with this I must say I have never been able to understand or appropriate a sentence of yours in the *Apologia* to the effect that all the diffi-culties in the world do not amount to one doubt. I cannot see what can be the use of difficulties, if no accumulation of them, and no amount of ill success in the attempt to solve them, is to make one doubt the truth of the proposition in connexion with which they arise. I suppose it was the multiplied difficulties in the way of the reception of the Ptolemaic system that led men, first to doubt it, and afterwards to give it up. I daresay this is all very weak and I know I am speaking to one by the side of whom I am a mere child in intelligence and knowledge; still I cannot help recording the matter so.

'Oxford is still, as ever, a most interesting place,' he went on. 'I could not exaggerate the affectionate and admiring terms in which I hear you spoken of on all sides, by men of all parties.' This was information which would be useful to Newman when he had to decide, in the next year or two, whether to accept his bishop's offer of the Catholic mission in Oxford. In the event the plans came to nothing, but because of Catholic, not Protestant opposition.

Tom mentioned a report which *The Times* had printed from a Bristol paper to the effect that he had returned to the Church of England. It was not true, for he had taken no overt step, and attended no services but the university sermon, but he did not intend to contradict it publicly because he hoped to take his Master's degree – 'Which I suppose may be called in one sense "returning to the Church of England".' Newman quoted this in a letter to Fr Henry Coleridge, another Oxford convert, and a Jesuit, on 14th June.

Tom remained affectionately disposed towards Newman himself. On 15th October he wrote from Oxford to explain why he had not called to bid Newman a final farewell, when he was in Birmingham winding up his affairs. 'I think you will believe me that the omission arose from no deficiency or diminution of that respectful admiration with which I have always regarded you, and implied no forgetfulness or ingratitude for many kindnesses, but [from] my feeling that you would probably rather not see me. I shall bitterly regret as long as I live that I entered into somewhat close and intimate relations with you only at the last to cause you pain and annoyance, by abandoning the standard under which I had enrolled myself. There is nothing of course that I can do or say to lessen that pain; only I solemnly protest, before God and man, that my *bona fides* in the matter of this change has been complete and that whatever rumours regarding my motives have been flying about Edgbaston (and I understand that some have been flying about) I gave admission slowly, sadly and unwillingly to the doubts respecting Catholicism which assailed my mind. Why, what greater happiness can there be for a man than to believe it, if he can believe it? What does the cold shade of this world's science or sentiment offer that can be weighed in the balance for one moment against those glorious imaginings, if we can firmly convince ourselves that they correspond to realities? This conviction has at any rate in large part, failed me; and if I return to the national church in which I was born, it is only because such is the natural and obvious course; there is in fact nothing else to be done. I do not ask you to send any reply but if you do not forbid it, I should like from time to time to write to you; and speak about the state of things here . . .'

Newman answered at once, on 17th October. 'It did not at all come into my head to fancy it any neglect on your part not to call here before you left the place. I was sure your reason for not doing so was to save yourself and me pain.' On Tom's change of mind he said, 'A man must follow his own convictions and it is not I who am his judge. While I say this I must ask your indulgence also to say, which in honesty I cannot keep from saying, that I think such a step as you have taken a sin, and that I shall ever pray that you may some day recover it, and that I believe you will. Meanwhile, having said this once, I don't see why I should say it again. And if thus having said it once does not change your intentions, I assure you it will give me great pleasure to hear from you as you propose any Oxford news you have from time to time to tell me.'

It was only a fortnight later, on 2nd November, that Tom responded with a long gossipy letter, filling three folded sheets, of Oxford talk, clerical chat, music, Clough's posthumously published poem *Dipsychus*, and enclosing a satirical print about Oxford's refusal to have the railway. Newman was delighted with the latter, recognizing the caricatured faces immediately. After this, it is not surprising that it was to Newman that Tom was to turn, some ten years later, when he wanted to return to the Church.

But at present he was still drifting away. Newman was sent a letter Tom had written to a convert called Algar, now a priest teaching in the Petit Séminaire at Roulers, Belgium. Algar was horrified at this sudden communication from Tom, whom he had not seen, he said, for twenty years. On 3rd January 1866 Tom had written to Algar: 'I was a Catholic myself for some years as you have perhaps heard, and if your sentiments respecting apostasy resemble what mine once were, you must regard with great disgust my avowal that I am so no longer. Such is the fact; I somehow slid out of Catholicism when I could no longer put faith in the infallibility of the Church. The strange thing is that one's ordinary mental states and habitudes are so little changed. An old friend of mine, now dead, Arthur Clough, when in Rome during the siege by the French in 1849, wrote that "things went on in a besieged city much the same as in any other city." So, if one gets close enough to them, one finds that heretics are much like other people. Nor do I find myself less disposed than before to give credit to the Church for the great services she has rendered to mankind, or to dispute the great dignity and beauty of her worship compared with that of other Christian bodies. But when the great prop of the system – God-given infallibility – appears to be unsound, it matters little that minor supports remain. Disenchanted therefore, and sad enough at heart, I returned to the communion in which I was brought up; not doubting still that man must live by faith and not by sight if he would distinguish himself from the brutes and be and do what his maker designed him for – yet convinced that the moulds and grooves in which we would fain make the Divine thought and operation run, are all destined to be broken up and fired and recast, as human reason advances on its predestined way.'

This letter shows more clearly the nature of Tom Arnold's loss of faith than his hesitant remarks to Newman; Algar's sending it to Newman probably contributed to his insight into the minds of those for whom, eventually, he wrote *The Grammar of Assent*. Tom was logical in seeing the infallibility of the Church as the prop of the system, for it is on the authority of the Church (the continuing community of believers) that anything at all is known about Jesus of Nazareth – beyond the fact, recorded by Roman historians, that a man called Christus was executed in Palestine and had become the centre of a cult. The Gospels were composed for, and accepted by, the Church of the first century; it is in the community of the Church that Christ must be found. But when he came to doubt that the Church was a true witness to Christ and faithful interpreter of the meaning of his words and acts – that is, 'infallible' – Tom did not take the further step, taken by so many of his contemporaries, of doubting God altogether. There was a sense in which he never lost the deepest faith, but went on living as a Christian, while regarding all forms of belief as moulds destined to be recast by the advance of human reason.

It certainly seems strange that he did not find assistance with his problem in Newman's theory of the Development of Christian Doctrine, by which it is possible to distinguish between the divine revelation, which is Christ himself, and the Spirit-directed unfolding in the human understanding of this revelation, which is Christian theology. Newman, after all, was the pioneer thinker in the field of relating Christian doctrine to 'the advance of human reason'. Yet, in the Church as Tom Arnold knew it in the sixties, other voices than Newman's spoke more loudly, and they appeared to identify revelation and theology, in an unhistorical and falsely supernaturalized way, so that it could appear as if the whole elaborate structure must be taken as having descended from heaven like the new Jerusalem in St John's vision. And the infallibility of the Church, during the sixties, was narrowed to the infallibility of the Pope, with the more fanatical of the doctrinaires attributing infallibility to every papal utterance, as if the successor of St Peter had become an oracle. Great confusion was caused by this controversial crusade by men Newman called theopoliticians – not allowing them the title of theologians. He was to do much to assist in the process of discrimination which eventually followed the decree of 1870, but should have preceded it, and especially in his *Letter to the Duke of Norfolk* (on Conscience and Papal infallibility) which was published in January 1875, the year before Tom Arnold finally made up his mind to return to the Church.

The ordinary unintellectual Catholic lives without thinking much about the formulation of doctrine, which is why people in every generation are shocked by theological controversy; nevertheless the intellectual person also has a right to think about his beliefs and in the nineteenth century he was given very little help by the official theologians of the Church, intent as they were on preserving the formulae of past centuries, regardless of the fact that people were now asking different questions. And with scientific enquiry leaping ahead so successfully, it was natural that people should compare it with religious enquiry, not realizing that the subject matter was incommensurate and that the method of investigating the natural world could not be used unmodified in examining the spiritual. There was a sense in which Tom Arnold, like many others, did not go deeply enough into the nature either of science or of certainty, before concluding that in matters of religion there was no such thing as infallibility. The excuse must be that the behaviour of many churchmen suggested that what they proclaimed was not only not infallible, but absolutely incredible.

Newman was able to continue to believe in the infallibility of the Church because he had carefully thought out what the Church was, how it worked, and how the truth was preserved in it. He believed in it even while he disapproved the way in which its contemporary leaders identified orthodoxy with their own narrow views. But for Tom Arnold, as for many others, human fallibilities obscured the unfailing source of truth.

IX

The Death of the Young

Towards the end of the year 1867 Matthew Arnold was looking for a house at Harrow. This was partly because he had always felt penned up in London, partly because he could send his boys to school cheaply at Harrow, where being a day boy was common and not held as inferior. Mary Shelley had educated the poet's son in the same way.

On 16th November Matt wrote to his mother, of Basil, the youngest child, then about eighteen months old: 'Baby looks very delicate and has little or no appetite but he has had no return of the convulsions and the gaiety of his spirits is surprising.'

Sadly, this improvement did not continue and on 23rd December the doctor told both father and mother, separately, that the baby could not get through the attack. Yet reporting on Christmas Day, Matt told his mother Basil was more himself; the morning before, which had been Matt's forty-fifth birthday, 'I did not think he would have lived two hours. He was exactly like a person in a severe paralytic seizure.'

The child survived only a few more days. On 4th January 1868 Matthew was writing to his sister, Jane Forster: 'My dearest K – Poor little Basil died this afternoon, a few minutes before one o'clock. I sat up with him till four this morning, looking over my papers, that Flu and Mrs Tuffin might get some sleep, and at the end of every second paper I went to him, stroked his poor twitching hands and kissed his soft warm cheek, and though he never slept, he seemed easy and hardly moaned at all. This morning, about six, after I had gone to bed, he became more restless; about eleven he had another convulsion; from that time he sank. Flu, Mrs Tuffin and I were all round him as his breathing gradually ceased, then the spasm of death passed over his face; after that the eyes closed, all the features relaxed and now he lies with his hands folded, and a white camellia Georgina Wightman brought him lying on his breast, he is the sweetest and most beautiful sight imaginable.

'And so this loss comes to me just after my forty-fifth birthday, with so much other "suffering of the flesh" – the departure of youth, cares of many kinds, an almost painful anxiety about public matters – to remind me that *the time past of our life may suffice us!* – words which have haunted me the last year or two, and that we "should no longer live the rest of our time in the flesh to the lusts of men, but to the will of God." However different an interpretation we put on much of the facts and history of Christianity, we may unite in the bond of this call, which is true for all of us, and for me, above all, how full of meaning and warning.'

Two days later, on 6th January, he was writing to his mother, 'I shall never cease to rejoice that you so persisted in your invitation to our large party last autumn, and that we were all there together before this break; it will be one tie more, if that were wanted, to bind us to you and Fan and to dear Fox How.' At first Fanny Lucy wanted the child buried at Ambleside, but this was not possible, and so they chose Laleham, the old home.

'This morning he was photographed – we should else have had no picture of him whatever – and now he lies in his little gray coffin, with his hands folded on his breast and a little cross of double white primroses placed in them, looking sweeter and more touching than I can say.'

On 11th January, after the funeral, he wrote again at length and in somewhat morbid detail. 'We have just come back from Laleham and I have now barely time before the post goes out to tell you the last of our dear, dear little man. It has been something to see him all this week but if, even in his illness, it was not the real child we had known, how much less after his death. But still there was some satisfaction in going to see him at one's accustomed hours – directly I got up, when I used so often to see him in the day nursery in his nightgown, just brought in from the other room to be dressed. Then after breakfast, when he always came down, and used to like me to carry him round to all the pictures ... He looked beautiful, and so he continued to the last, though the colour got a deader and deader hue, and the parts round the eyes ceased to have the fulness of life; but the cheek and chin kept their roundness and smoothness to the last, and anything so perfect as the little waxen fingers crossed upon his breast was never seen. He had fresh flowers yesterday, double white primroses and lilies of the valley; at half past nine in the evening Flu and I looked at him for the last time and then he was brought down into the dining room, closed up in his little coffin, and lay all night on the table with the wax candles burning by him and one white camellia which Mrs Tuffin had brought him on his coffin . . . And now we have come back . . . and that little darling we have left behind us at Laleham; and he will soon fade out of people's remembrance, but *we* shall remember him and speak of him as long as we live, and he will be one more bond between us, even more perhaps in his death than in his sweet little life.'

Basil, the last and youngest child, died at the beginning of 1868; the eldest, beloved 'little Tom', died at the end of it.

Byron's house at Harrow was bought; it was theirs in March and they moved into it at once. Tom and Budge entered the school though Tom was not able to take full part in school life. However, he had always been delicate, and his parents were now so used to his state that they did not anticipate what was to come. While they were on summer holiday at Fox How he had a fall from his pony and after they had taken him home to Harrow, he had 'an attack of rheumatism' which confined him to bed. In October Matthew thought the attack was passing off, but on 23rd November 1868, Tom died. He was sixteen.

Matthew wrote to Lady de Rothschild, now a devoted friend, on 30th November: 'I imagine every one here thought he could not get through the winter, though they could give no special name to his complaint except to call it, with the doctors, "failure in vital power" following upon the slight shock given him by his fall from a pony in Westmorland. But his mother and I had watched him through so many ebbings and flowings of his scanty stock of vital power that we had always hopes for him, and till I went into his room last Monday morning an hour before the end I did not really think he would die. The astonishing self control which he had acquired in suffering was never shown more than in the last words he said to me, when his breath grew shorter and shorter, and from this, and the grieved face of the doctor as he entered the room, he knew, I am sure, that the end was come; and he turned to me and – his mamma, who was always with him, and whom he adored, having gone into the next room for a moment – he whispered to me in his poor labouring voice, "Don't let mamma come in." At his age this seems to me heroic self-control; and it was this patience and fortitude in him, joined to his great fragility and his exquisite turn for music, which interested so many people in him, and which brings a sort of comfort now in all the kind and tender things that are said to us of him. But to Mrs Arnold, the loss of the occupation of her life – for so the care of him really was – will for some time to come be terrible.'

Tom also was buried at Laleham, by his baby brother.

On his own birthday, 24th December 1868, Matthew, correcting examination papers as usual, put them aside to write to his mother from Harrow. 'Now I am within one year of papa's age when he ended his life; and how much more he seems to have put into it, and to what ripeness of character he had attained! Everything has seemed to come together to make this year the beginning of a new time to me: the gradual settlement of my own thought, little Basil's death and then my dear, dear Tommy's. And Tommy's death in particular was associated with several awakening and epoch-making things. The chapter for the day of his death was that great chapter, the first of Isaiah; the first Sunday after his death was Advent Sunday, with its glorious collect, and in the Epistle the passage which converted St Augustine (*Romans* xiii, 13). All these things point to a new beginning, yet it may well be that I am near my end as papa was at my age, but without papa's ripeness, and that there will be little time to carry far the new beginning. But that is all the more reason for carrying it as far as one can, while one lives.'

One fruit of this new beginning were Matthew Arnold's essays on religion and culture, the first of which appeared the following year in the *Cornhill* and were published in 1870 under the title *Of Saint Paul and Protestantism*. There were others to follow, but before that came one more terrible loss.

On 16th February 1872 Matthew Arnold's second son Trevenen, always known as Budge, died at the age of eighteen.

Two days later Matthew wrote to his mother: 'When I wrote last Sunday there was not even a trace of illness to be seen in Budge, though I hear now he had been much knocked up by running a mile very fast the day before; but he was entirely himself all Saturday and Sunday, and indeed particularly gay. When I came home on Monday evening Flu told me that Budge had

(158)

gone to bed with a cold and toothache. I saw him three times that evening and found him very sick and miserable. I concluded he had a bilious attack such as I often used to have when a boy, and that he had a cold with it. So it went on, headache taking the place of toothache, and I cannot say I was in the least uneasy. But, when Victorine called to us on Friday morning and I found him light-headed and wandering about the room, I was very uneasy; he knew me however, and said, "ah! papa!" but I went off at once for Dr Tonge, the doctor who lives nearest. When I came back he seemed dropping into a heavy doze. I had to go very early to London, and he seemed in the same heavy doze when I left him. The rest you have heard; when I saw him again at 2 p.m. all the doctors were there, besides Hutton, who had come down with me; and it was clear there was no hope. He never showed the least spark of consciousness till his breathing ceased with a sort of deep sigh. How fond you were of him, and how I like to recall this! He looks beautiful, and my main feeling about him is, I am glad to say, what I have put in one of my poems, the "Fragment of a Dejanira." '

These are the lines from the poem:

> But him, on whom, in the prime
> Of life, with vigour undimm'd,
> With unspent mind, and a soul
> Unworn, undebased, undecay'd,
> Mournfully grating, the gates
> Of the city of death have for ever closed –
> *Him*, I count *him* well starr'd.

The suddenness of the loss of this normally strong and happy boy numbed the shock at first, but the Arnolds soon felt they could not stay long at Harrow. 'Everything here reminds me of him so much . . .' A vault had been made at Laleham and the bodies of all three sons buried together, 'though if Budge had not died, I could not have borne to have disturbed the other two,' Matt wrote to his mother on 25th February 1872. 'I cannot write his name without stopping to look in stupefaction at his not being alive.'

In the next year his mother, Mary Penrose Arnold, died at the age of eighty-two, thirty-one years after the death of her husband, Dr Thomas Arnold.

In 1873 Matthew and Fanny Lucy Arnold moved to Pains Hill

Cottage, Cobham, Surrey, which they rented and lived in for the rest of Matt's life. He was fifty; his one surviving son, Dick, was in his teens, and the two little girls, Lucy and Eleanor, or Nelly as they called her, were thirteen and eleven. And Matthew Arnold was then at the height of his fame.

X

Literature and Dogma

In October and November 1869 and then in February of the next year, the *Cornhill* published the articles which Matthew Arnold brought out as *St Paul and Protestantism* in 1870. *Essays in Criticism* had gone into a second edition in 1869 and there had been another edition of the *Poems*; he had gained the attention of the reading public and the Victorian magazines were ready and willing to publish what he wrote. Ever since the furore in 1861 over the Anglican collection *Essays and Reviews*, which resulted in the prosecution for heresy of some of its authors, religion had become one of the favourite subjects of debate – a debate as much concerned with criticism of the Bible as with Darwin's theory of the Origin of Species, which nevertheless started a ferocious Science *v.* Christianity tournament which was to continue into the twentieth century.

Matthew Arnold joined in this discussion at the age of forty-seven – the age Dr Arnold had been at his death, a fact that Matt was much aware of, as his letters show. Encouraged by the reception of *St Paul and Protestantism* he went on to a fuller exposition of his views, which became the considerably larger book *Literature and Dogma*. This too started in the *Cornhill* but was stopped after two articles. It seems hardly likely that the editor, Leslie Stephen, would have objected to Matthew Arnold's unorthodoxy, but the publishers may have done. It appeared as a book in 1873.

Literature and Dogma is still readable and interesting, and at the time provoked wide and varied response, from France, Germany and Italy as well as from England and America. But unfortunately Matthew Arnold decided to answer objections and the result was *God and the Bible*, which is very long and very long-winded and makes one think that even Matt's hated theologians would be less of a burden to read. Finally, in 1877, he published *Last Essays on Church and Religion*, quite a small book, which included two lectures given at Edinburgh on *Bishop Butler and the Zeit-Geist*, which are up to the author's best form.

It is curious that Matthew Arnold is said to have been a bad lecturer, for his written style is exactly that of a popular lecturer, with all the repetitions, mental headlines, key texts, striking analogies and humorous tone which go down so well in a crowded hall.

In *St Paul and Protestantism* he performed an original rescue operation, extracting the Apostle of the Gentiles from the hands of doctrinaire Puritans who had, in the English scene, held almost a monopoly. A century later it is quite difficult to realize how Victorian Christianity, in its popular forms, was dominated by a particular theory of redemption, presented in Lutheran or Calvinist dress, which was derived from part of St Paul's epistle to the Romans. In *Literature and Dogma* Matthew Arnold hit on an amusing way of expounding this theory, which was the principal object of his attack, by using the name of the great evangelical social reformer, Lord Shaftesbury.

He supposed that believers imagined 'a sort of infinitely magnified and improved Lord Shaftesbury, with a race of vile offenders to deal with, whom his natural goodness would incline him to let off, only his sense of justice will not allow it; then a younger Lord Shaftesbury, on the scale of his father and very dear to him, who might live in grandeur and splendour if he liked, but who prefers to leave his home, to go and live among the race of offenders, and to be put to an ignominious death, on condition that his merits shall be counted against their demerits, and that his father's goodness shall be restrained no longer from taking effect, but any offender shall be admitted to the benefit of it on simply pleading the satisfaction made by the son; and then, finally, a third Lord Shaftesbury, still on the same high scale, who keeps very much in the background, and works in a very occult manner, but very efficaciously nevertheless, and who is busy in applying everywhere the benefits of the son's satisfaction and the father's goodness.' Although he thus makes fun of the popular theology of redemption, Matthew Arnold insists that it is not degrading; it is merely unverifiable.

In the first book he shows how mistaken it is to take this as the whole of St Paul's idea of Christianity. St Paul's language is not scientific, not philosophical or metaphysical; it is poetic, *literary.* The language of the Bible is all of this kind, and the Bible deals with human experience, and particularly with moral experience; it is concerned with righteousness, with conduct, which, Matthew Arnold reiterates again and again, is three-fourths of life. He had already made the distinction between Hebrew and Hellene, the one concerned primarily with moral action and the other with intellectual culture. Here St Paul was a Hebrew, and what set him in motion was the desire for righteousness, and he derived his religion psychologically from experience, not theologically from authority. He was converted to *Jesus*, and 'Have faith in Christ' did not mean accept some theological system but 'Die with him!' Die to sin, as Christ did, and live the eternal life with him, by identifying with him in spirit. The three Lord Shaftesburys are irrelevant; though even in St Paul there is a good deal of what Matthew Arnold called *Aberglaube* – extra-belief or fairy tale. Salvation did not lie in the 'magical and mechanical' idea of pleading Christ's sacrifice but in sacrificing oneself with him, as St Paul himself teaches.

Matthew Arnold called this self-renunciation Christ's *'secret'*. His *method* was 'inwardness' – converting the old, external, communal morality of Israel into something personal, concerned with thoughts and motives. The medium of both the secret and the method was his mildness, his *epieikeia*, a word Arnold is fond of, and translates as 'sweet reasonableness'. Self-renouncement, inwardness and sweet reasonableness: this *is* Christianity, which developed ideas about the three Lord Shaftesburys just as Israel had developed theories about the coming of a victorious Messiah, as fairy-tale explanations of, and compensations for, the patent injustices of the world, where the wicked and not the righteous too often flourish. Christianity is to follow Christ in dying to selfish desires and living in sweet reasonableness for the kingdom of God.

God! But what does 'God' mean? Matthew Arnold starts *Literature and Dogma* with mockery against the Bishops of Winchester and Gloucester, who had expressed their determination to 'do something for the honour of our Lord's Godhead'. They are taken throughout as representatives of learned theology and they are trounced again on the very last page. Arnold's point is that 'God' is a term without any verifiable meaning, which is used by theologians to mean a thinking and loving personal governor of the universe, and by the populace to mean an infinitely extended Lord Shaftesbury, 'a magnified and non-natural man'.

Matthew Arnold's own definition of God, repeated *ad infinitum* in these books is: *The Eternal not ourselves which makes for Righteousness*. He maintained that this alone was verifiable from experience. We all have a knowledge of good and bad, right and wrong; we discover that to do right gives, ultimately, satisfaction; that this is so was not invented by us, and it continues to be so for every generation. Thus it is eternal, it is not ourselves, and it makes for righteousness. Matthew Arnold was aware that this was similar to Newman's argument from conscience to God; he referred often to Newman in these books and always with respect, while politely insisting that he was wrong in imagining that the whole system of the Catholic Church could be developed from this basis.

Arnold was attempting two things at once in his books on religion: to show that religion, and in particular Christianity, is based upon facts of experience, human moral experience; and to show that the metaphysical explanations of these facts are unnecessary, misleading and untrue in a scientific sense. Dogmatic statements are intended to be scientifically true, or verifiable; but they are not. Religious statements, however, such as are made in the Bible, in the poetic language of experience, *are* true.

In thus taking on two enormous subjects it is inevitable that the work should emerge as uneven; it is full of insights, but also full of moments when the reader wants to interrupt and say, 'Aren't you forgetting . . .?' It was just what Arnold's readers did, and he could not resist going on with the argument, and so we have *God and the Bible*, which has the tone of a schoolmaster riding his hobby-horse, uncaring whether the bell has gone for break or not.

But still, in 1870, it was a tremendous point to make, about the literary, rather than scientific, language of the Bible, a point which many Christians had not reached at the middle of this century. Arnold's actual excursions in re-interpretation strike one as the brilliant but idiosyncratic attempts of an amateur, but that is because we now have had about fifty years of hard work put in by Biblical scholars on the subject.

In his other aim, to demolish what he called the *Aberglaube* or fairy tale of dogma, I feel that Matthew Arnold was sometimes carried away by his irritation at the three Lord Shaftesburys and their faithful propounders, the Bishops of Winchester and Gloucester. Tiresome as these good gentlemen may have been, it is not possible to blow them into space by ridiculing them as hopelessly out of touch with the *Zeit-Geist*. It is the *Zeit-Geist* which sounds like a mythological deity today and there are Bishops still at Winchester and Gloucester.

Man is a thinking being and is bound to think about religious and moral facts, as about every other form of his experience. St Paul certainly did, even if the Lord Shaftesburys represent a travesty of his thought. And so we shall always have theology, organized thinking *about* the divine, as well as contemplation, which may be called thinking *into* the divine, and morality, which is thinking in action *with* the divine. Even Arnold's careful statements about righteousness provoke a response of *thought*. To give but one example, his insistence that 'To righteousness belongeth happiness' surely needs more proof than he gives it, though possibly one is more aware of the gaps since the work of Freud and other great psychologists.

Again, even if doing the right thing brings some people happiness, that self-renunciation does so is not self-evident. It did not bring Jesus happiness but crucifixion, and he promised the same to his followers. Christians of the tradition find joy through the resurrection: the conquest of death, evil and time, which sets us free from their apparent finality. But to Matthew Arnold the resurrection is simply a *miracle* – and the *Zeit-Geist* has pronounced that miracles do not happen. He calls it the resuscitation, and this shows that what he refused to accept was the naïve idea of the resurrection admittedly current in the popular mind – that Jesus simply got up out of the tomb and walked away. But this is as much a travesty of the resurrection as the three Lord Shaftesburys are of the Father, Son and Spirit of the divine community. Just as Arnold dismisses the scholastic idea of trinity-in-unity, the reformation theology of redemption, without studying the experiential descriptions in the New Testament of the action of the divine in Jesus, in that which he called his father, and in the spirit which inspired the community of believers – just so he dismisses the Gospel accounts of the appearances of Jesus after his death. Yet from these it is clear that, though the body could be touched as well as seen, it was totally transformed and operating in a reality normally beyond human senses. It is merely a scientific mistake of ours to think that the reality transmitted by our senses is somehow more solid than any other. What the friends of Jesus saw of the body which had been raised from death was as much as human senses could take in of a reality far greater than ours. If the schoolmen tried to express this in terms which sound quaint today, that need not prevent us from finding modern terms. The *event* is what Christians have always believed: that Jesus, the whole man, lives beyond death and has power to bring others to life, now.

Matthew Arnold has made me argue with him, just as he made his readers argue in the eighteen-seventies; yet to read *Literature and Dogma* is to discover, powerfully displayed, the image of Jesus: Jesus the prophet of the kingdom of God, with his absolutely clear eye for the failings of men, his secret of discovering love by disowning self, and his unshakeable *epieikeia*, whether we call that sweet reasonableness, or meekness, or mildness, or just goodness, in the sense of 'he was good to me'. Whatever Matthew Arnold believed or did not believe of God, there is no doubt but that he believed in the man Jesus of Nazareth as the moral ideal of all humanity.

Reading Matthew Arnold's religious books must also, surely, lead the reader, even in the twentieth century, to consider what is, and what is not, essential to faith in Christ. Matthew's niece Mary, Mrs Humphry Ward, said he was a Modernist before his time; he has also been called the Father of English Modernism. In so far as Modernism was a movement which attempted a modernization of the language, or expression, of Christianity, this might be conceded. In his sometimes sweeping way of brushing aside miracles, dogma and God along with the Bishops of Winchester and Gloucester, Arnold acts rather as some English liberal Protestants were to do; in suggesting that liturgy should be enjoyed as poetry and that the Mass was much more universalist than an infallible system of doctrine, he was perhaps like some of the Modernist Catholics. Christianity, to him, was the best way of educating men to be loving, reasonable and peaceful, and he was annoyed with the three Lord Shaftesburys and the resuscitation of the body of Jesus because he thought metaphysics and miracles, which had become incredible, made people throw aside religion itself. And this though he realized the nature of the popular mind well enough; for, as he scornfully observed, if a man walks on the sea 'the mass of mankind will believe about him anything he chooses to say', and 'to think they know what passed in the Council of the Trinity is not hard to them; they could easily think they even knew what were the hangings of the Trinity's Council chamber'.

Yet Arnold did not want that mass of mankind to lose the Bible, because with it they would lose the method and secret of Jesus, and the knowledge that God is the Eternal not ourselves who makes for righteousness. But if the *Zeit-Geist* made them lose faith in miracles and metaphysics, they could only keep the Bible if it was interpreted anew for them. So instead of the Bishops of Winchester and Gloucester, one is tempted to think they would need a procession of Matthew Arnolds. Yet this is just a case of new interpreter being old theologian writ large – or writ modern. And indeed ordinary Christians do find it hard to keep up with Biblical interpreters to this day, whether or not they are bishops.

Matthew Arnold is of his time in being a great individualist. He insists that what Christ did was to remove morality from society to the individual, and this he praises, as 'inwardness'. He thinks that the Eucharist originally was entirely addressed to the individual person and that the Church institutionalized it with doctrines of the Real Presence, the priesthood, apostolic succession and so on. But historically one might well come to the conclusion that all the doctrines of the Church have grown out of that communal ceremony which *is* the sacrifice of Jesus, as he made it for his friends. We may feel that Matthew's father has a deeper understanding of this communion, even though he did not believe in priesthood or Real Presence, because he saw it as the means of loving one's neighbour.

Matthew Arnold thought that Catholics had kept the 'secret' of Jesus by maintaining the self-renouncement of monastic life, and that Protestants had kept the 'method' of inwardness, personal accountability. Perhaps he felt *epieikeia* had too often got lost in transit. His idea of community, as with so many attached, however vaguely, to the Church of England, was co-extensive with society. He had grown up at the very end of the era when, so far as the English were religious at all, they were Christian, and his quarrel with Dissenters was precisely his father's – that a mere theological opinion was no good reason to separate yourself off from the rest of men. So that, in a national sense, he was not an individualist, in that he believed 'church' was a useful moral institution in the life of society – and he himself went to church with Fanny Lucy and enjoyed the *true* poetry of the Bible even if not the *Aberglaube* of the Creed.

When one looks back over a century, and sees how little was done by educated Christians to distinguish between faith and theology, how rigid were the interpretations of doctrine, how unhistorical were the minds that taught them as immutable truths, one is inclined to salute Matthew Arnold's freelance charge, even if it only confused the simple souls on whose behalf it was undertaken. At least one does not feel particularly sorry at the rout of the worthy Bishops of Winchester and Gloucester, who wanted to do something in honour of our Lord's Godhead, when what was needed was a clearer understanding of his humanity.

XI

A New Scene at Oxford

Mary Arnold, eldest child of Tom and Julia, first saw Oxford in the long vacation of 1865, when she was fourteen, but consider-ed that her intellectual awakening began two years later, when the whole family were reunited there at the house which Tom had built on Banbury Road. What did he call it? 'Laleham' – after the unforgotten first home of the family. The house was made large, to accommodate pupils as well as the family. It later be-came the home of Wycliffe Hall, an evangelical theological college.

Mary described herself, arriving in England at the age of five, as a black-haired, dark-eyed child. Because she had almost at once gone to school with Miss Clough, Arthur's sister, at Amble-side, she had grown up separated for long periods from her brothers and sisters, as she was afterwards to remark to Willy, the nearest to her in age. She took holidays with them, at Fox How and in Ireland, or later at Edgbaston, but she was sixteen before she lived all the time at home, an unusual fate for a girl in those days. Barely five years later she was married.

Mary was a clever, observant child, able to sympathize with the passionate feelings of her mother, but with an Arnold mind, capable of directing a strong will and controlling her emotions, intense though they might be. She early became aware of the tensions in her parents' marriage and though inevitably irritated, at times, by one or the other, remained able to sympathize with both. This balance of personality was no doubt assisted by her early and successful marriage to Humphry Ward. Her own life was not overshadowed by the troubles of her parents. And in the crucial years of her adolescence they were united as they had not been before, since Tom had abandoned the Church so much feared and hated by his wife and was living what seemed to Julia a more normal life among his peers at Oxford.

Money was still a problem, with so large a family to support. Besides Mary there were Willy, Theodore, Arthur (born at Fox How on the return to England) Lucy and Frank (both born in Dublin), Julia, known as Judy, and Ethel, the youngest: eight in all. The boys were all taken away from the Oratory School when their father left the Church. Except for Tom's reference to Lucy's birth I have discovered nothing more about her, whereas there is constant reference in Mary's letters to Judy and Ethel, who lived with their mother in Oxford. Willy was sent to a preparatory school for a year and then to Rugby, winning a scholarship to Tom's old college, University, at Oxford in February 1872, just about the time Matt lost his son Trevenen (Budge).

Tom Arnold, now in his forties, coached pupils and undertook the editing of early English texts for the Rolls Series, and other academic writing in the field of literature. He was on the lookout for an academic post but none suitable came within his reach till the creation of the chair of Anglo-Saxon in 1876, which he lost by his return to Catholicism. This was over ten years after his return to Oxford.

Oxford was the scene of Mary's youth and the influences there determined her development. She was at first a serious, not to say earnest young person. At school, she related in her *Recollections*, she had met 'a gentle and high-minded woman, an ardent Evangelical, with whom, a little later, at the age of fourteen or fifteen, I fell headlong in love, as was the manner of schoolgirls then, and is, I understand, frequently the case with schoolgirls now, in spite of the greatly increased variety of subjects on which they may spend their minds'. The last trace of this emotional Evangelicalism, Mary recalled with amusement, survived in her earnest determination not to 'dress' on Sundays, so that she went to spend the evening with the Pattisons at Lincoln College wearing a high-necked woollen frock.

Such priggishness did not long survive these visits to the Rector, Mark Pattison, a clever and bitter man (supposed to be the original of the scholar Casaubon in George Eliot's *Middlemarch*), and his beautiful restless wife, who smoked – unusual for a woman at that period. Mary remembered the Rector's high cackling laugh and the long conversations on learned subjects. Mark Pattison advised her to 'get to the bottom of something', to choose a subject and know *everything* about it. Mary accordingly chose early Spanish church history and was allowed to work in the Bodleian Library, under the kindly patronage of the Librarian, Mr Coxe.

The Pattisons continued to invite her to their Sunday suppers and she met interesting people there. She long remembered one occasion in the spring of 1870 when George Eliot (Marian Evans) and George Henry Lewes came. Mary did not like Lewes, who talked all the time, while George Eliot hardly talked at all. But she remembered the novelist taking Lewes's arm to show him the arresting sight of the beautiful Mrs Pattison looking down from a window of the Rector's lodging, into the quadrangle. And later, discovering that Mary was studying early Spanish, she made the girl sit down beside her and told her all about her recent visit to Spain. It was a recital, not a dialogue, but a fascinating one.

Then there was Benjamin Jowett, who became the Master of Balliol in 1878, but long before that a friend of the Arnolds; he had great sympathy for Julia Arnold and an evident liking for Mary. She remembered a dinner party of his at which the poet Swinburne was present, and how annoyed he was by the heat of the fire, his place being too near it for his comfort. Uncle Matt was at that party too. Mary was extremely fond of her uncle Matt, though she only came to know him well after her move to London in 1881. Until 1867 he was still Professor of Poetry and came to Oxford to give his statutory lectures.

Matt wrote to his mother after one of these lectures, on 28th February 1866: 'Tom was all right, dear old boy, and we had an hour's walk by the Cherwell which did me more good than any walk I have had for a long time. If I had Tom near me he would be the greatest possible solace and refreshment to me.'

The final lecture, since Matthew was not standing for a third term of office, came in June the next year, 1867. Tom and Julia pressed him to bring his boys with him – it was the year before the deaths began. The two brothers of the older generation took their sons boating in Port Meadow. Dick, Matt's third son, had a canoe 'which he managed very well', said his father, 'and had long wanted to try on the river at Oxford'. There was a big dinner at Balliol for Matthew and an evening party afterwards to which Tom and his wife came. Matt reported that the pupils living in Tom's house took to the boys, so that 'little Tom' and Dick were 'in great bliss'. This was the year of the publication of *Essays in Criticism*; Matt was forty-five and becoming well-known for his trenchant articles in the great magazines of the day, so much more influential than any magazine is now.

In November Matt told his mother of a magnificent present of a box of 400 Manilla cheroots. 'I do not smoke, but I am delighted with the present, as I shall give it to dear old Tom for his birthday. Such a jolly present for him – creature comforts and not books and head work, of which he has too much.'

Mary was only twenty when in the summer of 1871 she became engaged to Thomas Humphry Ward, a fellow and tutor of Brasenose College, the son of a clergyman and unrelated to other and more famous Wards of the time. On this important occasion Mary received tiny neat notes from her grandmother, Dr Arnold's widow, still at Fox How and still, at nearly eighty, very much alive and interested in all that went on in the family. Mary was the first grandchild to be born and the first to marry.

The wedding was on 6th April the following year, 1872, with the bride still a few months off her twenty-first birthday.

Arthur Stanley performed the marriage ceremony and Mary recalled with amusement that as he had recently buried the theologian Frederick Denison Maurice, his speech at the wedding breakfast was 'quite as much concerned with "graves and worms and epitaphs" as with things hymeneal'.

She was nevertheless very fond of Stanley and left a vivid, description of him, 'his small spare figure, miraculously light, his delicate face of tinted ivory – only that ivory is not sensitive and subtle, and incredibly expressive, as were the features of the little Dean; the eager, thin-lipped mouth, varying with every shade of feeling in the innocent great soul behind it; the clear eyes of china blue; the glistening white hair, still with the wave and spring of youth in it; the slender legs and Dean's dress which becomes all but the portly, with, on festal occasions, the red ribbon of the Bath crossing the mercurial frame.' When she was a child he would shoot questions at her, such as: 'Where did Henry IV die?' And when he was made Dean of Westminster and she visited him there, he said, ' "Come and see where Henry IV died!" And off we ran together to the Jerusalem chamber.'

So Mary was married, and as fellows of colleges were now allowed to retain their university posts after marriage, the young couple settled in one of the houses in the new suburb of North Oxford, growing up to fill the needs of married dons: 5 Bradmore Road. They had about £500 a year. 'Yet we all gave dinner parties,' she recollected, 'and furnished our houses with Morris papers, old chests and cabinets and blue pots.' They were the young generation of the seventies and the women wore dresses of 'Liberty stuffs, very plain in line but elaborately smocked, evening dresses "cut square" or with Watteau pleats, often in conscious protest against the London "low dress" which young married Oxford thought both ugly and "fast".' Young married Oxford! This was the first generation that had known such a thing.

It was a curious combination of advanced thinking and old-fashioned habits. Mary remembered that when the young married dons went out to dinner, the husband would walk, while the wife sat in a 'bath chair drawn by an ancient member of an ancient and close fraternity, the "chairmen" of old Oxford'.

The old chests and cabinets and blue pots were no doubt encouraged by Mary's neighbours, almost opposite her in Bradmore Road, Walter Pater and his sisters. Pater brought out *Studies in the Renaissance* in 1873, the year after Mary's marriage. Pater was then in his first reaction against Christianity and Mary recalled a dinner party at which he had said that no reasonable person could govern their lives by the opinions and actions of a man who had died eighteen centuries ago. Whereupon a Professor and his High-Church wife, highly offended, made haste to depart.

Pater was also a fellow and tutor of Brasenose; his sister Clara later became Vice-President of Somerville College. Mary admired this pioneer of higher education for women; she was in many ways a feminist and yet was to come out strongly against votes for women.

By the later seventies Pater's attitude had changed. Mary remembered a conversation in which she had said that orthodoxy could not maintain itself long against its assailants, especially from the historical and literary camp, and that they would live to see it break down.

'He shook his head and looked rather troubled. "I don't think so," he said. Then with hesitation, "And we don't altogether agree. You think it is all plain. But I can't. There are such mysterious things. Take that saying, 'Come unto me, all ye that are weary and heavy laden.' How can you explain that? There is a mystery in it – something supernatural." '

It was from such discussions at Oxford, particularly with T. H. Green, the philosopher upon whom she modelled the 'Grey' of her novel *Robert Elsmere*, that Mary built up the ideas she expressed in later years. Another friend was John Richard Green, once a curate to Humphry Ward's father, who had given up his orders on losing his faith. Consumptive and affectionate, he too contributed much to the formation of Mary's mind.

Then there was Mandell Creighton, whom Mary had first seen on a reading party her father had taken to Lynton in North Devon, noticing his 'tall slight figure in blue serge, the red-gold hair, the spectacles, the keen features and quiet commanding eye'. Later, she met him in his beautiful rooms at Merton College, and his married home was near hers. Mandell Creighton, a more robust character than some of her other acquaintances, managed to remain both a clergyman and an historian; he was to become a bishop and publish a history of the papacy, more understanding of the delinquencies of former popes than the liberal Catholic Acton.

The most revered historian in Oxford was Stubbs – also, later, a bishop. Mary tells a pleasant story of the time when she was writing on early Spanish kings and bishops for an historical dictionary. She was surprised one day to find that the very obscure books she was using were out, and as she left the Bodleian Library saw no less a person than Dr Stubbs himself walking off with 'Johannes Biclarensis' under his arm. A fellow-worker on the dictionary told her, with awe, '*Stubbs* has been going through our work!' The editor had wanted an *imprimatur* and had said, 'Can't expect anybody but Stubbs to know all these things!' Later, Dr Stubbs stopped Mary in the Broad and remarked with a smile that Johannes Biclarensis was quite an interesting fellow. And Mary received a friendly letter from the editor of the dictionary. What a feather in the cap of a girl of those days!

Like a true Arnold, Mary launched into pamphleteering early. She had heard the Revd John Wordworth's Bampton Lectures on 'The Present Unsettlement in Religion – the moral cause of unbelief'. Mary was so convinced that the causes of unbelief were more often intellectual than moral that she wrote her pamphlet: 'Unbelief and Sin, a Protest addressed to those who attended the Bampton Lecture of Sunday March 6th,' had it printed and put on sale at once in the High Street bookseller's. But on a certain Dr Foulkes's threatening the law because there was no printer's name, the bookseller hastily withdrew it. But Mary had the satisfaction of being congratulated and thanked by her hero, Professor T. H. Green.

Mary's children were all born in Oxford, in 1874, 1876 and 1879 – two girls, Dorothy and Janet, and one boy, christened Arnold. The Christmas of 1874 was spent in Paris, where they saw Sarah Bernhardt acting and met Madame Mohl, still as alert and intelligent as ever at eighty-one. And there was Dr Lushington, Byron's adviser, who, at the age of eleven, had been in the theatre the night the news reached London of Marie Antoinette's execution (October 1793); it was given out from the stage and the audience instantly broke up. Such historical links must fascinate anyone, but especially a novelist.

XII

Returns

I

As an old man, writing *Passages in a Wandering Life*, Tom
Arnold said of his wavering in the faith: 'The instability and
weakness of my proceedings I do not mean to palliate or under-
estimate. The only plea I can urge is, that I acted in good faith,
and that the taint of self-interest never attached to what I did.
With folly, weakness, obstinacy, pliancy I may be charged, and
more or less justly; but no one can say that any one of my changes
was calculated with a view to worldly advantage. If it were not so,
I should not feel that I had the right to hold up my head among
honest men.'

It was only too true that Tom lost, not gained, by his changes
of belief, each time losing either a regular job or the chance of
one. By becoming a Catholic in 1856 he lost the school inspectorship in Tasmania; by leaving the Church and his connexion with
Newman's educational projects, he had to try to build up a new
career at the age of forty-one, when he settled in Oxford in 1865;
and finally, in 1876, at the end of which year he was fifty-four,
he forfeited his chance of becoming a Professor at Oxford by
returning to Catholicism.

In fact, it was the possibility of his being elected to the new
chair of Anglo-Saxon which forced him to declare himself, for
he was incapable of accepting a position under false pretences.
For some time his mind had been working its way back to the
Catholic faith but, knowing what his wife's feelings would be, he
had till then taken no overt steps to reverse the decision of 1865.
The story goes that his children would hear the sound of Latin
prayer from his study and suspect what was coming. He may
have been reciting the Hours, a practice which in any case was
followed by some Anglicans. Certainly Julia had no idea of the

disaster impending when, at the beginning of the year 1876, Tom first broke his intention to her. The details have to be picked up from the letters remaining, and Tom was not a great keeper of letters.

On 6th February 1876 Mary wrote to her father from 5 Bradmore Road, Oxford: 'With regard to my mother your letter should I think bring her some little relief but she is very unhappy, mainly I think from the remembrance of your last interview in London. She bids me say that she deeply regrets the bitter things she said and she promises that for the future she will do her very best to abstain from saying bitter or wounding words. She was in a state of frenzy from a feeling of loneliness and lovelessness and hardly knew what she said. And she also bid me say that if when the children are a little older and your prospects are more assured, you decide to become a Roman Catholic she will feel it "her bounden duty not to oppose you". So my darling father let there be peace between you for your children's sake. We shall all understand that it is your intention to make an open profession of Catholicism as soon as your doing so would not do grave injury to those nearest you. It is very possible that if this Manchester work comes and if it suits you, money matters may look better for you than they have done for some time and in a year or two you may be able to take this step with less misery to those around you . . . I feel most tenderly and keenly for you, my dear father. I know how hateful it must seem to you to put off an open profession of belief for any worldly reasons. Look upon them as reasons of affection and pity to those dependent on you and the whole matter looks differently. It is a great sacrifice, but God will reward it. – Ever, my beloved father, your most affectionate daughter, Mary A. Ward.'

Tom Arnold did postpone his return for some months, but he could not allow himself to be put up for election to the chair of Anglo-Saxon as a member of the Church of England. Religion still played an important part in academic politics and his letter to Newman, after his reception back into the Church, indicates Tom's feelings on this subject. It was written from Woodhouse, Loughborough, the home of his sister Mary, after her second marriage, and dated 20th October 1876.

'My dear Father, You must let me call you so, for truly "in Christ Jesus you have begotten me through the Gospel". I think I shall bless God through all eternity for having brought me to your doors last Monday, and for the charity with which you received a wanderer for whom there was so little excuse, and whom God might so justly have condemned to impenitence.

'I am here, corresponding with my daughter and son-in-law at Oxford. The state of my wife is very sad and it seems likely that it will be found the best course for me to remain in London for a while. I think of taking lodgings somewhere near the British Museum, where I can find plenty to do. If any of the Fathers know of good and cheap lodgings in that part of London I should be very glad to be informed of them.

'I cannot make out exactly how the election to the Anglo-Saxon chair would have gone had I not acted as I did. In a note I have received from Montagu Burrows, he says that Earle would anyhow have been elected by a large majority; on the other hand I hear from Oxford that Liddon has said I would have been elected. I enclose a note from Liddon, (which please return) as you may be interested in seeing what he says about the policy of his party in filling university posts. It implies a formal defiance to the spirit and intention of the University Tests Act: but I cannot think it will be as successful as it is bold. No electing body at Oxford – at least as to the majority of its members – really objects to the appointment of a freethinker, if intellectually qualified, provided he behave himself with decorum. And, from what I see, this is likely to become more and more true.'

Liddon's party was Pusey's – once the embattled remnant of the Tractarians but now on its way to becoming the strong Anglo-Catholic movement of the end of the century. Pusey was fighting a rearguard action to preserve the religious character of the university; Liddon was to be his biographer, as he was already his chief aide. It can be seen from Tom Arnold's remarks to Newman that he did not approve their methods, or even their object. In general matters he remained a liberal, whether or not a Catholic.

The day after writing to Newman, Tom wrote to his daughter, a letter which must be quoted at length, since it gives the fullest explanation of his return to the Church.

'My dearest Mary, – I hardly know what to make of your letter, ... I had better not return home at present, if your Mamma cannot bear it. A life of wrangling would do no good to anyone. I could not feel with more painful keenness than I do, the bitterness of the disappointment and shock which what I have done has caused your mother. Would to Heaven that she were linked to someone more capable of satisfying the ambition and aspiration of her nature than I am. And yet, I must own to you, that when I look back, the horror of the thought of the mental state into which I must have fallen had I let myself be elected through Liddon and his friends avowing – as he himself has avowed to me – that the policy on which they vote in university elections is guided by their views and hopes for "the religious future of Oxford" – the horror of this thought, I say, makes me even now tremble and shudder. You cannot tell, nobody who has not had experience can tell, what a world of conceptions and emotions is opened out in the Catholic faith and life. This experience, you must remember, had been mine; however I wished it, things could not be to me as they are to one who has never been a Catholic. On the borders of this shining universe I had been hanging and haunting for years, looking up to the glorious orbs within, sighing for a day when I might regain what I had forfeited, harrassed evermore by a self-accusing voice. Suddenly the prospect comes before me of violently tearing myself away from those borders of a land of light and establishing myself firmly in the depths of the desert outside. How could I do it, when all my nature told me that that bright world was God's world, and that in fleeing from it, I was abandoning Him? Dreams, fantasies, you will say. Well, nobody can know, so as to prove to another, whether they are or not. Yet "if there is any consolation in Christ" if that is not a fantasy, or if it is – then I have known that consolation, real or fantastic, since I obeyed the law of my conscience. When I say "if it is", I do not mean that I myself have any doubt of its reality.

'But all this is "selfishness" your Mamma often says. Well, if to think that a soul has one life – one eternity – and must before all things order the first with reference to the last – if that be selfishness, then I am selfish. I cannot put such thoughts away from me; it is my nature to entertain them and always was. But if I am found in any other sense preferring my selfish interest to that of my wife and children, then let all reprobation and scorn justly fall on my head . . .'

In his recollections, in describing what by that time appeared to him as a lapse from the Church (in 1865) Tom indirectly gives some indication of the manner of his return. He recalled how 'the misgiving which had long slumbered in my mind, that no clear certainty could be obtained as to anything outside the fields of science again assailed me. Again the mists of Pyrrhonism . . . closed round me. Nevertheless I cannot doubt that this period of uncertainty would have passed away in due time if I had adopted the means proper to it. One of those means, indeed – labour – I did not put from me, and this was my salvation in the end; but the weapon of prayer – being attacked by a certain moroseness or disgust, and weariness of existence – I began unhappily to use less and less . . . Only after a long time, and with much difficulty and pain – pain, alas! not mine alone – was I able to return to the firm ground of Catholic communion.'

His reconversion, in fact, seems to have followed the same lines as his original conversion; he recovered faith in the Church as the community which held the truth about Christ and mediated his life through the sacraments, and thankfully replanted himself in that common life, that 'bright world' that was God's.

But Julia Arnold could never bring herself to accept her husband's return to the Church. In spite of her promises through her daughter, she could not control her feelings when he was with her, so that he was able to live very little at home.

Over three years later, on 23rd January 1880, Mary was writing to her mother: 'For you and Papa to see much of each other just now, seems to me to be running a dangerous risk on your part – whatever mental worry you may have when he is away, you have double as much when he is at home, mainly from the mere fact that he is there and that his presence is constantly exciting you to think about topics which if he were not there you might forget, or at any rate not take to heart in such a wearing and painful way – Papa knows that I think this, and I think it more than ever after this last vacation. My earnest wish is that Papa should come down for a short time, say a day or two days, at fairly short intervals, but that he should not stay long in the house for at any rate three or four months to come, that Mr Baneker's treatment may have a really fair trial. I know you find it hard to make up your mind to this, but I am sure dearest that for some little time to come at any rate it is the right course, as much the right course as avoiding any other risk would be. *Short* visits I think would very likely be only good for you, as there would be no *daily* rub to fear.'

The treatment was for breast cancer, which was eventually to kill Julia Arnold, in 1888.

But Mary could attack her father, at times, in defence of her mother. On 20th May 1880 she wrote to him, 'I do indeed think that you are rather too hard on Mamma about money matters. She seems to have been too passionate to make her meaning plain to you here, but I cannot quite understand your returning the statement of accounts with the comments you have written upon it.'

Julia, as her daughter had to admit in June, was no judge of prices and quantities and had 'notoriously no aptitude for that kind of work'. Mary thought her sister Judy ought to be in charge of the household expenses.

The money troubles went on and on; Tom Arnold could not live in his own house because his wife made herself ill by her violent disagreements with him; and he struggled to keep up with the debts by the hack work of academic life until, in 1882, he was appointed Professor of English Literature in the Catholic University of Ireland – as Newman's university had become. This partly solved the problem of occasional residence, though not that of Julia's debts.

On 14th August 1883 Mary, then resident in London, where Humphry Ward was working on *The Times*, wrote to her father after an altercation, 'I am very sorry you should think us unjust, my dearest. I only feel that it is very difficult for two such different temperaments as yours and Mamma's to understand each other. But I do trust things will go more smoothly now.'

They did not. On 11th March 1885 (when Tom Arnold was sixty-one) Mary wrote to him: 'You might just as well give her something deadly to drink as write letters to the tradesmen about her. Every such proceeding on your part shortens her chance of life. There is the plain truth as your children see it, and they feel that in the treatment you have adopted to her lately, whatever may be the faults on her side, you are incurring a very heavy responsibility. Of course I can feel for your difficulties too. But then you seem to forget that Mamma is no longer in a state in which it is possible to her to carry out your demands upon her. If she were a strong woman capable of standing over her servants in the kitchen or of walking about Oxford in search of the cheapest food market, there might be reason in your finding fault with what seems to you an over expenditure of a few shillings per week. But you know that she cannot do these things.'

Mary thought that the household expenses for 'two hard-working girls', a boarder and 'an invalid who ought indeed to have far more dainties than she ever allows herself' were not out-rageous. 'I don't think you in the least realize the perpetual malaise and discomfort of Mamma's life, or you surely would try to make things easier to her. I hear of you as being very much in request in Dublin, very popular and much liked – you have work that interests you, you are among people who are congenial to you, your health is good, and you are necessarily less worried by small things than a woman is. Surely all these things ought to make you more tender and forbearing towards one who has suffered what Mamma has suffered, even were the provocations given greater than they are. – There – I have said my say.'

Tom may well have felt that his daughter was now too hard upon him, since it was only Julia's fault that she was not sharing his second life in Dublin, and he had to keep himself there as well as the big house in Oxford which could no longer be home. He must have defended himself, for two days later Mary wrote again. Her mother had written to her in gentler mood and it was reflected in the daughter's letter to her father. She suggested that money matters should always be discussed with Judy or Ethel instead of their mother. 'She cannot control herself and every scene is so bad for her.' And Mary added, 'I hope with all my heart that you do like Dublin and that you do get society you like there. The only thing I grudge is that others should have so much of you and I so little! When do you come home, dearest?'

In fact, there was no home. The marriage had been destroyed by passionate feeling about deep religious conviction.

2

On Trinity Sunday in the May of 1880, young Mrs Humphry Ward (she was not yet thirty) went to the Catholic church of St Aloysius in Oxford, newly built just beyond the point where the Woodstock Road leaves St Giles, to hear Newman preach. Newman was seventy-nine and had been made a Cardinal by Pope Leo XIII the year before. He had been ill in Rome and this spring had fallen and cracked two ribs. Nevertheless in May he carried out the two great celebrations his friends had arranged for him, a reception in London and another at Trinity College, Oxford, where he had been an undergraduate and which had made him its first Honorary Fellow in 1877.

In her *Recollections* Mrs Humphry Ward wrote: 'The sermon at St Aloysius was preached with great difficulty and was almost incoherent from the physical weakness of the speaker. Yet who that was present on that Sunday will ever forget the great ghost that fronted them, the faltering accents, the words from which the lifeblood had departed, but not the charm?'

The next day, Trinity Monday, she went to the reception at Trinity College, 'where the Cardinal in his red, a blanched and spiritual presence, received the homage of a new generation, who saw in him a great soul and a great master of English, and cared little or nothing for the controversies in which he had spent his prime. As my turn came to shake hands, I recalled my father to him and the Edgbaston days. His face lit up – almost mischievously. "Are you the little girl I remember seeing sometimes – in the distance?" he said to me, with a smile and a look that only he and I understood.'

Mary had never been allowed to come near him in her childhood, when she had received the impression from her mother that he was the cause of all their troubles; it is pleasant that before she left Oxford she was able to meet him in the place, as she truly said, which 'he loved so well'.

Matthew Arnold had already met him, at the Duke of Norfolk's reception in London. The Duke had been a pupil at Newman's school and it was to him, as the senior Catholic layman in English society (though he was so young) that Newman had addressed the pamphlet he wrote on Conscience and Papal Infallibility, in answer to Gladstone's attack on the Church after the First Vatican Council. The *Letter to the Duke of Norfolk* had come out early in 1875 and Newman's careful distinctions between what was actually intended by the definition, and the exaggerated interpretations popularized by such Ultramontanes as W. G. Ward and Henry Manning, Archbishop of Westminster, had been accepted by the English reading public and calmed a rising storm of anti-Catholic feeling. Newman's moderate exposition may well have helped Tom Arnold on his journey back into the Church. Newman was sure a later Council would correct the imbalance of an over-emphasis on the function of the Pope in relation to the Church, as he told many worried private correspondents; he understood better than most the historical nature of conciliar decisions and definitions, and the function of theologians in interpreting the formulations of faith as the knowledge of men increased and became discriminated over the ages. That Second Vatican Council was not opened till 1962, but when it began to open up the doctrine on the Church, many people felt that the spirit of Newman was presiding behind the scenes – he was even called 'the invisible Father at the Council'.

In his own day, Newman's greatness was often realized more by Protestants and agnostics than by fellow-Catholics. Matt was dining before the reception (for which he had a ticket) with Dean Stanley who, when he heard of it, was deeply interested and hurried him off the moment dinner was over, saying, 'This is not a thing to lose!' Matt told the story to his sister Fan, writing on 15th May, and how Lady Portsmouth (the Barbarianess!) who was a relation of the Duke's, had 'carried him through the crowd'. Otherwise, he said, 'I should never have got to Newman at all.'

It was necessarily a brief meeting. 'Newman was in costume – not full Cardinal's costume, but a sort of vest with gold about it and the red cap; he was in state at one end of the room, with the Duke of Norfolk on one side of him and a chaplain on the other and people filed before him as before the Queen, dropping on their knees when they were presented and kissing his hand. It was the faithful who knelt in general, but then it was in general only the faithful who were presented. That old mountebank Lord — dropped on his knees, however, and mumbled the Cardinal's hand like a piece of cake. I only made a deferential bow, and Newman took my hand in both his and was charming. He said, "I ventured to tell the Duchess I should like to see you." One had to move on directly, for there was a crowd of devotees waiting, and he retires at eleven. But I am very glad to have seen him.'

It was really only chance that Matt had not seen Newman before, since he had been in touch with him by letter for over ten years; he had once planned to visit the Oratory when he was in Birmingham to deliver a lecture, but in the end there had not been time.

Their correspondence had started in the sixties. Matthew Arnold sent Newman a copy of his *Essays in Criticism* and Newman responded with a copy of his own Poems, which had recently been published, after the success of *The Dream of Gerontius*. On 20th January 1868 (only a few weeks after little Basil's death), Matt wrote to thank him. 'I value the gift more than I can well say. I think almost all the more important Poems I was already acquainted with, but I am glad of any opportunity which makes me read them again. In addition to their other great merits, I find their simple clear diction come very refreshingly after the somewhat sophisticated and artificial poetical diction which Mr Tennyson's popularity has made prevalent.'

This is interesting, in view of Matthew Arnold's own practice, which also has a clarity and simplicity unlike that of the more famous Victorians. He went on: 'But the more inward qualities and excellences of the Poems remind me how much I, like so many others, owe to your influence and writings; the impression of which is so profound, and so mixed up with all that is most essential in what I do and say, that I can never cease to be conscious of it and to have an inexpressible sense of gratitude and attachment to its author . . .' He ended: 'Believe me, my dear Sir, with great truth and respect, sincerely yours, Matthew Arnold.'

On 29th November 1871 he sent Newman a copy of the *Cornhill* containing the lecture he had delivered at Birmingham and in the course of the letter he said: 'We are all of us carried in ways not of our own making or choosing, but nothing can ever do away the effect you have produced upon me, for it consists in a general disposition of mind rather than in a particular set of ideas.' He felt that in his conflicts with modern Liberalism and Dissent he recognized Newman's work, and was very much pleased when people said that in reading him they were reminded of Newman.

He then asked Newman two questions, one on Bishop Butler and the other related to Newman's remarks on Lamennais, written many years earlier at Oxford, and recently reprinted in a collection of *Essays Critical and Historical.* Arnold wondered whether 'what is Tory and anti-democratic in the Church of England' was not a great danger to her at the present time, and one from which the Catholic Church was 'much more exempt', for though the 'R. Catholic Church may in fact have been anti-democratic in modern times on the Continent, there seems nothing in her nature to make her so; but in the nature of the English Church, there does.'

In his reply Newman thanked him warmly not only for his letter but for his recent writings, even though he could not but be 'sensitively alive to the great differences of opinion which separate us'. He then took up the point about the Church and democracy, agreeing with what Matthew had said. 'It was one of Hurrell Froude's main views that the Church must alter her position in the political world – and when he heard of La Mennais, he took up his views with great eagerness.' Newman himself had written similarly, basing himself on the Fathers, that 'we must look to the people'. But, he said, 'Froude had seized upon it from the intuitive apprehension he had of what was coming, and what was fitting. We both hated the notion of rebellion and thought that the Church must bide her time.' It was a favourite idea of Newman's that impatience often ruined a good cause, but after expatiating a little on this he observed: 'Perhaps La Mennais will be a true prophet after all. It is curious to see the minute tokens which are showing themselves of the drawings of Papal policy just now in the direction of democracy. Of course the present Papacy is (humanly speaking) quite unequal to such a line of action . . .' Yet he thought it possible that after a 'season of depression' the Catholic Church 'may at length come out unexpectedly as a popular power. Of course the existence of the Communists makes the state of things now vastly different from what it was in the Middle Ages.'

This was the year after the First Vatican Council, the siege of Paris, and the Commune; Newman's letter (he was seventy) shows very well what Matthew Arnold meant by saying he was influenced by his 'general disposition of mind'. Newman's mind eminently showed the qualities of sweetness and light, and of *epieikeia* too, which Arnold regarded as the proper end of culture.

In February of the following year, 1872, Newman sent Matthew 'a book of odds and ends' (*Discussions and Arguments*) which contained some of his most interesting Anglican essays, including the series on education and religion, published under the title *The Tamworth Reading Room*, which first appeared anonymously in *The Times* in 1841, when Newman was forty and writing in an amusing polemic style not unlike that of Matthew himself.

Matt received his book during the short illness of his second son Trevenen (Budge), the third of his sons to die within a few years. He sent it back for Newman to write in it; when it was returned, Budge was dead. On 7th March Matt wrote: 'I find your book with its kind inscription awaiting me on my return home after a period of much family trouble. To read you, always gives me high pleasure; and it always carries me back, besides, to some of the happiest places and times of my life; so the book is particularly welcome to me just now.'

In return he sent Newman his own arrangement of the Biblical

Prophets for School reading, which prompted an exchange in May 1872 on what children could take in of the Bible and the best way of presenting it to them, which still has interest, since there is something to be said for both the views expressed. A further exchange took place in January 1876, this time on the subject of the Irish university. Newman wrote a very long letter of eight pages in which, among other things, he took Matthew up on the constitution of the Church. 'I think the people are the *matter*, and the hierarchy the *form*, and that both together make up the Church,' he said, using Aristotelian terms familiar to Oxford men. 'If you object that this virtually throws the initiative and the decision of questions into the hands of the clergy, this is but an internal peculiarity of the Catholic Religion. The Anglican Church is also made up of a like form and matter, though here, in consequence of the genius of Anglicanism, the power of the matter predominates.' This was a way of looking at things which Matthew Arnold could readily understand.

'As to your other volume, your edition of Isaiah,' Newman added later, 'I will only say that it is a most attractive book – and your (excuse me) standing aloof from Revelation does not mar its reality. It is that sympathy you have for what you do not believe, which so affects me about your father. It is one of my standing prayers that you and your brother may become good Catholics.'

Matthew, of course, never did become a Catholic; but it was later in this year that Tom returned to the fold, and returned by going to Newman in Birmingham.

On hearing the news of the Cardinalate, Tom wrote on 23rd October 1879: 'My dear Cardinal Newman, – You cannot conceive what a pleasure it is to me to be able to write to you again as formerly, and to feel that I am one with you. Of my own dear father also I think a great deal, and have the most inward assurance that, if God reveals to him what is passing here below amongst his children, he sees with joy the son not the least loved following Jesus Christ to the utmost of his small strength, although by a road from which he, according to the light which he had, drew back with aversion and dread.'

Tom Arnold's remarks on his father, written when he himself was nearly fifty-six, ten years older than Dr Arnold at his death, are interesting, both as his thoughts and as an assessment of the senior Thomas Arnold.

'My father, as you know well, was extremely unlike Stanley,

upon whom it is the fashion to say his mantle has descended. My father loved *truth* before all things: if he was for Comprehension it was because he thought that all parties were holding much that was untrue or only half-true and that by repression they were made to cling affectionately to this worthless part of their possessions; while lenity, giving them time for careful examining, would ultimately lead to the discarding of what would not stand all tests. Thus, as he imagined, all parties, if let alone, would come eventually to his own standpoint – a very simple, highly moralized, non-sacerdotal form of Christian doctrine. Believing this, he never sacrificed his allegiance to truth; but it is difficult to think the same of those who know well that their party differences have not diminished and are not diminishing, yet rather pride themselves upon them, as marks of freedom of thought!'

All religious movements take much longer to work out their implications than observers, even acute and interested observers, imagine. The last quarter of the nineteenth century – and indeed the twentieth up to the cataclysm of the First World War – though a time when God and Christianity were increasingly doubted, was also a time when believers were still passionately committed to what were called party differences; it was, paradoxically, the heyday of sectarianism, with splits in every denomination and chapels and halls going up all over the place.

The spirit of unity works in ways unexpected of men. Lenity to Dissenters, which at first led them to greater dissidence than ever, did eventually soften the barriers between them and the Established Church, though it did not bring them towards Dr Arnold's moralized and non-sacerdotal Christianity. Because, faced with the scientific and historical critics, all Christians were forced to study their origins, and in a clearer understanding of the Bible and the Church, they began to rediscover the *mysterion*: the Eucharistic expression of the sacrifice of Christ. And, curiously enough, since he did not believe in this mystery as something real, Dr Arnold's son Matthew played a part in this renewed understanding, because, in essays very widely read, he showed ordinary people the way to take the language of the Bible, the language not of science, but of poetry – which is also concerned with truth.

Poor Tom ended his letter to the Cardinal: 'I am living here because I find living at home impossible.' He was in London, lodging in the Fulham Road, working with a friend on a Catholic Dictionary which became known as 'Addis and Arnold'.

XIII

Departures

Dr Arnold's widow died on 30th September 1873. Matthew wrote of her to Lady de Rothschild: 'She had a clearness and fairness of mind, an interest in things, and a power of appreciating what might not be in her own line, which were very remarkable and which remained with her to the very end of her life.' That this was so is shown by his own letters to her; to her and to Fan he spoke quite freely of ideas which he knew they did not altogether share.

Mary Arnold had remained at the centre of the family web and all her sons and daughters brought their children for holidays at Fox How. Fan continued to live there, and Fox How remained beloved and visited for yet another generation of Arnold's descendants. Mrs Arnold was eighty-two when she died and as her husband had been younger than herself he might well have survived into the eighteen-seventies. It is difficult to imagine him in the second half of the century and one wonders what he would have made of Matt's religious books even more than one wonders about his possible comments on Tom's conversion to Catholicism. But he would have been over ninety had he survived to witness his grand-daughter Mary's sudden fame as the author of the novel *Robert Elsmere*, which was published in February 1888, when she was within a few months of thirty-seven.

Since the Wards' removal to London in 1881, Mary felt, she says, an 'intensification' of life, from living in the great city, though she was glad to escape from it, quite often, to a farmhouse they rented near Godalming in Surrey. Humphry Ward covered the arts for *The Times*, and Mary, besides their busy social life, found time to undertake such work as examining in Spanish for the Taylorian scholarship at Oxford, which she did in 1882 and 1888 – the first woman to do so. She continued to work on the early Spanish period at intervals, but put most of her energy into translating Amiel's journal. Her first novel, *Miss Bretherton*, came out in 1884.

It was during these London years that Mary really got to know her uncle Matthew; they met not only in town but in Surrey, where Matt spent as much time as possible at Pains Hill Cottage, bought after the deaths of his sons. Mary left an amusing account of Matt in this country retreat where she loved to visit him; the only drawback, she said, was the way in which the dogs, two dachshunds called Max and Geist, 'were always *in the party*, talked to, caressed or scolded exactly like spoilt children'. She remembered breathless chases after Max, 'where the little wretch was harrying sheep or cows, with the dear poet, hoarse with shouting, at his heels'. Besides these 'dear dear boys' there was always a cat, almost equally dear. 'Once at Harrow the then ruling cat, a tom, broke his leg, and the house was in lamentation.' The vet's treatment was not approved and so 'Uncle Matt ran up to town, met Professor Huxley at the Athenaeum and anxiously consulted him'. The result was that T. H. Huxley came down and dealt with the cat's injury himself.

Huxley's son Leonard married Mary's sister Judy in 1885. Judy, born on 11th December 1862, grew up in Oxford. It was said that Lewis Carroll (Charles Dodgson) wrote *Sylvie and Bruno* for the three Arnold sisters; he also took photographs of Judy. She grew up a tall raven-haired girl, and clever; she was one of the first Oxford Home Students and later went to Somerville College on a Clothworkers' exhibition. She gained a first in English Literature in 1882. Leonard Huxley was at Balliol and they had to wait a few years before they could get married, till he got a junior mastership at Charterhouse, Godalming. Here in 1887 their first child, Julian Sorell Huxley was born. Two more sons, Trevenen, who died young, and Aldous, the writer, followed, and a daughter, Margaret, was born in 1899. In Mary's letters there are many references to Julian, his sayings and his character. But the story of these famous grandchildren of Tom's – great-grandsons of Arnold of Rugby, does not belong to this book.

Judy was to start a school of her own; she died comparatively young of cancer, a loss which is reflected in several of the novels of her youngest son Aldous, to whom it came as a deep shock.

Tom's eldest son, Willy, went up to Oxford on a scholarship in 1872. He was a tall, good-looking Arnold, clever and hard-working. He and his sister Mary were not close in childhood, having spent so much of it apart, but became friends when they were grown up and married. Willy was barely twenty when, on holiday at Fox How, he met Henrietta Wale, daughter of his father's first love, Henrietta Whately; they were so young that no engagement was allowed till December 1873, and it was not till June 1877 that they were able to marry, when Willy, who had only gained a Second Class in 1876, decided he could earn a living coaching and lecturing to the women students at Oxford. He redeemed his academic reputation by winning the Arnold Essay Prize with an essay on Roman Provincial Administration. Roman History became his chief interest and hobby – not a life work because in 1879 the famous C. P. Scott, talent scouting in Oxford for the *Manchester Guardian*, succeeded in carrying him off to the North, where he became devoted to that celebrated organ of high-minded progressive thinking. Although he had spent some time at the Oratory School, and remembered being given a prize of guineas by Newman himself, he had shaken off his Catholicism with relief; his religious beliefs seem to have been uncertain, though he had a strong moral idealism. He and Henrietta lived in Manchester; they had no children, but liked to invite a succession of nieces and nephews to stay.

After his early death in 1904, Mrs Humphry Ward collaborated in a memoir of him, prefaced to a posthumous book: *Studies in Roman Imperialism*. In this she recalls him 'standing before the fire in the drawing room of the pleasant house in Nelson Street, alert and vigorous, his broad shoulders somewhat overweighted by the strong intellectual head, his dark eyes, full of fun and affection, beaming on the guest who had just arrived, perhaps, from the South – delighting in the family gossip . . . or listening with quick sympathy to literary plans and projects'.

She also described him with his father, after the time when Tom had become a Professor of the Royal University of Ireland, for he would often stop at Manchester on his journeys between Dublin and Oxford. 'Father and son were both of those spirits whom the world cannot tame, and so were linked through all division, whether of occupation or opinion. The spiritual face of the father, his gentle, hesitating ways, were in sharp outward contrast with the rugged intellectual strength of the son; yet no doubt Arnold owed some of his most characteristic qualities to his father.'

Willy became ill with some spinal affection in the late nineties (before his father's death) and had to give up his place on the staff of the *Guardian* in 1898, when he retired to an invalid life in London and abroad. When his father died, in 1900, he wrote a memoir of him which appeared in the *Century*, but he himself died only a few years later, in the June of 1904, aged fifty-two. Although he had had many religious doubts he seems to have retained a basic religious orientation, and on the day before he died Mary heard him saying, 'I love God – I love God.'

Another brother, Frank, who became a doctor, had also settled in Manchester, to be near Willy; the bond between them was close. After a broken engagement he married Annie Wilkinson, whom his family liked much better than his first choice. But it was the daughters, rather than the sons, of Tom Arnold, who have made their names remembered.

Matthew's only surviving son, Dick, went up to Balliol in 1874 but alas, though perfectly charming, Dick was not a hard worker. He ran up debts in Oxford and eventually was found a job inspecting not schools but factories. He was devoted to his father and looked after him when Matt came lecturing in the North, but financially he was a liability. He married Ella, daughter of Dr Ford of Melbourne, Australia; they had no children. In later years he became a friend of Edward Elgar's – he got his musical ability from his mother, not Matt – and lived at Salcombe in Devon, fishing and yachting. It was partly to pay off Dick's debts that Matt undertook his first lecture tour in America, which began in the winter of 1883 and lasted until the summer of 1884.

In this year Matthew retired from his long stint at the schools, enabled to do so by the grant of a Civil List pension of £250 a year, which he was persuaded to accept from Gladstone. Thus he was free to spend months in America. As a lecturer, his chief disadvantage in large halls was inaudibility; after the first occasion he took a few lessons in voice production and improved somewhat, but it was his fame as a writer, not as a speaker, which brought people to hear him. His elder daughter Lucy fell in love with an American, Fred Whitridge, whom she was to marry. As the party travelled at reduced rates on theatrical tickets, these were stamped 'Matthew Arnold Troupe' – much to Matt's amusement.

Matt was always able to take a laugh at himself. In December 1882 he had rashly published in the *Pall Mall Gazette* a little poem on the death of a canary – 'Poor Matthias'. This was too much for one of the wags, who contributed some verses to the *World*, which amused the subject of them.

> Poor Matthias! many a year
> Has flown since first upon our ear
> Fell that sweetly doleful song
> With its ancient tale of wrong.
>
> But the burden never falters,
> But the chorus never alters;
> Those smooth periods no more vary
> Than the song of your canary.
> Won't you give us something new?
> *That* we know as well as you.

Matthew brought out a book of his American Discourses in 1885 and in 1886 went back for a second tour, when the great attraction was Lucy's first child, a little girl. 'My Lucy's baby is a real pleasure to me and I nurse it a good deal,' Matt wrote to his sister Fan, still living at Fox How. 'It is such a refined, calm looking little thing.' He used to call in at the nursery on the way to the bathroom in the morning, just as he had with his own children, and the baby clutched at his eye-glass and played with it.

But it was during this visit that Matthew Arnold had a first warning pain across his chest – when he was bathing and a wave had carried him against a taut rope under water. He felt it for about a week and afterwards, when he was home in England, he was conscious of some difficulty in climbing hills. Yet he was, as ever, full of energy, writing articles, writing letters, and congratulating his niece Mary on her novel *Robert Elsmere*, which he had begun to read and which was making such a stir everywhere, because it treated of something so much in people's minds – the uncertainties about religion.

Robert Elsmere is a very long novel, overweighted, as Henry James observed, with minor characters and incidents. James met Mrs Humphry Ward in 1882 when, she recalled, her daughter Janet, then about five, had climbed on to his knee and gone to sleep – a somewhat unusual view of 'the Master'. The whole of the first 'book' of *Elsmere* is taken up with the meeting in West-morland of Robert and Catherine, whom he marries, though the main part of the action is at Robert's parish in Surrey and in London where, on leaving the ministry, he founds a humanist

New Brotherhood. Robert, whose days at Oxford are sketched in a long recapitulation of his early life, is finally given the psychological push to disbelieve by the unbelieving Squire Wendover – an unusually intellectual squire, partly drawn from Mark Pattison, the Rector of Lincoln, who had recently died. What destroys Elsmere's faith is the historical criticism of the New Testament; its miraculous element seemed to show up the unreliability of the authors. Mary's is a similar approach to Matthew Arnold's, but his niece had not, at that time, Matt's ability to isolate from the miraculous element a convincing image of the real Jesus, with a real and new and ever valid message for mankind.

Matthew was enthusiastic about this novel, though, as Mary records, he had only read the first part. Writing her *Recollections* at the end of the First World War, when she was older than Matt had been in 1888, she doubted whether he would have liked the second and third 'books'. Although she declared that he was 'a Modernist long before his time' Mary added 'but to the end of his life he was a contented member of the Anglican Church, so far as attendance at her services was concerned, and belief in her mission of "edification" to the English people. He had little sympathy with people who "went out". Like Mr Jowett, he would have liked to see the Church slowly reformed and "modernised" from within.' And then Mary concluded by saying that as the years had gone by, she had come to agree with him. But that was after the whole Modernist movement, in which she took a great interest, had blown up, and with the advent of the Great War, blown out.

In 1888 she thought, with Elsmere (who dies at the end of the novel), that there was a future in the kind of humanitarian fraternity he creates in the East End of London. She herself planted (in 1897) a less pretentious but more enduring community effort in the Settlement in Tavistock Square.

The novel came out in February 1888 and all through March 'the tide of success was rising'. And Mary's mother, Julia Arnold, was dying. She had long been ill with breast cancer, and before the days of operations for this, it could be a very long illness indeed. She was a year or two over sixty; Tom, usually now in Ireland, was sixty-four. Mary spent the last week or two in Oxford, just about Easter time.

By a curious chance, Gladstone was there too, staying with friends, and he had been given a copy of *Robert Elsmere* by

James Knowles, the editor of the *Nineteenth Century*, who was anxious for him to review it. Gladstone was deeply interested in the book and when he heard its author was in Oxford, wanted to meet her. They did meet – the day after Mary's mother died; they had a long conversation on the evening of Sunday 8th April, and another, a regular argument, the next morning. Mary jotted down her recollections of it and wrote off a rapid account to her husband. Gladstone felt she had not given traditional Christianity an *intellectual* chance; the arguments for it were all merely emotional – all the intellectual ideas were on the other side. Mary felt that Gladstone did not understand that her objections were *historical*, and based on her own reading of fourth- and fifth-century authors, when she had worked in the Bodleian on West Gothic Spain.

In the midst of this Arnoldian ferment of mind Mary was called to endure the pathos of her mother's death. She died on 7th April 1888. Willy had come to see her but had had to leave before the end, and it was to him Mary wrote, 'It was the most profoundly piteous thing. I feel as if I should carry the pity of it in my heart all my life. In the afternoon yesterday she was much the same as when you left her, conscious at times but generally sleeping. When Ethel and Julia and I came in after dinner she looked at us with recognition. I bent down to her and said, "Say Mary once, dear" and she said at once with a sweet look of the eyes, "Mary, *darling*" and then "Ethel" " Julia" in the same way. Then she spoke of you and Frank, just your names.'

At ten they all went to lie down but were called again at two. Julia was then restless and in pain, moaning. 'She said twice, "Papa!" and when he came, he thought she knew him.'

Mary thought Julia's death 'a childlike rendering up of the soul'.

'In her conscious moments,' she wrote to Willy, 'she seemed as Judy said, "all love". Nothing else was left but the intense affectionateness which was the basis of her character: "the love to love" and be loved – then there was the extreme sincerity of all she said about religious matters. She took what others said with gentle docility; she said nothing herself but what meant something *real* to her – "I love God" she said once on Thursday, and again, "God will be merciful". But there was no acquiescence in things as it were for *safety's* sake, and not the smallest terror of death. Truth and love – what can one want more?'

So died Julia Arnold and her body was taken up to Fox How for burial.

On 16th April, as Mary was, in her own words to her father, 'weeping over the photographs of Mamma's grave of which the proofs came this morning and over your dear letter, when Humphry came in with the telegram' – the telegram which announced the sudden death of Matthew Arnold.

'This is indeed sorrow upon sorrow,' she wrote to her father, Matt's brother. 'A heartbroken little note has just come from Lucy Whitridge. "Darling Papa," she says, "fell down and died in the street this afternoon as he was coming into Liverpool to meet us from New York . . . Mamma *alone* was with him. You may imagine the awful shock to her but she is so wonderfully brave and calm, I fear for her health. We are all heart broken. Such a homecoming!" '

Just before, Matt had been rejoicing at the prospect of seeing Lucy and 'the midget' again.

Yet Mary was probably right to say that for him it was not tragic to be spared the 'slow decay' of his brother Edward, who had died in 1878 at the age of fifty-two, 'and even grandpapa's short sharp struggle'. Matt was sixty-five when he fell down dead in Liverpool on 16th April 1888. They buried him at Laleham.

*　　*　　*　　*

After Julia's death, Tom Arnold had a peaceful Indian summer at the end of his life. The house in Oxford was sold. In 1890 he married Josephine, daughter of James Benison of Slieve Russell, County Cavan, and settled in Ireland.

In the April of 1888, after his first wife's death, and Matt's death too, Tom had been to see Newman in Birmingham. In *Passages in a Wandering Life* he wrote of this last meeting with one who had been so great an influence in his life: 'He received me with the greatest kindness and we had a long conversation, chiefly on the Irish University question. I noticed then, and not for the first time, how much more distinguished his features had become, for regularity, dignity and even beauty, since he had become a very old man. There was not the least sign in his talk of the infirmities of age. When I rose to go I spoke of the pleasure it had given me to find him in such comparatively good health and strength. He replied, with a smile, "But you know, Arnold, I am so *very* old." '

Two years later, at eighty-nine, he died, and Tom Arnold was one of the many hundreds, of all religious persuasions, who followed his funeral procession in Birmingham, to the little burying ground beside the Oratorian holiday villa at Rednal.

In 1898, when he was in his seventy-fifth year, Tom made a pilgrimage to Sweden, to visit first the tomb of St Brigit, whose life, picked up years ago in Tasmania, had drawn him towards the Catholic Church, and then the site of the Old English poem of *Beowulf*, which he had translated in 1876. Tom greatly enjoyed this expedition and no doubt it stimulated him to make another the following year, to Rome, staying with the Humphry Wards, who had taken a villa near Castel Gandolfo.

'Never before throughout all his ardent Catholic life,' wrote his daughter in her *Recollections*, 'had it been possible for him to tread the streets of Rome, or kneel in St Peter's. At last, the year before his death, he was to climb the Janiculum and look out over the city and the plain whence Europe received her civilisation and the vast system of the Catholic Church.'

Tom, of course, hurried off to view the scenes of St Brigit's visits to medieval Rome, but he was scarcely less interested in the Rome of classical times. 'I remember well,' Mary recorded, 'that one bright May morning at Castel Gandolfo he vanished from the villa, and presently, after some hours, re-appeared with shining eyes. "I have been on the Appian Way – I have walked where Horace walked." '

Tom went home to write *Passages in a Wandering Life*, which came out in 1900 and offended no one. In November of that year he became seriously ill and Mary went over to Dublin, writing to her brother Willy that their father had difficulty in getting down food, was sleeping heavily, but woken by his cough. When she came in he knew her and said, 'Mary!' with a look of pleasure, opened his arms and said, 'God bless you.'

Later they talked of Leonard Huxley's book – the life of his father, T. H. Huxley – and Tom Arnold said it would rank among the 'massive' historical or scientific books of the time.

He had already received Viaticum – the last communion for the traveller out of this world; the last sacraments of the Church preparing him for the journey. He was not in severe pain, or even distress, Mary reported. She found 'veneration for him here, increased by the sympathy and sweetness of his book, bless him.'

On 10th November she wrote again to Willy: 'Alas, our dearest father is just fading away very peacefully and steadily. He lies with his beautiful grey head a little raised, the sunshine coming freely in through a large south window.'

She asked his blessing for all his absent children by name, which he gave affectionately. ' "And your blessing to Theodore?" I think he understood this, though I am not so sure.' Theodore seems to have been unsatisfactory in some way, though later Mary mentions a nice letter from him on his farm, so all may have been well in the end.

Arthur, the only one of the boys who had returned to the Catholic faith, had been killed, quite young, in the South African war, in 1878. He was 'incurably loose about money matters', his father sadly told Newman, in a letter dated 13th January 1879. He had died owing money to the Catholic bishop out there. 'It was not a large sum, however, and the bishop writes kindly and tenderly and does not seem to have thought seriously the worse of him for it.' Arthur, called after Clough, born at Fox How on their return from Tasmania, could only have been about twenty-one or -two when he died, shot in the lung, giving as his last message 'God's blessing to his family' and so vague about his religious affiliation that, the authorities not knowing it, 'the Anglican service was read over him'.

Now, twenty-two years later, his father was on his deathbed, had come to the end of what Mary called his 'life of constant labour and many baffled hopes'.

She wrote in her letter to Willy: 'Then I asked him a little later if he loved me and forgave me everything and he made a motion as if to put up his hand to my cheek, with a sweet faint smile.'

He died on 12th November 1900, just short of his seventy-seventh birthday.

They put up a tablet to Tom Arnold in Newman's university church on Stephen's Green and lettered on it: *Domine, Deus meus, in Te speravi.* O Lord, my God, in thee have I put my hope.

* * * *

The generations of Arnolds lived on, but the nineteenth century was ended. It was just over a hundred years since Thomas Arnold had been born in the Isle of Wight.

Sources

Since this book is intended for the general reader I have not given detailed references but, apart from the Arnolds' own works mentioned in the text, quotations can be identified from the following list.

The Life and Letters of Thomas Arnold DD by Arthur Penrhyn Stanley (1844) – for Dr Arnold's own letters.

The Life and Letters of Dean Stanley by Rowland E. Prothero (1893).

Additional material from:

Dr Arnold of Rugby by Norman Wymer (who used much family material), Robert Hale (1953).

The Doctor's Disciples by Frances J. Woodward, Oxford University Press (1954).

(This includes a study of Arnold's son, *William Delafield Arnold*, from which the letter quotations in 4 (iii) and 5 (ii) are taken.)

Arthur Hugh Clough: The Uncommitted Mind by Katharine Chorley, Oxford University Press (1966) – for Clough's letters to friends other than Arnolds.

The Letters of Matthew Arnold 1848–1888 edited by G. W. E. Russell, 2 vols. (1895.)

The Letters of Matthew Arnold to Arthur Hugh Clough edited by Howard Foster Lowry, Oxford University Press (1932, 1968).

Unpublished Letters of Matthew Arnold edited by Arnold Whitridge, Yale and Oxford University Press (1923) – for letters to Newman.

Other quotations from the Newman correspondence from MSS at the Birmingham Oratory.

Charlotte Brontë: The Evolution of Genius by Winifred Gerin, Oxford University Press (1967) – for Charlotte Brontë's letter on Matthew Arnold.

Matthew Arnold's Books: towards a publishing diary by William E. Buckler, New York University, Geneva (1958) – for quotation from Macmillan letter to Matthew Arnold and his reply.

New Zealand Letters of Thomas Arnold the Younger edited by James Bertram, University of Auckland and Oxford University Press (1966) – for all quotations from letters of Tom Arnold to his family until his marriage. Also for quotations from Clough's letters to Tom till this date, which are printed in full. I have relied entirely on Professor Bertram's annotation for New Zealand and Tasmanian affairs.

Passages in a Wandering Life by Thomas Arnold, MA (1900), sometimes referred to in the text as his recollections or memoirs, when quotations are made from it.

Tom's letters to Newman are taken from unpublished MSS at the Birmingham Oratory and will appear in Professor Bertram's second volume. Tom's letter to his daughter Mary on his reconversion in 1876 is taken from a copy given to the Oratory by Mary Moorman.

A Writer's Recollections by Mrs Humphry Ward (1918), sometimes referred to simply as her recollections, when quotations are made from it.

Mrs Humphry Ward's letters to her father, Tom Arnold, and her brother, William Thomas Arnold (Willy), from unpublished MSS at Pusey House, Oxford.

Memoir of William T. Arnold, by Mrs Humphry Ward, prefaced to his posthumous work *Studies of Roman Imperialism*, Manchester University Press (1906).

Newman's Letters are taken from the relevant volumes of *Letters and Diaries of John Henry Newman* edited by Charles Stephen Dessain, (1961–) or from still unpublished MSS at the Birmingham Oratory.

Index